INSIDE THE PELOTON

INSIDE THE PELOTON
RIDING, WINNING & LOSING THE TOUR DE FRANCE

GRAEME FIFE

MAINSTREAM
PUBLISHING
EDINBURGH AND LONDON

For
John & Angela
and
Nick & Jan

First published in Great Britain in 2001 by
MAINSTREAM PUBLISHING COMPANY (EDINBURGH) LTD
7 Albany Street
Edinburgh EH1 3UG

ISBN 1 84018 400 0

A catalogue record for this book
is available from the British Library

Typeset in Garamond and Univers
Printed and bound in Great Britain by
Butler and Tanner Ltd, Frome and London

ACKNOWLEDGEMENTS

I have many people to thank for help in the preparation of this book. As ever, thanks to my friends Nick and Jan for their hospitality, generosity and practical help on several occasions when I went down to their Guest House in the Ariège to ride and conduct interviews; also for use of their library, in situ and via e-mail and telephone. Another friend, John, as usual gave me invaluable advice at a critical stage of writing; he has encouraged and furthered the work throughout. Luke Evans, editor of *Cycle Sport* in whose pages some of this material made its first appearance and to whom I owe especial thanks for use of several photographs – gave me my first chance of an interview and thus planted the idea of this book. Thanks to the irrepressible John Deering for setting up my visit to the Giro d'Italia and securing me press accreditation on a couple of occasions when jumping barriers or sweet talk would have been wholly impracticable. Phil Liggett, although he is a subject of one of these chapters, has been a mine of information, uncomplaining about what anyone else might have taken as importunity; a friendly companion in the course of many conversations and bike rides. Jenny Daly, Gennie Sheer, Jayne Kendrick, Ron Webb and everyone at the Jacob's Creek Tour Down Under were indefatigably amenable, helpful, friendly and good fun to be with: their intelligent good humour made the work in Adelaide a joy. Thanks to Keith Wong of *Bicycle Express*, Adelaide, for the generous loan of the red Colnago for my use when I was in town; David Sharp for illuminating – and stimulating – exchanges in the press car and the press room; Terry and Veronica in Tea Tree Gully outside Adelaide, where the last two chapters were written. Marguerite and Lisa-Jane in Paris for hospitality; Daniel Carlier, for that lift to Roubaix station and for kind permission to quote his poem about the *pavé*; Molly and M. Arcenay of the Office de Tourisme, Combloux, for their generous assistance and faultless organization in helping me arrange my visit to the Arc en Ciel week. Finally, thanks to all the riders mentioned in these pages: their riding provided the first inspiration, their readiness to talk to me the continuing stimulus, their generosity the example to make it as good a book as I possibly could. Any flaws are entirely my responsibility.

Graeme Fife,
Sevenoaks.

CONTENTS

FOREWORD

I saw my first bike race at the World's Road Race weekend, Belgium 1975. Hennie Kuiper broke away on his own two laps (was it?) from the end to win the professional title. After the race, I joined the straggle of spectators ambling up the road towards the finish. Threading their way back down came Eddy Merckx and Lucien Van Impe, faces streaked with sweat and grime, slack with fatigue. They had missed out on their home soil and were caked, body and bike, with a liberal daubing of it. The finest professional cyclist ever to have pushed a pedal and the little climber whom Cyrille Guimard convinced he could be a giant passed so close I might have said 'hello', 'bad luck', whatever. They were, for the moment, just two bike racers from the bunch in quest of a hot shower. That curious anomaly between the fame and the very ordinariness impressed me again and again when I was talking to the men whose experiences fill this book. They were, each one, open, courteous and, however rich their *palmarès*, very far from grand. It is the peculiar character of bike racing, at whatever exalted level, that the riders are there, with notable exceptions, accessible to public and press alike. I enjoyed no privilege other than the extraordinary fact that I met men whose names resonated in my consciousness. I asked for and was granted interviews; turned up on doorsteps and enjoyed the company of some remarkable sportsmen. Professionals all, riding the machine we can all own, from bog-standard to deluxe, they typified what I have encountered all through in my dealings with cyclists: what the French call '*politesse*', a quality they demand of their sportsmen: an essential good manners which seems to emanate from a sense that the conduct of sport can match the conduct of life; that meanness in the one will spill over into the other. André 'Dédé' Darrigade said that when he was a young pro taking the train from home in Dax, south-west France to Paris to ride the spring classic one-day races, he got into conversation with someone in the same carriage. What did he do for a living? He replied that he was a racing cyclist. The response was immediate: had he ridden the Tour de

France? That was when he realised that the real proof of being a cyclist was to have lived that adventure, a ride to the summit of cycle racing. For those of us who never have or never will share that unique privilege, its fascination nevertheless does not wane and imagination dips into something of the mystery. Here is my version of it.

1. BY WAY OF AUTOBIOGRAPHY

I started on a trike in Dudley Road in Finchley, a 200-metre downhill cut from Briarfield by the cricket ground to Rosemary Avenue. When the milkman came round with the horse and cart, my father would cry: 'bucket and shovel!' and off we'd race to get there first in front of the rest of the street for the horse's droppings, a bucketful of fresh manure for the garden. The pavement was my trike piste: flat-out to the bottom and a left-hand, right-angle turn, no brakes. I did it solo, but the best was with Diana Muncaster, who lived next door, crouched over me, feet on the back axle, hands on the bars, the only solo-tandem trike team in north London and maybe further, hurtling towards the corner, shrieking like ghost-train passengers, into the bend at a mad speed and a 90° side-cast jink so sharp and fast it took a second for your heart to spring back into position. We were both five and when her family moved away the dare-devilry lost some of its poignancy without her to share it. I outgrew the trike, mastered gyroscopic motion (or rather it mastered me) and began to explore the territory way beyond the backwater of my childhood. I had already in those waking years assimilated two things which became central to my life: a passion for the bike and the companionship of cyclists.

The writing came much later, though I do remember an adaptation of the 'Tweedledum and Tweedledee' chapter from *Through the Looking-Glass* which I wrote and put on at my primary school. I made cardboard armour and dragooned the rest of the cast into rehearsals – an early flourish of the theatre work ahead. And there were the long stories in rhyme which I made up, in the manner of waking dreams, but never transferred to paper. In fact, I hadn't really grasped the secret about writing: that it has to be *done*. I had it all in my head, what need to extricate it? For other people?

Sartre writes in *Les Mots* that his first writing – stories about cowboys, adventurers, derring-do and knights of old – was always done in a rush and, once done, never looked at. It was when for the first time he re-read something he'd written that, he realised, he launched himself as a writer. For me, I should say it was when my English teacher set the class the weekly essay and then came up to me and said:

'You're lazy. You never write any more than a page and you've got a lot more pages in you. I want at least six.'

She got her six pages and I got going. Eventually. It took time because I never really *believed* it; I could write, maybe, but so could hosts of others. Why me? *Believing* it – the talent, the drive, the need, whatever – is what underpins the true, the profound, the peculiar desire to *do* . . . whether it be as a racing cyclist, which I never was, or a writer, which I am still learning to be. But learning is life's central task and, however big or small the talent, any talent is unique to the individual and deserves – requires – his or her unique attention and energy. 'Get to it' is the only answer.

Meanwhile, I cycled everywhere and the bike then, as ever since, was more than a mechanical convenience; it represented – *symbolised* – independence. Every time I mount my bicycle, whether the town bike for routine journeys or the silver Goblin which is my best racing bike, or the old handbuilt Shorter which my friends the Flanagans keep for me at their guest house in the Pyrenees, the feeling is the same. I'm boarding a vehicle of liberty, a particular liberty which I associate with nothing else. I may have had a racing talent; it's too late to say and I don't ponder the ifs. (There is no place in my life for pondering the ifs. Say 'if only . . .' and you are already beaten.)

When I was 14, I joined a school cycling expedition to Belgium and Luxemburg. I was riding an old Coventry Eagle, a gift from one of my father's cousins when I was about eight years old and far too titchy to mount it.

'Lightest bike on the road' he told me. It may have been once, though I doubt it, and by the time I'd grown onto it weight was the least of its antique demerits. But I could pedal; we rode into the Ardennes mountains and, one bright, warm morning, onto one of the highest climbs in the range. I went ahead and thought nothing of it, I got to the top feeling fresh and dismounted to wait for the others. They arrived at last, on foot every one of them, two masters included – pink, puffing and pooped. One of the boys, a 16-year-old good club cyclist, Perkins, was so outraged that he unstrapped his saddle bag, cycled halfway down the climb and – spluttering – rode back up again.

I attribute whatever speed I developed from the Saturday night rides back from my girlfriend's; a round trip of around 32 km and the home run was always *seriously* against the clock. If I wasn't in by 11 p.m. and my father was on the prowl I'd get a belting, like as not. Needless to say, the lingering pleasures of the doorstep at one end generally outweighed the risk of a rough welcome at the other, and the trial – on legs, lungs and nerves – was worth the difference.

At university in Durham I switched to rowing – another sport you can sit down at. My bike, an unlovely roadster, was nicked from the boathouse and I hardly pushed a pedal for some long time, apart from the annual trike race round the square on Palace Green. There I took on the university cycle club hot-shots, on their souped-up trikes – high seat pillars, regular bars, gears, probably. Our team mounted the kids' trikes which regulations (read to the letter) demanded. I had, though, that precious advantage of experience. I could out-corner the fast men and, once, racing for the crown of the right-angle turn, I took one of them on the inside. He overshot and came off, the crowd cheered (the professionals weren't popular . . . this was, after all Rag Week) and I raced on round the circuit driven by the raucous applause, past a bewildered professor of Greek who had just delivered a lecture I should have attended.

I resumed cycling when I went to live in Norfolk. (And it's *not* 'very flat, Norfolk'. That's the southern erstwhile fashionable end, near the racing at Newmarket.) I bought an old decay-green Raleigh with shopping-basket bars, chain-guard, rod brakes – a granny bike to ferry me to and from the school where I taught. One day I had to go to the local hospital for a routine chest x-ray. I returned to school to coach the school first XV and when I came back to change was told to report back to the hospital next morning as a matter of urgency.

The consultant showed me the x-rays. There were shadows all over my lungs; on this evidence it was a wonder I could walk, let alone charge about the rugby field. They kept me in for two weeks of tests. I felt fit, strong – not in the least bit ill. Finally, they wheeled me in for a general anaesthetic and conducted a bronchoscopy (a robot camera crew squeezes itself down the bronchial tubes, like a caving expedition, and comes back with a film of the trip). I woke up feeling ghastly – my lungs on fire, my throat sore, my entire chest aching. The consultant said: 'You're fine, you can go home.'

'Oh,' I croaked, 'thanks.'

The shadows were scars from benign sarcoidosis, an infection of the tissue. They had no idea what had caused it but assured me that my lung capacity would be severely reduced and that I would have to limit my athletic activities, such as they were. To aggravate the debility, I had an irregular heart rhythm (and a very slow pulse rate) which, in that form of medical opinion which passes for wisdom, they said wouldn't help either. (But then I know doctors who refuse to believe that Miguel Indurain has a heart rate below 30.)

'Sod warnings like that,' I thought and when a bike was advertised for sale a couple of weeks later I drove over in the pitch-dark of rural Norfolk in November to inspect it. The frame was orange and the name on it was Eddy Merckx.

And so it began, this thing with cycle racing. People have asked me how long it took to write my history of the Tour de France (*Tour de France: the History, the Legend, the Riders*, Mainstream Publishing) and it's a question I can't answer precisely – except that it really dates from the moment I loaded that mass-produced bike emblazoned with that one-off name into my car. On it I rode everywhere, a huge mileage – on one memorable occasion 150 miles in a day from Dieppe to my French girlfriend's house in the country south of Châteaudun. Once there, I rounded the corner of the drive at 10 o'clock at night and nearly collided with my girlfriend's grandma who was rounding it from the other direction into the cone of light shed by the outdoor lamp. Being *au fait* with French bikie slang I said:

'*Je suis cuit*' (an expression Bernard Thévenet had used in a Tour report that year).

Mamie's eyes flared and she sing-songed:

'*D'alcohol*?'

Cuit means 'cooked', 'knackered', but also 'drunk'.

The next day, we set off to cycle into the local town and, a mile up the road, my left crank fell off, the spindle worn through. It must have been hanging on through that long ride by a sliver (like me, indeed) but knew it had to get me there.

Years later, on a short cycling holiday with my then-wife, the downtube sheared; it was Easter Saturday but as we cycled past a garage, the loose stump of the tube clunking like Long John Silver's wooden leg on the hollow deck, I spotted a gas bottle and thought: 'Aha, welding'. The garage man obliged with a bronze solder like a metal neck brace and the frame lasted another 15 years before the weld gave out and the bike was, finally, beyond repair.

I learnt about racing on the water, in fours and eights – surely as punishing a sport as cycling, but far shorter in duration. One and a half miles at searing pace on various rivers in the north-east; grim interval training on the Wear in Durham; the Head of the River race (Boat Race course in reverse) – murder. I have never raced formally on the bike – save that, like many of us, I hate to be overtaken and am ready to crucify myself if necessary not to be. On one occasion, I put on a play at the Edinburgh Fringe Festival and was doing a round trip of 50 miles to digs in Haddington each day. Coming back along the coast road before cutting up west into the hills, a young guy on a mountain bike had the nerve to overtake me. I nearly let him go and he got a hundred yards or so on me before I turned it on. I came up onto his wheel, pulled a banana out of my back pocket, sat up, peeled it and, eating it one-handed, flew past. A few hundred yards on, nearly asphyxiated with effort and the mouthful of banana, I turned right and hit the gradient thinking *if he chases me I'm pumped.* He didn't.

For competitiveness is innate in me, and I love the thrill of riding out of my skin; in company best. Most recently, I rode the Raid Pyrénéen with three others, 720 km over 18 cols – the entire range of the Pyrenees from the Atlantic to the Mediterranean in four and a half days, and had some of the best riding I have ever had, through extended periods out of the comfort zone, at a peak of mental and physical concentration. It's a state of mind and body which transcends ordinary limitations, where the pleasure subsists in the simple fact that you are doing it, that you can do it, that the challenge you never set yourself before has presented itself whereat the joy of embracing it, meeting it and surmounting it is supreme. The climbs up the Pyrenean giants into the Circle of Death release strange anxieties rarely plumbed into hostile regions of time from which you think you'll never escape. And then, against all expectation and reason given the state of your legs and head, you're there – at the summit.

The first bit of writing I had published was about cycle racing – an article under that title for the *Everyman Encyclopedia.* Whatever expertise I have in prosing on the subject was certainly nurtured by a superb French monthly magazine, now alas defunct, *Le Miroir du Cyclisme.* The level of writing in it was markedly superior to anything I could find in English: intelligent, wide-ranging, above all *continental.* The parochial nature of all the other coverage – even of the European racing scene – was narrow, hidebound and, it seemed, endemic. The Brits simply did not understand professional racing, nor did they want to, apparently. One promising young rider of the period won a race on the continent and failed (through ignorance of the rules) to register at the finish. Someone phoned him some hours later: he was in trouble, under suspicion of trying to dodge the dope controls. What should he do? he asked. Call your own Federation, pronto, they said. He rang the BCF offices, explained his predicament, could they please vouch for him?

'In France?' said the voice at the other end, 'Sorry, you're on your own,' and put the phone down.

In the *Miroir*, I encountered an approach to sport which is, I think, peculiarly French: cycle sport as a subject worthy of serious intellectual analysis. To the French the Tour de France isn't a mere bike race but a test of courage, morale and character like none other; a forum for epic individual combat, for a clarification of the rapports between men and between man and Nature. It is a testing-ground where each rider discovers more about himself through submitting to the twin obligations of personal performance and sacrifice, of *collectivité*. This is a word much favoured by the French to express something rather beyond plain teamwork. It digs into much deeper wells of sacrifice, both physical and psychological – even spiritual. It's a word used to describe the ties of family, of blood, of loyalty which supersedes affection or even compatibility.

Highly-regarded French writers have observed and written about the Tour de France, its mythic proportion, its unique power to express and liberate the French nation (yes, they claim that), a testing-ground which draws out a chivalric ideal of action and endurance. There was, for example, Antoine Blondin, who refused to stray beyond his immediate neighbourhood quarter in Paris *ever*, save only to follow the Tour de France; Colette, who wrote in mischievous paradox about the 'imbecilic and unconquerable desire to come first'; Roland Barthes, the philosopher, most of whose writings about the Tour are pretty unfathomable (myth of expression, myth of projection, reality and utopia, moralities of combat, the magic interplay of natural elements and elemental powers, the hierarchy of supermen and domestic servants . . .) yet who rhapsodises about the epic stature of the race – these are part of a great French tradition of reason, of rationale.

This tradition can get wearing. But it can produce some delicious humour. Example:

A Frenchman tells me that he has no interest in religion; he's an atheist. But what he can't understand is this: why, if Jesus was *born* on a fixed day, why is it that he never *dies* on the same day? Every year a different anniversary.

They love their paradox and La Rochefoucauld is the master. 'Our virtues are, for the most part, no more than vices in disguise.' One of his maxims addresses one of the major themes of this book: the fear of success. 'It takes far greater inner strength to endure good fortune than bad.'

The need to explain, understand and analyse everything is nigh on instinctive in the French, from the nature of existence to the complex ingredients of cycle sport: the rage to win, the calvary of distress, the moral landscape of athletic achievement, the lure of the bike race. The excitement is for them as much an intellectual phenomenon as it is a sensual pleasure. Well that's not very endearing to us down-to-earth Anglo-Saxons, maybe. Why complicate things? The allusions are not part of our cultural reference. However, Albert Londres is different.

2. DEVIL'S ISLAND AND
THE TOUR DE FRANCE

Two years ago, I borrowed an old friend's apartment in Paris while she was away. I needed to do some research in the Bibliothèque Nationale. She left behind a present for me – a slim volume by Albert Londres: *Tour de France: Tour de Suffrance*. I knew about him. He had followed the 1924 Tour for *Le Petit Parisien*, a much-respected newspaper of the day, and written despatches – amongst them one celebrated report about an abandoning of the race by the Pélissier brothers. Like all great journalists, Londres not only reported news, he seemed to have an uncanny knack of being around when sensational news broke, and the Pélissiers did cause a sensation. Londres wrote up his interview with them in the café, including a lurid passage about the kind of pills and dope they routinely took to dull the pain of up to 20 hours in the saddle in the worst imaginable conditions. I used that passage in my earlier book. But here was the whole text. I translated it onto paper as I read.

Londres knew little about the Tour de France and it shows in a wide-eyed amazement at what the riders were asked to go through. He has an astonished quirkiness of style, a boyish adulation of the heroics he witnessed. But Londres was no *naïf*. Indeed, it is his track record as a journalist which made the choice of him to cover the race remarkable and it was testimony to the seriousness with which the French have always viewed the event.

Londres may fairly be called the father of investigative journalism. The subjects he covered compel admiration. The books he wrote, the reports he filed, are gems of reportage, insight and humanity. The first journalist to enter Soviet Russia after the October Revolution – *Dans la Russie des Soviets*, 1920, he had come to prominence with two devastating reports on the *bagne*, the French colonial penal camps on the Iles de Salut, off the coast of Guyana (one of which, Devil's Island, came to be a byword for hellish confinement) and in Cayenne on the coast. Established by

Napoleon as dumps for the dregs of society, for villains beyond redemption for whom the guillotine was too mild a punishment, the *bagne* epitomised 'out of sight out of mind'. The French public remained ignorant of the vile conditions in which the transported prisoners lived, and Londres' reports (*Au Bagne*, 1920) provoked an outcry. The colonial ministry were compelled to investigate and as a result the camps were eventually closed down. From the *bagne*, Londres went to the military penal battalion in north Africa, (known colloquially as *biribi*) where the bestial treatment of the prisoners made the camps in Guyana look almost generous. In *Dante n'avait rien vu*, 1924 (*Dante saw nothing*, in reference to Dante's vision of Hell) Londres produced a marvel of controlled reportage. His outrage is plain but it is never allowed to spill onto the page. He was concerned, always, that the reader should make up his or her own mind. It was not the job of a journalist to condemn or judge – only to report as accurately as he could. Despite the detached tone of his writing, his humanity and compassion is plain. There is none of that self-righteous moralising which mars so much contemporary 'crusade journalism', save through the savage irony of the satirist. He thereby conveys a profound sense that pity is more honourable than judgement and understanding more valuable than condemnation.

He even records the conversations he had with his editor, Elie-Joseph Blois, a man whom he revered as 'un grand capitaine des reporters que nous sommes'.

'What if I went to the *bagne*?'

'Go.'

(Eight months later:)

'What if I set out for *biribi*?'

'Leave now.'

(When he came back from *biribi*.)

'What if I did something on the insane?'

'Do it.'

He published *Chez les Fous* in 1925, a study of the notorious French mental asylums – which no one else had ever been permitted to enter, unless they were certifiably insane. Londres passed himself off as crazy and it was with this reputation that he produced *Avec les Forçats de la Route* in the same year; the text recently published as *Tour de France: Tour de Suffrance*. *Forçat* was the word for a prisoner condemned to hard labour and Londres applied it, not without irony, to the riders in the Tour de France. The father of the Tour, Henri Desgrange, was furious. Not because he thought it inappropriate. Quite the opposite. He had used the same phrase about the men he always thought of as *his* riders a few years earlier, but he'd meant it as a compliment. These were the real heroes: the tough men, the modern demigods, like Heracles, Odysseus and Jason. Londres, apart from being a stranger to the business was not a dedicated sports journalist either and had no right to pronounce in such high-falutin' style on a subject about which he knew nothing.

Londres' articles make fascinating reading. He saw his duty, in whatever he wrote, as to write in a way that an outsider could understand, in a manner that would allow full scope to independent reaction. Few of his readers can have had even the faintest notion of what the *bagne* was like; he filed his copy on the great bike race in much the same expectation (thus revealing his own ignorance) but no matter.

EXTRACTS FROM *TOUR DE FRANCE: TOUR DE SUFFRANCE* BY ALBERT LONDRES

STAGE ONE: PARIS – LE HAVRE, 381 KM

LE HAVRE, 22 JUNE 1924.

They were still eating dinner yesterday at 11.30 p.m. in a restaurant near Porte Maillot. [On the western outskirts of Paris.] You could have sworn it was a Venetian banquet – from a distance, these men in their striped jerseys looked like festive lanterns. They took one last drink and tried to walk out, but the crowd chaired them off in triumph; for these were racing cyclists about to start the Tour de France.

I myself took the Argenteuil road at one o'clock in the morning. I passed smartly-dressed ladies and gentlemen pedalling through the night. I'd never have believed there were so many bicycles in the department of the Seine. Tram number 63 wanted to get on with its job, conveying passengers to Bezons Grand Cerf, but the ladies and the gentlemen held it up, yelling at the driver: 'Watch out. They'll be here soon.'

The riders were actually just along the road, riding into Argenteuil for the start. In no time, the whole suburb was alive: open windows bedecked with spectators in night-gowns . . . crossroads seething with impatient onlookers . . . old ladies who normally go to bed at the same time as the sun perched on chairs in their doorways . . . and if I didn't see mothers breast-feeding their babies it was only because it was too dark.

'Look at those thighs' people shouted. 'That's what you call thighs.'

The riders pulled off at a section of the road where it enters the forest; they waited here for an hour. One of them erupted: 'Are we going or not?' he spat.

Another said: 'There's no point getting worked up.'

A commissaire arrived and read out the names of the riders. The French answered: 'Présent'. The Italians responded with 'Presente'. Whatever it was the Belgians said made no sense to me.

At last, the commissaire gave the signal: 'Go'.

A woman in the crowd piped up: 'Good luck, Tiberghien' and 157 riders began the Tour de France. A quarter of an hour later, I saw number 223 on the pavement, changing a tyre. The first casualty. I drew up in my Renault. 'Puncture?' I said 'hard luck.'

He replied: 'Someone's got to be first.' But suddenly people were shouting: 'Dungheap! Flash bastard! Fat arse!' I feel obliged to relate that I was the sole object of these three insults. My car was in the way of an impassioned throng of people sprinting after the riders at a speed worthy of Olympic athletes. [The Paris Olympics were on at the time.]

It was still dark; we'd been going an hour and, on the open ground between the road and the woods on either side, bonfires were burning, as if they'd been lit by jungle tribes who'd heard there was a tiger on the prowl. But no, these were Parisians, standing around their braziers, waiting to see the 'giants of the road' go past. I saw a woman in a light-grey evening cloak standing by a tree, shivering, next to a man in a fold-up (opera) top hat. It was 3.35 in the morning. Day broke and we could see that nobody in France had been to bed this night. The entire region was standing in doorways, its hair in rollers. The riders plough on. Number 337 is the first to get the knock in his stomach. He dips a hunk of bread in wine lees and wolfs it down.

'Don't eat bread' calls out an old hand, 'it blows you up. Eat rice.'

LES SABLES–D'OLONNE, 28 JUNE 1924.

There are certain freaks who swallow bricks, others who eat live frogs. I've seen fakirs tucking into molten lead. These are normal people. The real nutters are certain lunatics who left Paris on 22

June to tuck into dust. I know them well; I'm a member of the club. We've scoffed 381 km between Paris and Le Havre, 354 km between Le Havre and Cherbourg, 405 km from Cherbourg to Brest. It didn't satisfy us. When you've got a taste for it, you can't get enough. Even the waiter at the hotel in Brest, registering what an appetite we had, was sympathetic. An hour after midnight, he knocked on our bedroom door.

'It's 1 a.m.' he called. 'Time to eat our dust.'

'How many kilometres have we got today?'

'412.'

'Hurray!' shouts everyone, tumbling out of bed, drunk with joy.

We crossed Finistère and on through the departments of the Morbihan, the Lower Loire and the Vendée. The dust of the Morbihan is poor stuff compared to Finistère's and the Lower Loire dust is a bit more tangy. As to the Vendée dust, it's a real delicacy. I only have to think about it and my mouth waters. I just hope that the dust in the Landes – next Monday – is as good.

The crusaders of the Tour de France have reached their fourth station. They career down into Landerneau at breakneck speed in the middle of the night. It's the only town since the start where there's no noise to be heard. It's 2.30 in the morning. Landerneau is asleep. It's cold. Châteaulin is asleep. The wheels of 100 bicycles crunch over the ground. By Quimper, the whole of Cornwall is hanging out of its windows. One Breton, thrilled by the sight of them, said: 'It's sad. We lay out 250,000 francs on a horse for a 2½ minute race and men who work a lot harder than any horse get chicken feed.' The sun settles in on the horizon.

'No way we can ride with God's gold medal glaring in our eye' drawls Alavoine. The *peloton* rides in a body down into Lorient.

We pass a wild beast at the side of the road, ferociously devouring rubber. It's the yellow jersey, Bottecchia. He's punctured. To get the tyre off more quickly, he's tearing at it with his bare teeth. Bellenger remounts after puncturing. He calls out as he goes past: 'They're blowing it apart at the front.' It's Thys shaking things up. He escapes with two accomplices, Frantz and Archelais riding elbow to elbow. A touch of drama. Frantz has been instructed to keep the tempo high. I don't really know why Archelais is there. He's a shadow man, a rider without a stable, riding for himself since the start, no manager, no thighs, no calves, no nothing. At the finish of each stage he's in such distress he weeps like a child, but he's always in at the finish with the 'aces'. [Aces were the riders sponsored by bicycle manufacturers, as opposed to the independents, or 'shadow men', who rode without sponsorship.] You feel like giving him a push on the bike, whereas Frantz is brutally strong. If Frantz dared to say 'I'm tired' the telegraph wires by the road would convulse with laughter. Result? We wouldn't be able to telegraph our reports through from Brest to Nantes.

One rider in distress. 'My backside's killing me. I've been hardening it up for six months.' And in a burst of anger: 'Who'm I riding against? My backside.'

At Roche-Bernard, a shadow man goes past. He's badly behind; he's punctured more times than he can count. He calls out cheerily: 'I'm not getting off any more to go looking for bracken.' The leaders are running true, that's to say they're piling on the pace.

The Marquis of Priola, alias M. Hector Tiberghien, [the Marquis de Priola: a character in boulevard comedy, byword for dandyish and well-groomed] isn't going to ruin his reputation for anything so trivial as riding in a straight line. Whenever he sees a pretty woman by the road, he blows her a kiss in the name of cycle sport and Velocipedic France.

Into the heat. The *peloton* gives off a strong smell of hot rubber; the riders grab their bidons and tip them over their head; faces streaked with dust and water, very handsome they look.

TOULON, 7 JULY 1924.

As soon as they got off their bikes, the 'marshall' resumed his role. The marshall is Alphonse Baugé. He is commander-in-chief of all racing cyclists . . . those who race in the Tour de France, the Six Days, the Classic races, on road track. Alphonse Baugé is the life and soul of cycling in France. He is, I believe, the only man alive today capable of working a miracle. He'd have a young boy riding a bike without saddle or handlebars. One day, Alphonse Baugé will be canonised. He wears a dark-blue uniform, cut like pyjamas, with red wool piping round the jacket. You can't mistake him: he's got a dentifrice Mistinguett smile. [The famous film star with the radiant smile had just arrived back from a visit to Hollywood.] He follows the race in

23

a closed car, and it's not only his car that's closed, it's his mouth, too. At every start, the secretary general of the race sews his lips together with brass wire. The other day, out of pity, I thought I'd push a straw into the corner of his mouth to give him some air. He refused. He's a stickler for the rules. At the end of the stage, the secretary general takes a pair of scissors from his pocket and cuts the wire. Alphonse Baugé takes three deep breaths, declares that his heart is still beating, pauses to take stock then goes off to the riders' hotel. In Brest, I'd hardly crossed the threshold of the Tour de France dining room when I heard: 'So, you say it makes no difference to you whether you sing at the Opera or the Batignolles?' Baugé was talking to Curtel. Curtel wanted to abandon the race, complaining that he'd ridden 1,200 km and only earnt 650 F. 'In Marseille,' he said, 'I got 500F for 300 km.'

'Well, no, you're not a great artist; you're happy to be a provincial baritone playing in knockabout comedy.'

'What?' replied Curtel. 'I'd rather get 100F at the Batignolles than 5F at the Opera.'

'Have you no self-respect? Haven't you got even that?' He put his hand over his heart. 'Don't you maybe think how proud your old parents are?'

'Hang on,' said Curtel 'my parents aren't that old.'

'You don't want to know, you've closed your mind. Listen, I'll give you an example. You know Kubelik, the great violinist? Right. You think Kubelik would drop the violin because he'd only earned 650F? No. Kubelik is an artist. So then. You too, you're an artist of the pedals. For the first time you have the honour of riding the Tour de France, this beacon flame of cycle racing, and for some story about 650F you'd let that go?'

'If I kill myself for 650F, what am I going to live on afterwards?'

'Stop: you're no better than a hack, a dumb labourer, a boot-shine boy, a dish washer-upper. You understand nothing about the beauty of the handlebars. Suit yourself. You disgust me.'

We arrived in Bayonne. The assault on the Pyrenees started the next day. Five or six riders were faltering with nerves. In comes Baugé to the hotel foyer to see what's going on. 'You're going to abandon, you with your system for the Pyrenees?'

'What? I haven't got a system for the Pyrenees, Monsieur Baugé.'

'Of course you have a system for the Pyrenees: you're going to quit when the whole world is waiting for you on the cols?'

'Oh no, Monsieur Baugé, no one's waiting for me on the cols.'

'I tell you the whole world's waiting for you, you know that as well as I do. Your old Pyrenean grandmother will be handing you flowers on the summit of the Tourmalet tomorrow.'

'I don't give a f . . . for flowers, M. Baugé, I tell you, I've got no tendons left.'

'It's not a question of tendons.'

'What am I supposed to push with, then?'

'Go and find your masseur. He'll give you tendons. Listen, son, have you got heart?'

'Yes, but I don't have any tendons.'

'Don't think about that. Think about your success, about your name in the big Paris papers. Think about the hero's welcome they'll give you at the station when you get home if you finish the Tour.'

'For heaven's sake, M. Baugé. I keep telling you . . .'

'Yes, yes, you tell me you've got no tendons. Understood. Very well. So, be an undertaker, not a racing cyclist, you understand me? Goodbye.'

Next time, it was Luchon. When the guys arrived they were as cold as a decomposing corpse. They went off for a bath. They came back for dinner. 'You think this is any kind of profession?' they were saying. Baugé put his head round the door. 'It's not a profession, it's a mission.'

'Our mission' said Collé 'is to be with our wives, not to work till we drop.'

'Your wife,' replied Baugé, 'is your bicycle.'

By Perpignan, of 46 aces, only 20 were left. Sellier and Jacquinot had abandoned in Bourg-Madame; they were suffering too much.

'I understand that, my boys' said Baugé, 'but you know, don't you, no rider becomes great without great hardship.'

Between Perpignan and Toulon, two routiers went under the wheels of a car and were left unconscious on the road, Ugaglia first, then Huot. Their fellow-riders weren't amused.

'My friends' said Baugé, 'I've taken falls, too. I've gone under the wheels of a car, too. I was brought up in the business. I know what it's like. There are crosses to bear in our profession, like any other. You know what I'd do if I were you? I'd read Duhamel's *Life of the Martyrs*, it will put heart into you for tomorrow's stage. Take it from me.'

'Can you get it in Toulon?'

'You can get it anywhere.'

'Great. We'll go and buy a copy . . .'

STAGE 10: NICE–BESANÇON 275 KM
WINNER: GIOVANNI BRUNERO 12H 51M 7S.
STAGE 11: BESANÇON–GEX 307 KM
WINNER: NICOLAS FRANTZ
12H 3M 51S
GRENOBLE, 12 JULY 1924

They call these stages simply 10 and 11. It avoids complications. When you organise the Tour de France in 15 stages, it's natural that one day after the 10th stage you come to the 11th. Thus the event proceeds according to an established order. However, there is one trifling detail to add: the crossing of the Alps. It would have been absolutely fine if these 60 men nailed to their bikes had not behaved without conscience today: they *didn't* go up and plant themselves on the top of Mont Blanc. So, what makes them virtuous?

Well then, this is what I observed on the ascent and descent of the Izoard and the Galibier. Crossing these cols, they seemed no longer to be pushing on the pedals but tearing up huge trees by the roots, heaving with all their might at something invisible hidden deep in the earth, something that refused to budge; grunting 'Ghanh . . . Ghanh . . .' like bakers kneading their dough in the middle of the night. I didn't speak to them; I knew them all but they wouldn't have replied. When their eyes caught mine, it reminded me of a dog I had, staring imploringly at me, just before he died, because he was so profoundly sad at having to leave this earth. Then they lowered their eyes over the handlebars once more, and rode on, their gaze fixed to the road as if to find out whether the drops of liquid they were sprinkling over its surface were sweat or tears. This spectacle is part of what they call pleasure. That's what the regional papers have decided it is. The people of the Dauphiné and Savoie départements will be setting out for the Galibier tonight at 12.45 a.m.. At the summit they'll be able to get a cold supper and a glass of champagne for 45F all-in.

The riders are still climbing. The Italian, Brunero, riding his first Tour, croaks a question: 'Is it a lot further, the Galibier?'

'I think we're nearly there,' I say.

Ten minutes later, I hear him ask Thys the same question. Thys replies: 'Yes' with a nod of his head. 'Yes, it's a lot further.'

The year before, Alavoine fell on the descent of the Izoard, knocked himself out and lost the race. He remembers: 'I'm scared' he calls out to me. And, anxiety written in his eyes, he freewheels onto the descent, cutting into the wind. I stop at the foot of one steep section and watch them hurtle down, one by one.

'I'm scared' a routier calls out to me in a quavering voice. And another: 'I'm scared.'

They think I'm waiting at this corner ready to gather them up in pieces.

Another comes down at such a speed I feel the rush of the wind as he goes past.

'I'm scared' he calls out.

One of them brakes, zigzags across the road . . . he's going to go over the edge, he hurtles into the rock face, which planes a slice off his leg, but the rock brings him to a halt. I go over to him. His chain is broken. 'I had a small lead today. What a disaster.' He looks at his chain: 'How am I going to mend that? I'd need an anvil.'

He finds one big stone, one small: the big one for an anvil, the smaller for the hammer. 'If I can fix it, I'll get drunk at the finish.'

The repair doesn't work.

'Something like this and you have to abandon.'

He's a routier, Ercolani, a native of Froges. [An Alpine village just north east of Grenoble, so he was on familiar terrain.] His wife's about to have a baby.

'If it's a boy, I'm going to call him Benjamin.'

'Why?'

'Because I'm the Benjamin of the Tour. I'm 21.'

He succeeds in repairing the chain. 'I'm happy' he says.

Other routiers go past downhill. It reminds him of his unhappiness.

'I started well today. I could have moved up a bit in the classification . . . anyway, now I'm back on course.'

His chain fixed, as he puts his wheel back he asks me: 'You're not a doctor as well, are you? You'd be able to tell me why the baby hasn't arrived yet. I ordered everything, all the medicine, from the pharmacist before I left. It'll go bad.' He leaps into the saddle. 'Ah, they won't let me ride the Tour de France again. I'm too young; it's cleaning me out. I'll come back when I'm 25.'

But he rides off, quick as a zebra who's spotted a creepy lion. If Ercolani doesn't get a telegram in Gex, I'll forge one for him: this anxiety about the baby has gone on too long.

Further up the road, a giant devil waves his arms at me. His bicycle's on the ground; his right knee is bandaged up in a jersey. I go up to him. His legs are a mass of deep cuts. It's Collé.

'What stinking luck. I was keeping something in reserve for the day after tomorrow.'

Collé is from Geneva. They all save themselves for the stage going through their home territory. So, Muller gets ready for Strasburg, Goethais for Calais, Collé has his eye on Geneva – Gex, that is.

[Geneva is in Switzerland; Gex, famous for its blue cheese, is 14 km away, over the border in France.] The Genevans are crossing the border in their thousands to see Collé win.

'. . . God's sake, I collided with a wagon. What rotten luck, mister, what rotten luck.'

'A car?'

'No, a yokel with his moke.' Collé shows me a doctor's certificate:

Extensive swelling to the knee, multiple wounds.

'What do they expect me to do with that? What luck. This job's a death ride. I only hope they still make a benefit collection for me in Geneva.'

Collé is out of the race. What's to become of a man who can't ride any further? I give him a lift in my car. In accepting, Collé has, apparently, committed a grievous infraction. When a rider can no longer ride he must at least walk. Otherwise, he gets hit with a 500F fine. In his place I'd have killed myself on the spot. That way there'd be no infringement of the rules. Ahead of us is the 'lanterne rouge', the name they give the man who is last overall. It's Rho, alias D'Annunzio. Difficult to say whether Rho is skinnier than he's stubborn. He is replacing a tyre and appears to be deep in thought. 'What are you thinking so hard about?'

'I'm thinking about signor Bazin . . .'

Bazin is the timekeeper. At 21 hours, 41 minutes and 3.25 seconds, M. Bazin presses a small object under his table, a timepiece which cost 2,500F. Then he calls out: 'Gentlemen, the control is closed.' He might see D'Annunzio three metres away, crawling in on his stomach and, with an exaggerated shrug of desperate commiseration, signal that he is not going to bend the rules. M. Bazin knows the vital significance of a tenth of a fifth of a second. M. Bazin is a sort of cuckoo who inhabits a clock.

STAGE 12: GEX–STRASBOURG 360 KM
WINNER: FRANTZ 15H 51M 2S
STAGE 13: STRASBOURG–METZ 300 KM
WINNER: ARSÈNE ALANCOURT 11H 36M 27S
STAGE 14: METZ–DUNKERQUE 432 KM
WINNER: BELLENGER 20H 17M 51S

Dunkerque, 18 July 1924. For the penultimate ordeal it was another story. It lasted exactly 20 hours and 45 minutes: it was undoubtedly one of the jolliest of the circuit. This other story began precisely on the dot of midnight at Metz and finished at 8.45 p.m. in Dunkerque. Let's start at the beginning. It was pouring with rain and there was a howling wind; you wouldn't put a guinea pig out on the balcony in such weather. The riders shuffled up, one by one, dragging their bikes, and they were given the 'off' right into the teeth of the wind. Think what that would do to you: from midnight till four in the morning. The men pedalled through the night, chilled to the bone, in pouring rain. A sight to see. As soon as the sky began to lighten, the blackness slipped onto the men. I can tell you, these men who'd been white when they set off at midnight were black by 4 a.m. It's true.

My Belgian colleague couldn't help blurting out: 'My God, what do you look like?'

The riders didn't respond. The riders were right. Think what they could say a few hours later. This time it wasn't dust the cars spewed up at them, it was jets of mud. My friends had turned into real draggletails . . . It grew more and more overcast and gloomy. The roads in the north are paved with stone blocks remarkable for their irregularity so the 60 surviving pilgrims of the Tour de France, a tour which they're also calling the Tour of Sufferance (suffering), rode along the pavements, changing line constantly to escape the roughest sections. We went through a region where the towns are not unknown – Sedan, Lille, Armentières. On signposts we read 'Ypres, 17 km.' Then we crossed the river Yser. In short, it took us back some years to our youth. Yet this was no war we were engaged in; it was a race. Judging from appearances there was no very great difference in the faces of those taking part.

STAGE 15: DUNKERQUE–PARIS 443 KM
WINNER: BOTTECCHIA 14H 45M 20S
PARC DES PRINCES VÉLODROME, PARIS

Sixty are going to make it. [Actually 62.] You can come and see them – these are no fainthearts. For a month they have fought with the road. The battles have taken place in the middle of the night, the early hours of the morning, through midday, groping their way through fog so thick it makes you retch, into headwinds which laid them flat, under the sun which, as in the Crau, spit-roasted them on the handlebars. They have taken the Pyrenees and the Alps by the throat. They'd climb into the saddle at 10 o'clock one evening and not climb off till the following evening at 6 – between Les Sables d'Olonne and Bayonne, for instance. They used roads not intended for bicycles. People barred their way. They've had level-crossing gates shut in their face. Cows, sheep, dogs have run into them. Yet, this was not the great torture. The great torture started from the moment they left and will last till the moment they ride into Paris. And there were the cars. For 30 days, these cars have driven alongside the riders and planed a layer off the road surface. They've planed it uphill, they've planed it downhill and thrown up a copious waste of dust. Eyes burning, mouth parched, the riders have suffered the dust without a word of complaint. They've ridden over flint. They've devoured the coarse *pavé* of the north. When it was too cold at night, they've wrapped up their stomachs with old newspapers; by day, they've tipped pitchers of water over themselves, fully clad, and gone on watering the road until the sun had dried their jerseys out. When they split open a leg or an arm in a fall, they climbed back on the machine. At the next village, they searched out the pharmacist. It might be a Sunday, as at Pézenas, where the pharmacist told the injured man: 'I'm closed for business.' And, instead of shaking him by the neck till his teeth rattled, the rider replied: 'Okay, sir' and carried on riding.

Albert Londres wrote indefatigably on a wide range of subjects. He was consumed with professional curiosity; a man of admirable generosity and humanity. There could be no better rôle model for a seeker after truth in contempt of self-interest or *amour propre*. He wrote about the scandal of slavery in colonial Africa in *Terre des Ebènes* (1928); about the Jews in Europe and the Zionist movement in *Le Juif Errant est Arrivé* (1929), about the turmoil in the Balkans, *Les Comitadjis* (1932) and described his purpose always as 'dipping the pen in the wound' – his own wound, his own pity, his own distress. He claimed:

> A journalist is not a choirboy and his rôle does not consist of walking ahead of the procession, dipping his hand into a basket full of rose petals. Our job is not to entertain, nor to injure but to dip our pen into the wound.

Londres is a hard act to follow, but it is worth the effort. On his way home from China, presumably with another controversial book in his case, Londres lost his life. The small merchant ship in which he was sailing, the *George-Philipar*, mysteriously caught fire; everyone on board perished. It was a sad, ignoble end for a fine spirit who, in 1924, devoted his pen and passion to a mere bike race. He was 40 years old and is commemorated in an annual prize for journalism, bearing his name, inaugurated in 1946, the year of my birth. I hope that's not the closest I can get to him.

3. CHARLIE HOLLAND'S SOLO RIDE

For when the One Great Scorer comes
To write against your name,
He marks – not that you won or lost –
But how you played the game.
(Grantland Rice, *Alumnus Football*)

Henri Desgrange, the father of the Tour de France, said that Charlie Holland had all the characteristics of the English people: 'courage, tenacity, strength and a fine physique'. Desgrange invited Holland, winner of the 'UK Best All-Rounder' competition in 1936, to ride the 1937 Tour de France, expenses paid. Yielding to increased commercial pressure from the bike manufacturers, Desgrange had finally dropped his favoured category of *touristes–routiers*, unsponsored independents who, owing no allegiance to manufacturers or collective team tactics, gingered up the racing in the hunt for the day's prizes. The 1937 Tour was, however, opened to 31 'individual' riders, among them Holland – bronze winner in the team pursuit, Los Angeles Olympics of 1932, and star of the domestic racing scene. Desgrange was always on the alert for novelty, and a British champion would be a real catch for his posse of Tour singletons. However another English rider, Bill Burl joined the Midlander in what would be the first ever GB 'team' (the big outfits had 10 riders apiece). Up popped a French-born Canadian unknown to the Brits, Pierre Gachon, and the trio was dubbed a 'British Empire' team.

Some two months before the race, Holland broke his collarbone in the Wembley Six and cracked it again just before a race at Crystal Palace in early June, but, as soon as he could ride again, he was training hard – 100 miles per day. He'd recently turned pro with the Sturmey–Archer organisation but, given the chance of riding the Tour, he deferred that commitment to the autumn. Then – bad news. The French press leaked a shirty rumour that Holland and the others *wouldn't* be riding after all: they hadn't signed any contracts. A telegram to the organisers at *L'Auto*

32

in Paris, though, ironed that out; the contracts *had* been signed and on Sunday, 27 June, Burl and Holland caught the boat-train at Victoria. A sign at the station told them if the Channel was rough or calm; the steamer (always hosed down after a rocky, puke-strewn crossing in the choppy waters of the narrow sea lane) pulled away from the White Cliffs of Dover on the first leg of the great adventure, up to four hours to Calais. Despite Holland's experience of the 1932 Los Angeles and 1936 Berlin Olympics and the first Isle of Man race in 1936, he and Burl were basically amateurs, largely ignorant of bunch racing, wholly unblooded in the merciless arena of continental pro bike-racing; innocent of the rules, the ethics, the dodges. They were about to take on a bunch of hardened Tour men, past masters of the massed-start style of racing which the British NCU had turned its back on right from the beginning on the grounds that massed-start races were *slow*. Compare the time for a 50-mile closed-circuit race in Dublin – 2 hours, 15 minutes and 20.36 seconds – with Thorpe's unpaced record of 2 hours, 3 minutes and 38 seconds. Racing was not at all true athleticism or fair play: it put too high a premium on cash, luck and opportunism. Amateur, 'lover of the sport for sport's sake', was the true test of character, though in 1878, when the Bicycle Union was founded, cyclists at once adopted a definition of 'amateur' which embraced *all* competitors and not, as originally, only those 'gentlemen' who had private means. Not all sports were so egalitarian. In the year Holland rode the Tour de France *Cycling* recorded how:

> At last the Amateur Rowing Association has decided to fall in line with other athletic bodies and to alter their amateur definition in the spirit in which other bodies regard amateurism. They are expunging that blot on their constitution which prohibits rowers who were engaged in manual labour or menial occupations (whatever that may mean) from participating in first-class rowing.

(The trouble had been that on the big rivers of England, rowing had been a professional sport for years, practised by the working class, of course.)

Five years before, the pukkah England and Surrey gentleman Douglas Jardine had been encouraging his 'body-line' bowlers to take out Australian batsmen in a ruthless campaign of rank gamesmanship. When one of them went down, felled by a vicious ball to the chest, Jardine drawled: 'Well bowled.'

Holland and Burl, working class, stout English yeomen, resolutely 'fair play' as the French say, true Corinthian in spirit – were champions of the amateur code about to encounter a very different convention, a much darker notion of probity, a game with very peculiar rules.

In Paris, they met Gachon and went to the organisers' office to collect their bikes: standard Tour issue since 1930, to curtail the influence of manufacturers on the outcome of the race, and to equalise competition. They had uniform, welded frames in a range of sizes to suit most riders (made by Alcyon – Desgrange and the Alcyon boss were big friends), were painted yellow with black stripes with *L'Auto* on the head tube and the rider's name on the cross tube. The forks were raked more steeply than Holland was used to, the frame itself larger (no more than 4 inches of seat tube protruding). This altogether more extended and rigid set-up originated in Italy where all the long races traversed either the Apennines or the Dolomites. Italian makers, already ahead of the field, tailored their machines more precisely for perfect balance on rough roads and high passes *and* to allow riders to let go of the handlebars to take food without fear of toppling over – something that the extreme crouch posture of time-trialling took little account of. A handy comparison here might be between the posture of a racing jockey and that of a cross-country rider.

Each bike was fitted with standard rims, brakes, tyres and gears – Desgrange had allowed the '*derailleur*' for the first time in the Tour, having resisted it previously, with some justification, on the grounds that such a flimsy item was bound to break down and need specialist repair. (More eccentrically, he also reckoned that it would impair the true test of tenacity and strength on the big climbs.) Riders took their own handlebars and saddles (invariably a leather Brookes 17), but though there were official mechanics, none offered to assist Holland and the others. They had to borrow tools to fit their bikes themselves.

Time pressed. Although the machines still needed expert attention the Race Director was at a banquet and couldn't deliver the requisite permission for a Tour mechanic to overhaul them. The Brits would have to make do. They wobbled off for a test ride on Tuesday and went back to their hotel room and decided on team tactics: stay together till 20 km from the finish and then go for as many points and as much prize money as was on offer as they could, individually.

Wednesday 7.30 a.m.

The entire field, 66 'team aces' (a category which, with some irony, included the British Empire men in blue jerseys emblazoned with the Union Jack), and 29 'individuals' rode round Paris, the streets thronged with dense crowds, cheering and applauding. The city was in the grip of 'Tour fever'. It was a royal send-off, a marvellous occasion; a taste of the enormous popularity of the Tour de France. They even rode up the great avenue of the Champs-Elysées, then past the Arc de Triomphe and west into the suburb of Le Vesinet where at 9.30 a.m. 'Tonin' Magne (winner in '31 and '34) fired the gun for the off.

Gachon must have been stunned into amnesia by the detonation. He went AWOL – or got lost – somewhere along the route, never arrived in Lille and was eliminated as a defaulter. The truth is, he hadn't taken the race at all seriously and must have taken fright when he realised just what he'd let himself in for.

On that first stage, across long stretches of the terrible antique, cobbled tracks known as the 'Hell of the North', (much reduced nowadays) Burl had a nightmare ride. He crashed into a rider who'd skidded and fallen on the greasy *pavé* but managed to stagger on, supported by Holland, whose headset was only adjusted finger-tight because he'd had no wrench to secure it. He scarcely reached the finish – one lap of the horse-track in Lille and his front wheel was wobbling all over the place and, when he climbed off, he found two long splits in the head tube. He had been that close to losing his forks.

There were a number of official Tour mechanics: one to every five or six riders and one service *camion* following the riders to provide no more than basic help at the roadside. This help tended to be selective: top riders who punctured were frequently handed wheel and inflated tyre complete while the 'proles' had to change and pump up their own tyres (they carried two spares).

Thursday 11 a.m. start

There's chaos: rain, tramlines, riders weaving about in search of clear road, blocking, crashing, pitching-off. Round one corner, Holland's tyre burst and he went down on his left (injured) side. Luckily the collarbone held up but the bars had dug into and bruised his ribs. His gear got stuck in a low ratio and a tube in his frame fractured. Teaming up with Paul Chocque, the only rider in the bunch who spoke any English, he began the long chase. Doing 'bit and bit' they rejoined a small group at the back of the race. On being told that they were only 15 km from the finish, Holland

35

decided he'd give it a go. He attacked. There was no reaction from the others: they watched him fritter himself for a while and coolly reeled him in. Again they did nothing when he belted off again, merely paying out rope for him to hang himself by. He'd been duped, of course. There had been, in fact, more like 30 km left. Holland eventually gave up but, smarting from the fun they'd had at his expense (a very British way of putting it), he 'slammed in the top gear' and out-sprinted the rest through crowds pressing so close there was room for only two riders abreast.

It brought a short-lived satisfaction. Having missed the control, he was penalised 18 minutes. Worse, Burl didn't make the time limit and was eliminated. With 18 stages, nearly 4,000 km left to ride, Holland was on his own.

Under-trained, a novice to the routine rough-trade amongst these continentals, bruised from his crash, shocked by the poor state of the machine that he had had to struggle with in the two arduous hauls across the wretched cobbles of northern France, Holland must have felt horribly isolated. The comradeship of Chocque (chatting amiably to him about the ferocity of the mountains that lay ahead of them) and a loose alliance of individuals (which, naturally, didn't survive self-interest in the chase for prize money) can only have been small comfort. However, surrender wasn't in his make-up. The British bulldog tenacity kicked in; he certainly was *not* going to quit the race. Quite early on, his cheerful acceptance of what to most must have seemed a forlorn effort, impressed the rest of the bunch – particularly the French riders, it seems. The gallant, handsome, dogged 'roast-beef' was obviously a rider of class, if a bit green. His courage was never in doubt and, as the race went on, he rode himself into peak fitness.

Average times for the stages of this Tour were already raising eyebrows. For example:

> Paris – Lille 263 km:
> *1936*   7 hours, 6 minutes, 18 seconds
> *1937*   6 hours, 57 minutes, 48 seconds
> Lille – Charleville 192 km:
> *1936*   5 hours, 32 minutes, 21 seconds
> *1937*   5 hours, 18 minutes, 31 seconds

The new variable gear gave the riders better developments as well as easier changes on the move. Hitherto, they had had to stop and swap the rear wheel around for a choice of four freewheels, two either side of the hub.

Another complaint, though: the specialist sprinters – a fixture in the national teams – were in lively action too, a fact lamented by some team managers who bemoaned their inclusion in place of more hill climbers. Sprinters were of no help in the race overall, good only for popping up at the finish to snaffle the glory and the prizes. *Plus ça change . . .*

The increased pace caused a higher than normal rate of retirements. At the halfway, over 30 had quit – but as the race moved into the Vosges, Holland at least was actually beginning to find himself in form. The sun had healed his wounds; the masseur (there was one to five or six riders) told him his legs had no signs of fatigue in them – even a time penalty and a fine had not daunted him. On stage four (Metz to Belfort) he punctured, changed the tyre and, when a car in front slowed down and the driver made signs to him to tuck in, he did. He'd seen several riders do the same already and there was such an array of cars – official and unofficial – straying across the road, that it was near impossible sometimes *not* to take a tow. Besides, a race *commissaire* had been watching him from his car, so he thought that he was doing nothing wrong. He was, however, fined 100 francs (roughly £10: a handbuilt Bates bike would cost nearly £9 at the time) and docked 18 minutes 'to show how strictly the rules were applied'. This was to show him but not the others, apparently. Holland was puzzled by the double-standards, the routine bending of very rigid regulations in the interests of keeping the race alive. He didn't want to cheat. He wasn't aware that he *had* cheated and on this confusion his Tour would, eventually, founder. He wanted to ride fair and square or not at all. That was *not* how it worked over here.

That fourth stage took the riders across one of the mythic climbs of the Tour: the Ballon d'Alsace. It was the first col ever included, a gruelling 10 km punishment of zigzags to 1,424 m. For a rider bred on the steep but short English hills, this was a rude baptism, a severe test of nerves and physique. Holland thought that climb would never end, the sun-scorched road twisting and turning through a haze of dense heat and choking petrol fumes. He was sprayed from head to foot with melting tar, cars stalling abruptly in front of him.

The next day, there were three sections – an oddity of those Tours. First, a massed start 175 km followed by a 34 km team time-trial, which Holland rode with the Italians, a high octane bunch who attacked the climbs like a boarding party and rocketed down the descents like skiers on a black run. He struggled in alone. The 'strange array of foodstuffs' they'd had for lunch had taken his legs away, he said. The third section was a 93 km slog over the Col de la Faucille – 'a worse climb than the

Ballon' – into Geneva. But Holland was beginning to flex his muscles: he rode in alongside the leaders, Sylvère Maes, (winner, 1936), Gino Bartali, (winner, 1938), Maurice Archambaud, (fifth, 1933) feeling good. His spirits soared; he even drank in the 'magnificent' scenery, one aspect of the Tour which has made it so durable: the majesty and abundant variety of the terrain it traverses.

The awesome sight of the Alps was looming ahead up the valley. The psychological impact of those monstrous ranges cannot be underplayed, and continual problems with gears made Holland's first taste of the high mountains difficult but not, he found, unmanageable. Indeed, he felt he could have ridden the Alpine stages harder. Prudently, he held back. There was a long way still to go; the Pyrenees lay ahead and reaching Paris was the sole aim.

Struggling on a 49" gear up through snow and cold mists to the Galibier, with dozens of riders strung out on the hairpins below him, his tyres sinking into mud and slush or skidding on loose stones, Holland finally rode through a crowd of spectators at the top who stood roaring encouragement above a cacophony of shrill police whistles. He'd conquered the mountain Desgrange rated *the* mountain par excellence, authentic *grand cru* vintage, compared to which the other cols, Tourmalet included, were 'colourless *vin de table*, gnat's piss'.

The descent was awful: through sheeting rain, his legs bruised by stones bulleting at him from spinning car wheels. His front tyre punctured and the wheel started to wobble violently as the tyre rolled off. He held on, brakes crimped tight and shuddered to a halt on the bare rim. His hands were so numb he could barely pull the flat tyre off and fix the new one on. (It was known for riders in such a plight to tear the blighter off with their teeth.) Then he was off again at last and into warmer air, but, alarmed by the tendency of the fresh tyre to creep and slither on the rim, he was forced to ease up on the bends. It was, as he put it, 'very unpleasant when a tyre comes off doing the knots down the mountains'.

The torrid heat of Provence and the roller-coaster of the Maritime Alps were a different sort of trial; there were times when he felt like falling off into the verge and staying off, but English holiday-makers and some bikie tourists cheered him on. This was, too, the celebrated Côte d'Azur: fashionable, chic and risqué. The road out of Nice was lined with tanned young belles in what passed then as scanty beachwear, ogling the tanned riders with bulging leg muscles and sunken eyes. There was distraction aplenty; life was pleasant for a while until they were back up into the hills, dancing, stamping and gasping. His chain started to clatter and jumped off once, twice. He was tempted to chuck the bike down the hillside and declared he would have done had it come off a third time, but the gremlin quit the machine, Holland weathered his mood and, at Perpignan, it was the blessed relief of a rest day. Time to read the fan mail from home – and a number from French schoolgirls, wishing him *bonne chance* . . . ('their letters indicated that they had obviously made a careful study of the Tour de France', which may, or may not, have been euphemistic).

Holland speaks with amazement at the French riders: they habitually spent up to a whole *hour* on dinner. Imagine. In fact there was little or no time to spare for much else but riding, sleeping, and eating, eating ravenously, too. In Perpignan they got up at 2 a.m. for a scheduled 3 a.m. departure (eventually 4 a.m.) and tucked into soup, fish, meat, ham, eggs, vegetables, fruit, beer, wine, coffee and mineral waters. The Roman gladiators were given a sumptuous condemned man's last meal, the '*sagina*'. Holland had just eaten his Tour version.

In the pitch dark, the first miles of the route – another triple-split stage – were hampered by long bottlenecks of farmers' carts and lorries coming to market; riders spilled in the crush. At daybreak, one jumped away, the bunch chased him down and the bosses of the *peloton* gave him a rollicking for his stupidity. They had to cover 325 km *in toto* over a giant's mogul field of mountains. Holland had caught a slight cold and was breathing heavily. By the col de Puymorens, halfway, his head felt clearer but on the descent his back wheel started to bump. He'd picked up a large boot stud in his heavy gauge rear tyre.

From lunch at Ax-les-Thermes, the race moved on to the col de Port. A short way from the summit, Holland, a bare 30 metres down on the leaders, punctured. The heat had warped the washer on his pump and he could only half inflate the spare tyre. He rumbled along a short way, begged another pump from an English-speaking journalist and crossed onto the descent. He punctured again: both spare tyres gone now. Then a third puncture. He had no option but to sit at the side of the road and wait – and hope – for the service lorry or something else to turn up.

Even in that remote Ariège region, the roads were commonly lined with locals from the hillside hamlets, tourists on bikes and in cars, all drawn to see the passing of the Tour and its heroes, the giants of the road. A friendly priest gave the lone British racer a bottle of beer, but the sacristy didn't run to bike spares. A cyclist spectator offered him a touring tubular; in the excitement of inflating it, thinking he was saved, Holland broke the rod of the pump. He begged and borrowed yet another pump and set off, but the tyre was too big, it squirmed loose on the rim – impossibly dangerous to ride. He cadged yet another tyre which did fit and went his way down the long Massat valley. It's a lovely ride (I know it well) but for Holland, anxiety gnawing at him, it must have been grim. Twenty-five miles on, the control in St Girons was closed: the officials had moved on. Disconsolate by the empty *commissaire's* table, Holland took off his number. His Tour was over. He'd been beaten by punctures.

A press car rolled up and he asked for a lift to the finish in Luchon. They gave him some spare tyres so he could ride on; a lift – even for an injured rider, was against the rules. He said the rules had already eliminated him; he'd pulled out. But he fitted a tyre and remounted. The press car drove alongside him, telling him, in broken English, there was no reason not to carry on; they even grabbed his jersey to tow him, assuring him that he'd be reinstated, that it wasn't his fault. But the Englishman baulked; penalised for missing a control, fined for taking a tow, he *wasn't* going to infringe regulations again. They insisted this was different. He didn't understand the workings of the race. But for Holland, the workings of the race were as impenetrable as if they'd been in code.

'I think they'd have done anything to keep me in the Tour' wrote Holland 'but I did not want to finish this great race unless it was by my own efforts'. One sympathises, but laments, too – an almost sullen pride, a certain obtuse stubbornness: Holland, it is clear, simply didn't know the game and didn't want to know. He finally got a lift from a private car.

His abandonment – forced but almost certainly reversible – was not only a huge disappointment for him but sorry news for the organisers. The lone Brit had captured the popular imagination; he was good copy for Desgrange's paper, *L'Auto*. To see him reach Paris would have been a spectacular coup. His heart, legs and courage were intact; he had conquered the mountains only to be beaten by mechanical failure. The press went to town on the legend of the lone hero squaring up bravely to massive odds. Stories flew that he had begged Desgrange to let him continue, (more likely the reverse); that his manager (he didn't have one) had pleaded with him to go on; that relays of sympathetic locals had pushed him from one village to the next. (Downhill?)

Reaction in the English cycling press had a less romantic turn, largely affected by the scandal at Bordeaux when the Belgian team were subjected to some ugly harassment by French spectators. On the previous stage the leading Frenchman, Lapébie, had been penalised for an infringement; the partisan crowd took it badly and deliberately tried to wreck the chances of Sylvère Maes, in yellow. They closed a level crossing gate to hold up the Belgian, who had punctured, and his team. The crowd threw pepper into their eyes, hurled stones. The Belgians quit and Lapébie took the race, which only 46 riders finished. *Cycling*'s editor reported:

> To put it mildly, the Tour de France just ended has been a sorry affair. It is a terrible race, even if one regards it as a sporting fixture which in truth it is not . . . However much he may hope to see the best man win the tremendous popularity of the race, the Frankenstein the organiser created has developed a chauvinism among certain elements of the French people . . .

A reader (German, judging by his name) weighed in with:

> As a sporting event the Tour de France is a fiasco. The rotten sportsmanship shown throughout by the French is enough to make any decent person sick . . . We'd do well to get the 'continental' bee out of our bonnet. At present the cycling game here is a clean one . . .

The reader snorted at the harsh penalty imposed on Holland, ('a single-handed beginner'), compared to the light punishment served on French riders for the same offence.

A clean game?

In a post-Tour report in *Cycling,* Holland spoke of overtaking 'a few riders who were taking "acid" . . . ' the current UK club slang for dope or 'go fast' and, in the same issue of the magazine, a cartoon shows an elderly woman berating a cyclist who is tipping his bidon out onto the roots of a vastly oversized sunflower: 'I wish you wouldn't empty your "dope" in the garden.'

The national UK press, to the dismay of cycling fans, largely ignored the drama across the Channel. Cycling, then as now, 'was not news' – even when a Brit was making it. But the papers judged the stature of the sport from the size of the crowds at the Herne Hill track and they were small. The golf Open came first. In France, of course, it was different. As Holland himself reported: 'The Tour just *gets* the French and Paris goes wild with excitement over the finish.'

Holland's response to the crusty British gallophobia was mannerly and composed; he was one of nature's gentlemen:

We can't censure *all* French people for the actions of a lunatic fringe. Cycling is their national sport. *We* don't condemn football and devotees of the game wholesale when we read of some referee being attacked by angry spectators or players having a free fight.

That he had ridden (with credit) so much of the race without support – mental, physical and, to his undeserved misfortune, mechanical – was a great triumph. Desgrange was impressed and asked him to come back next year. Could the English arrange a full team of ten riders, a manager, the whole caboodle? Whatever efforts were made to that end though, they came to nothing.

The War came, Holland retired, England cherished her unpaced flat-out soloists.

Before he left England, he weighed 11 stones; during the Tour he had gained five and a half pounds and a wealth of experience of pro racing. On the stage towards the Galibier, Holland remarked that he felt as if he were on a Tour de Luxe, the pace was so easy, the riders making no effort. But he soon realised that these were professionals; there was a purpose to everything they did and this day their purpose was not just to ride but to *race* over nearly 2,000 metres of wicked mountain. Economy of effort in the lead-up to extreme expenditure of effort was an obvious prudence.

The War effectively put paid to Holland's professional career. Serving with the army in France and Germany, he suffered a dreadful dilemma. He'd enjoyed the great fellowship of the Olympics in Germany and made friends there. To face the possibility of *killing* them was hateful.

After the War, forbidden by BCF rules to compete as an ex-pro with amateurs, the all-rounder Holland (who'd had a trial for Aston Villa as a teenager and wasn't far off playing cricket for Warwickshire) turned to golf, but when the restrictions on 'pro–am' competition were relaxed, the rather overweight, nicotine-stained newsagent ex-pro got back on his bike and got training. In the old days, he'd have been out on the special triple with his brothers, no slouch racers themselves. 'The Yellow Peril' they called it. They must have been a fearsome sight, three Hollands on two wheels coming at you like a three-up war-horse. In 1972, Holland, still a class act, delivered a string of Vets' records: 1 hour, 1 minute, 23 seconds for 25 m; 2 hours, 9 minutes, 6 seconds for 50 m and 4 hours, 40 minutes, 47 seconds for 100 m.

4. BRIAN ROBINSON

1953, Coronation year. Britain was beginning to emerge from a long period of post-war blues. On 30 August, a hot summer evening, a small group of Englishmen was sitting in Nino's café near Lugano in Italy. These were not tourists. They were members of the Hercules Road and Track Racing Team and they'd just watched a great day's cycle-racing. The *campionissimo* Fausto Coppi, twice winner of the Tour de France, had won the road race by over seven minutes to take the rainbow jersey of World champion. Behind him, Dave Bedwell of the Hercules team, became one of only two riders ever to have finished the World Championship course. He'd ridden the final 6 km on a flat tyre.

The Hercules racing team (sponsored by the cycle manufacturers of that name) were having a good year, making a bit of a mark on the continent. It was a sun-soaked evening, the wine flowed and with it the excited talk about the old dream: building a team to ride the Tour de France. It was past midnight when two members of the party, Peter Bryan and D.D. 'Mac' McLachlan, the Hercules PR manager, went round to the hotel where the veteran cycling journalist Jock Wadley was in bed, fast asleep. They summoned him to the foyer and told him they were all in one hundred per cent agreement: a Hercules team in the Tour, they were going to give it a go, straight into the deep end, they knew it'd be a slog, they were up against real hard men and it was all bound to be a bit amateurish to start with, but maybe in three years . . . and you know the continental racing scene better than anyone in UK, so what do you think, Jock?

Wadley hadn't even had time to put his teeth in.

British cyclists dominated continental cycling in the early days although the British establishment was sniffy about bikes from the start. In May 1869, an article in the London *Daily News* declared:

'The practice of riding or driving upon bicycles does not form any part of the Civil Service Examination.' Undeterred, James 'Jimmy'

Moore won the first ever bicycle race over 1,200 metres at St Cloud in Paris on Whitsun weekend 1868. Resident in Paris, which soon became the hub of bicycle racing, Moore, who by now had earned himself the nickname 'the Parisian Flyer' pocketed 1,000F (roughly £3,000 in today's money) for winning a race from Paris to Rouen on 'the horse that eats no hay' in November the following year: 123 km in 10 hours, 25 minutes, through driving wind and rain. He beat a field of nearly 100 other riders, including 6 women. A famous amateur (prize money notwithstanding) Moore was the first major star of a string of British riders who dominated the road-racing scene in France and at home towards the end of the century.

Riding an 'Ordinary' with the huge front wheel (around sixty inches) for which British cycle manufacturers were then noted, Moore soon switched to a two-wheeled 'Ariel' (48 inches and 22 inches, 51½ pounds in weight) designed by the brilliant James Starley for the Coventry Machinist's Company. On it he broke the hour record: 14 miles, 440 yards in 1873. In July 1882 Herbert Lidell Costis became the first man to beat 20 miles; plus 300 yards (i.e. 32.456 km). The Brits not only invented the concept of *time* records – which introduced the possibility of notional races between two riders not even in the same country; even the living against the dead – they monopolised what has become the blue riband of cycle records: the hour, in the early days. Chris Boardman has illustrious forebears. The early supremacy waned, however, and in 1893 the record crossed the Channel when a certain Henri Desgrange pushed it to 35.325 km and, because of his amateur status, was rather 'Englishly' obliged to refuse the bank notes (cashable as gold louis) which his manager offered him.

Thanks to the English enthusiasm, cycle racing became the rage and, with that imperialistic English fondness for bureaucracy (Civil Service attitudes) the Bicycle Union was formed in 1878. The Union Vélocipédique de France followed in 1881 but it was the British governing body (renamed the National Cyclists' Union) which ruled the continental roost, barring foreign professionals from strictly amateur races even on French soil, garrotting the sport with finicky rules and kowtowing to the establishment in a way that rapidly became almost a tradition. Their stuffy approach to professionalism was reflected in the divisive class-conscious British evaluation of the bicycle. *Cyclist* magazine even haughtily declared war on slang, 'strongly objecting' to current usage of 'jigger' and 'crock' for the bicycle (not please gentlemen, the scurrilous terms 'bike' and 'trike' employed by one Mr W.S. Britten) and 'sosh' for the sociable, a side-by-side machine for married couples. There was even a distinction of social rank attached to the tricycle, as outlined in a mandatory note which went the rounds of the tricyclists of the Bicycle Touring Club in 1883:

'It is desired by most Tricyclists to separate themselves entirely from the Bicyclists who are a disgrace to the pastime, while Tricycling includes Princes, Princesses, Dukes, Earls, etc. There are none of the upper circle who ride Bicycles.'

Cyclist (August 1892) defined the bicycling class as pre-eminently 'clerks and shop assistants', a social distinction which has bedevilled the British racing scene ever since. The bicycle was unarguably a machine for people in the *trade*. In France, a fundamentally rural, agricultural society, the bicycle was heralded from the start as a proletarian machine of liberty and independence; French working-class men and women took to racing for the money and the acceptance of and passion for cycle racing (particularly road racing) became deeply rooted in public esteem *and* popularity. A multiplicity of French journals clamoured to sponsor and report the sport. The British had *Cyclist* laying down the law about 'u' and 'non-u' vocabulary while the respectable press, the police and the public joined in a concert of rising indignation directed at cyclists 'hurtling recklessly' along the roads. Criminal charges of 'pedalling furiously' were brought against the rampaging hordes of anti-social wheelers and in 1895 the *Rational Society Gazette* reported that: 'the North Road has become a cycling track as well as a public thoroughfare'. On holidays it ceased to be a thoroughfare at all for non-cyclists. (Shades here of the notorious time-trial specialist of the '60s Alf Engers, fiendishly riding the central white line up the A1 carriageways, slipstreaming cars and lorries.)

In 1890, the NCU, prompted by the police and backed by the CTC, had forbidden any road racing and that ban persisted until well after World War Two. (An honourable mention is due here to the BLRC – the British League of Racing Cyclists – and the 1945 Victory Marathon, from Brighton to Glasgow in five stages, the first major road race in Europe after the armistice.) But the limited ardour for time-trialling – the British disease – had been seeded. Even the early stars of the continental racing scene snottily dismissed the foreign 'intruders'. G.P. Mills won the inaugural Bordeaux–Paris in 1891 leading in four other Brits, but refused to ride the first Paris–Brest–Paris later that year because they'd proved their point and, besides, French professionals were riding. ('Infra dig, old boy.') One of them, Charles Terront, won it. He had been employed by Mills' trainer, H.O. Duncan, who was an exception to the 'Britannia Rules' mentality. He knew Terront (charmingly nicknamed 'Frog-eater' in England where he had won a potful of races) and sponsored him on his St Petersburg–Paris ride (14 days, 7 hours in 1893) in partnership with Superbie. Their trademark was 'DS', 50 years in advance of that icon of French elegance and style, the Citroën DS (which the French pronounce 'Déesse' – 'goddess') 19.

But Duncan's sterling efforts were both lost on and alien to the homely British cycling scene. A Welshman, Arthur Linton, took the 1896 Bordeaux–Paris, crossing the line with the great Gaston Rivière, but the Brits had more or less bowed out. The next winner of that one was Tommy Simpson in 1965. The red white and blue of the French tricolour took over; and then of the Stars and Stripes. Zimmerman – amateur champion of the world, Chicago 1893 – turned pro, crossed the Atlantic and crushed Edwards and Baden, who had come to Paris expressly to hand the upstart Yank a walloping. It was, for a while, 'Zimmerman first, the rest nowhere' – and that 'rest' for many years to come included the English riders, flogging their talent up and down the bloody tarmac against the same bloody clock every bloody weekend.

The Hercules plan to enter an all-UK team in the Tour de France ripened and eventually centred on the talents of Brian Robinson, an amateur racer of exceptional strength and intelligence with a singular goal: to race on the continent. He'd ridden in the 1952 Olympics and the Worlds, and the domestic scene didn't interest him: the horizons were too narrow, ambitions too limited. The real action was in France and, in 1952, he had his first taste of it in the Route de France, a forerunner of the Tour de l'Avenir, a two-week stage race for amateurs aiming to enter the pro ranks. He found himself riding against French clubmen who were professional in all but name, and had been nurtured as such. It is the same nowadays: local French clubs are well-funded and run on professional lines; road races call on the sympathetic assistance of the local police; a long caravan of support vehicles strings out behind the race, and road-side crowds gather to watch. Robinson found himself floundering to begin with. The race organisation allotted him the service of a mechanic but that was his sole support. He had to do everything else himself. And there was a certain anarchy about the schedules. The race depart time might, capriciously, be brought forward by ten minutes. Robinson, stocking up with food in the grocer's had to spring out sharpish to catch the off when the gun went.

It was a 'very steep learning curve', as he put it; learning to wash his clothes every night, rolling the wet stuff in towels to help the drying. But, he said, he never disheartened. While struggling to assimilate this entirely alien code, to match the pace of events, to read the tactics of road-racing, to settle into the *peloton*, he reassured himself constantly: if the others could do it, then so could he. That pragmatic attitude, shorn of sentiment, is indicative of the mental toughness essential to what Robinson called '*faire le métier*', the evocative French phrase which means simply 'doing the job' but which is nevertheless the kernel of true professionalism in whatever line, in whatever trade.

'Trade.' That word so despised by the British establishment. The vulgarity of cloth-cap occupation, commercial work, grubbing for money in trade. That trigger of contempt, snobbery, class and background. Earning money by the sweat of one's brow was low. A noted cricketer of the '20s (Surrey, probably, I can't recall, but certainly England) when asked what he did, replied: 'Cricket'. But no, he was pressed, what do you *do*? (meaning how do you make a living). He replied, in astonishment: '*Do*? I don't *do* anything.'

When I was growing up, even middle-class households routinely mounted a small metal plate on their front garden gates: 'No hawkers, no circulars' and tradesmen were shunted to their own entrance by the back or side door and through a separate wicket. But in France, where an Emperor famously remarked that England was a nation of shopkeepers, 'trade', or rather *métier*, has different connotations. *Un homme de métier* is a craftsman; *gens de métiers*, experts; and the great technical school in Paris, home of science, research and technology, is the *Conservatoire des Arts et Métiers*. One French proverb says: *il n'y a pas de sots métiers, il n'y a que des sottes gens* – 'there are no stupid trades or skills, only stupid people', and there are other aphorisms in praise of honest trade.

British cyclists didn't lack talent – never have lacked talent – but they shone largely on the track, as they still do. In 1954, for example, British track riders took two World titles (one silver and two bronze) and two Empire Games golds. Eric Thompson won gold in the road race but the road race specialists were still novices in comparison with the continentals. Like the hapless Charlie Holland, they simply did not understand the workings of professional racing with its odd masonry of team loyalties, feudal structure and pecking order; the peculiar system of rules with built-in bypasses and running waivers. Rules which, it appeared, applied in varying degrees of seriousness to top riders and lowly *domestiques*, to French and to foreign. The Tour de France not only took place in another country; it was like a separate fiefdom, autonomous and entire of itself, compliant to its own sovereignty and none other. The few Brits who did cross the Channel to compete found that if the racing itself was rougher, faster and longer than anything they knew at home, the manner in which competition was conducted left little room for the traditional English reserve about 'play up, play up and play the game'. To this day the French talk about *le fairplay* as a uniquely British – and therefore rather quaint, if somewhat charming and praiseworthy – characteristic. Continental bike racing wasn't so much a game as a plain matter of life and death and the honour of victory came at a heavier cost than a mere amateur could, in general, cope with. In general the British amateurs had neither the head, the legs nor the stomach for it. Robinson for sure was, from the outset, under no illusions. Illusions, like sentiment, had no place in the continental *peloton*. He had a fight on but there was nothing else for it: he got stuck in. The Englishman, they say, is noted for his sangfroid, and never was 'cool blood' more necessary than in surviving the cruel heat of the baptism by fire in the hurly-burly of the *peloton*. It's not so much the ruthlessness of the racing, nor the speed and occasionally dodgy tactics, but more the absolute necessity of making yourself impervious to any inner hurt, distress or suffering. The mask of the professional hides any chink through which a rival might observe weakness. The rough-house need not turn a rider into an ignoble scrapper; real honour does not die in the cauldron, it is tempered. The one trait you cannot afford is any hint of vulnerability. That disguise has to be learnt or else you will show a constant slow puncture.

Robinson had a fight on but he got stuck in. He recalls the first time he saw the mountains. The race went into the Pyrenees and the giants lined the route up ahead: Aspin, Tourmalet, Aubisque. He looked up into the impossible altitudes where flashes of light winked against the heavy dark mass of the towering mountain flanks. He realised that this must be the sun glinting off car windscreens, and if there were cars, there must be a road – but how could a road wind up so high? It's a common enough experience and I share it, but Robinson was in a race. There was no time for introspection.

He was from the beginning utterly single-minded, hungry to succeed in this job of continental racing; there was *never* time for introspection. If the job was to be done it had to be got on with and done as dictated by local rules. Contemporaries of his in England had a more comfortable time of it. Dave Bedwell, for instance, a Hercules rider on a guaranteed salary, could afford to rest on his laurels. For Robinson and the other riders in the continental *peloton*, jostling for prize money and sponsorship, only hard work made money. This didn't deter him, rather it was the spur. He more or less based himself on the continent, determined to learn, to school himself in the hard craft of no-quarter professional racing, to match results to his undoubted talent as soon as he could – aiming, of course, for the big prize: a ride in the Tour de France. A pro since 1953, he announced his arrival most emphatically when he won the Schwenningen to Augsburg stage of the 1954 Tour of Europe.

He signed for Hercules early in 1955 and went straight to their training camp in Saint Raphaël on the Riviera, south of Cannes. Next door were Louison Bobet, winner of the Tour in '53 and '54, and his brother Jean. Jean, who could speak English, was friendly from the first. Louison, a man of prickly temperament, played the *grand seigneur* rather, until the Brits met him out training where two wheels could spin the familiar threads of fraternity between them. There was no feeling either that the Brits were trying to usurp the French. They slipped in with the fast crowd and the only judge of rank was, as ever, the road.

They rode in local races, built form in the hot competition with the French racers, gradually establishing their presence on the scene. They went to Italy for the Milan–San Remo and north for the Tour of Belgium and the Dauphiné Libéré (seventh stage over the dreaded Mont Ventoux). Robinson won the Mountains Prize in the Grand Prix de Cannes and, in the 8-day stage race (the Tour du Sud-Est, which started in Albi), he took the leader's jersey on one stage. Robinson was fourth in the Flèche-Wallonne, fifth in the Grand Prix du Moulin and tenth in the Grand Prix du Havre. His results were startlingly good for a newcomer. This certainly brought the Hercules team most prominently to the notice of the Tour organisers. The novelty of a British team must have held out a juicy commercial possibility, but the team deserved attention on its merits: it had riders of undoubted talent, especially its obvious leader, the by now seasoned 24-year-old Robinson. His depth of experience was unmatched in the rest of the team, although Bernard Pusey (25), Bob Maitland (31) and Tony Hoar, (23 and a one-year pro), had also crossed the Channel. Maitland had ridden various events in Europe, mostly Italy and France, including the 1953 Grand Prix des Nations; Hoar had taken a stage and come second overall in the recent Tour of the Netherlands. The rest of the team were largely untried on the continent when they arrived in France.

After three days of their début Tour de France, the Hercules team was reduced to seven. Pusey was eliminated on time after stage one. On the third stage – out of Roubaix, onto the *pavé* – the French, under strict orders from Bobet, who had a signed agreement of help from the whole team and was anxious to establish his authority against a *peloton* largely united against him, whipped up the pace. Bedwell and Bevis Wood lost time with punctures. Stan Jones, the consummate *domestique*, worked himself into the ground to bring them back, but by the afternoon they had lost heart and abandoned. Jones, one of those riders with a heart as strong as his legs and his will, went back and found them. They told him they'd packed.

'You can't,' he said. 'This is the Tour de France.'

'Well we have.'

The Hercules team was hard hit by punctures. Under the sponsorship contract, they were required to use Dunlop tubulars rather than the brand the individual riders favoured. The foreign riders routinely ignored contractual obligations; good equipment was more important to them than brand names. The British, in the Charlie Holland tradition, phlegmatically stuck to the rules. The Dunlops had not been cured (riders generally left a new tubular to mature and harden for at least a year). This probably accounted for the mass of blow outs, but Robinson was, and still is, scathing about time lost on such trifles. If you were in the lead, then a flat tyre was a blow; but if you were already half an hour down what did it matter? Change the tub and get back on. Do the job.

Jones abandoned, exhausted, on stage seven in the Alps; Maitland crashed, held on for another day but crashed again and retired. Hoar, adrift on his own for 120 miles into Monaco after a crash, missed the time limit but a *commissaire* ruled that he had been baulked by traffic and he was reinstated. Mitchell developed a saddle boil, rode on with great courage, but was finally forced out along with Fred Krebs. Bob Maitland and Ian Steel succumbed to exhaustion and wounds from crashes. Robinson and Hoar were on their own; by the rules of the race they no longer constituted a team and their mechanic, Bob Thom, was sent home.

Robinson always made sure to get from each finish to the hotel and into the bath as quickly as possible, and from there onto the massage table. Those times on the table were, he says, always the best times on the Tour: talking things over with the masseur, a light-hearted chat with this guy who acted as the team's confidant, absorbing some of the day's hassle as he soothed aching muscles. Recovery – mental as well as physical – was the vital task in a long race like the Tour. And on rest days there was the vinegar bath. A pint of wine vinegar and a kilo of sea salt dissolved in six inches of water as hot as you could bear. A five-minute soak and the veins on your legs stood out 'like chapel hat-pegs'. Blood coursing, driving out the toxins; a wonderful relaxant. It was all part of doing the *métier*.

Hoar adopted a very different approach; very laid back. He dawdled around at the finish of each stage and often turned up at the hotel an hour and a half later, slumped onto the bed and lay there without moving, completely knackered. But he was a great joker, he had a real zest for life and gave the more focused Robinson tremendous moral support. He soon became *lanterne rouge* (back marker), of the race and his genial manner endeared him to the French fans.

When the stages were routinely upwards of 250 km long, a bit of levity never went amiss; it helped to while away the tedious early kilometres and there were some noted pranksters in the *peloton*, like Roger Hassenforder, constantly set on lightening the mood. Journalists were always ready to grab the gift of a rider's *musette*, packful of goodies. One day Hassenforder found a dead cat, put it in his lunch bag and delivered it, with compliments, to one of the press cars. (He was no slouch, incidentally; he won eight Tour stages, four of them in 1956.)

Robinson says that he had the impression of hardly sleeping a wink the entire race. His heart pounding, body overheating in the airless summer nights, he was kept awake by an incessant noise from all-night revellers outside the hotels in the town centres drilling into his head. He must have slept, but was so revved-up it didn't feel as if he had. He was moreover tirelessly adapting himself to the rhythm of the race; wondering before each *départ* if this would be his day to go home. And, another day survived, would he make it to Paris? That had to be the overreaching goal; yet he wanted to have a go in the Pyrenees, to stretch himself, to see what he might be capable of in future. That desire is clear proof of his essential nerve: an innate attacking spirit coupled with a willingness to take risks, a quality without which any talent, however much it promises, can only ever be modest. What, though, if he cracked in the last chain of mountains; cracked and didn't make the end of the race? A simple answer to that: any day might throw calamity at him and finish him off. So, the risk must *always* be worth the throw. Caution does not figure.

Before the Pyrenees, they crossed Mont Ventoux, where the Swiss ace Ferdinand Kubler (winner in 1950) made his notorious attack. He had never ridden the climb.

'Careful, Ferdi, the Ventoux is not like any other' they called out as he accelerated onto the fearsome slopes.

'Nor is Ferdi like any other rider' he cried back. Several kilometres on, he was weaving across the road, delirious, cooked in the torrid heat on the bare slopes. Robinson saw him, some 300 metres from the col, zigzagging, sobbing, and rode past. As he did, Kubler moaned: '*Pushez Ferdi. Pushez Ferdi.*'

Robinson retorted with a pithy Anglo-Saxon expression and rode on. He reached the top in sixteenth position, nine minutes behind Bobet but half an hour ahead of the tail of the field. Later, in the Pyrenees, he showed even more strongly, riding with great courage and panache. He had ridden himself into the race and was ready to take on the big men in the *peloton*. The one thing he could not abide was the crowds on the mountains shouting and bellowing as the riders went by. It was like thunder in his head and he hated it.

On stage 18, over the Tourmalet and Aubisque, he finished a mere 2 minutes 45 seconds down on the winner, Jean Brankart of Belgium, (second overall and third in the Mountains competition) and only 19 seconds behind a group containing Bobet, the eventual winner; the great climber Charly Gaul, winner of the Mountains prize; Raphaël Géminiani, sixth overall and the redoubtable Stan Ockers of Belgium, the rider who inspired a young Eddy Merckx. It was a superlative performance. He had overcome a bout of sickness on the last climb, and amongst those who congratulated him at the finish in Pau, was André Leduc, winner in 1930 and '32.

'Well done,' he said 'you climbed splendidly and descended like a devil. With your class and a good team to support you, you could finish in the top 15 next year.'

Robinson, so tired he could hardly speak, commented dourly: 'I've learned how to descend in this race.'

Robinson finished the Tour in 29th position. Hoar, who beat him by over a minute in the final time-trial, rode onto the Parc des Princes track as *lanterne rouge*, the crowds chanting '*Or-ah*', their pronunciation of his name. The following day the two Britons lined up at the first of the post-Tour criteriums in a field containing the yellow jersey Bobet and the *campionissimo* Fausto Coppi. Riders avoid this gruelling circuit as far as they can nowadays, but in the past this was where the racing men, riding independently for a month or so, could double or treble their season's take.

The Hercules people were jubilant. 'Mac' McLachlan said: 'We've broken through the Tour de France barrier' but in 1956 there was no Hercules team. Robinson returned to France and joined the newly-formed L Perle team, riding what the French call *à la musette* (no wages, just the bike and the chance of a bonus for a win). Half the French pros and independents were riding on similar terms and that is the commitment Robinson made to further his ambition in his chosen trade. Most British riders were not prepared to do it – to live in France, learn French, steep themselves in the demanding, unforgiving life of the continental *peloton*. It has ever been thus and all the British riders who have crossed the Channel and stuck it out in Europe have had to match the pioneer Robinson's lead. He rode the 1956 Tour in Gaul's team. Team orders were vague to begin with and the leadership undefined so he did get some chance to ride for himself. However, although Gaul rode the early stages 'like an amateur' in Robinson's words, throwing away the real chance of overall victory, his lesser objective – the King of the Mountains prize – gradually took precedence over individual interests and the team effort consolidated. (Robinson's irritation at Gaul's amateurism was as much professional as personal. The team winnings were paltry whereas, had their leader been more pugnacious, they might have been substantial.) Yet Robinson *did* finish in the first 15; he came 14th, by mistake. Gaul had asked him to stay ahead on the last stage and take the unlucky 13th place. Robinson didn't see Gaul ride past. The bad luck didn't stick, apparently. Gaul did win overall in 1959.

Team orders were a constant irritant to a rider of Robinson's class, but an unavoidable factor in the job. Attacking in the 1957 Milan–San Remo, he was called to heel by his team manager. Robinson's duty was to ride for Miguel Poblet. Poblet arrived in company with Fred de Bruyne and Robinson took third place. A few weeks before he had shown what cracking form he was in by beating Louison Bobet in the Grand Prix de la Ville de Nice. A small revenge, maybe, for having to knuckle-under in his first round of post-Tour criteriums in 1955. Bobet had rounded on him, telling him not to be so bumptious. It was his job to show how good Bobet was, not to ride him off his wheel. 'I win,' said Bobet. One is reminded of W.G. Grace refusing to walk in a cricket match not once but three times. He turned to the irate umpire and, with perfect disdain, said: 'They've come to see *me* bat not *you* umpire.'

Robinson rode seven Tours all told, finished five and in 1958 won the seventh stage in Brittany by over twenty minutes – a monumental solo victory, and took a second stage win in 1959.

Of course he was saddened by the Hercules withdrawal of

sponsorship. 'We proved there was a chance of doing something' and it took another five years before that something was done. I asked him whether the Hercules bikes sold in France, as a result of their showing in the Tour. He paused.

'They sold a hell of a lot in Egypt' he said. (The RAF held a series of championship races in Egypt at the time.) In his last two Tours, Robinson helped realise the larger Hercules dream. *Grande Bretagne* entered a team once more; in its ranks was a young rider who became the first Briton to wear the yellow jersey: Tom Simpson.

Robinson not only led the way into Europe; he proved himself a true, outstanding exemplar of the professional code and the professional attitude. Every pro rider is, in the very noblest sense, a self-made man. There is no other way. Robinson inspired a generation of riders and established an entrée to pro racing which, though it is ringed with fire, is by his own terms less daunting now because he proved it was within reach.

5. RAYMOND POULIDOR

I told Raymond Poulidor that we would arrive some time after lunch but couldn't say exactly when – we had a long drive from the Pyrenees to the village in Limousin where he lives. Nick, my friend who lives down in the Ariège, had offered to take me. Just to meet the man promised some reward for 14 hours behind the wheel. We set out at 7.30 a.m. and didn't get there till after 3 p.m. I had the address but the three people I asked hadn't a clue where the road was.

'Raymond Poulidor's house' I said.

'Ah. Easy.' (That's a country thing: people figure; house numbers and street names don't – and the instructions were, let us say, rustic.) But we found him at last, sweeping the leaves away from his paved drive. Raymond Poulidor, 'Poupou' or 'the eternal second' as they called him is the man who should have won the Tour de France but never even wore the golden fleece; the victim, (though perhaps 'victimised' fits better) of the retrusive Jacques Anquetil. Abandoning the Tour in 1966, Anquetil made sure, before he packed, that his protégé Lucien Aimar was secure in yellow. Anything to block Poulidor.

Anquetil had five years' professional experience when Poulidor, who was two years younger, joined the *peloton*. The new man was strong and fast, brimful of confidence. He posed a clear threat and Anquetil, already the lofty champion, was wary of him – not least because of his genial manner. As Merckx said, 'you can't *like* a rival', but Poulidor was not easy to *dislike*. The rivalry with Anquetil: the country-boy from Limousin versus the bourgeois from Normandy, like all such rivalries exacerbated by the conflict of personality, lasted only through the first half of Poulidor's career – but it shaped the rest of it; imposed on him 'a legend', as the French put it, from which he never wholly emerged. Indeed, his feelings when Anquetil retired were coloured by a bewildered sense of loss. The defining element had gone.

Poulidor: 'the eternal second'?

In truth, the sobriquet 'eternal second' better fits the Dutchman Joop

55

Zoetemelk (six times second to Poulidor's three) but it was a popular perception: Poulidor never quite living up to expectation; foiled constantly by the cold-hearted, vengeful egotism of Anquetil. In 1964 he came as close as he ever came and lost by a measly 55 seconds after crushing his rival on the ironbound slopes of the Puy de Dôme; the famous elbow-to-elbow duel, Poulidor on the ravine side, Anquetil forced into the mountain wall. Poulidor missed yellow that day by nine seconds. 'If he had taken the lead' Anquetil confessed 'I would have gone home that night.' In the final time-trial, Anquetil (the 'bird of prey swooping on his quarry') wrenched another 46 seconds out of him and with that a record fifth Tour win. Poulidor was no slouch in the test against the clock. It was a skill he had to learn and did so to become one of the best. He even whipped Maître Jacques memorably in the Paris–Nice and in 1963 took Anquetil's prime event, the Grand Prix de Nations (first win aged 19; he eventually won it a record 9 times). But Anquetil was always prepared to drive himself way beyond imagined limits on the bike, especially when Poupou had to be beaten. And after Anquetil came another implacable tormentor, Eddy Merckx. But Poulidor, indestructible it seemed, phenomenally motivated and strong, was still in contention even at the twilight end of an illustrious career. He came second to the Belgian in 1974, aged 40.

I have thought much about him, about the apparent psychological flaw which cheated him of the laurels and especially the Tour de France victory which eluded him. How much ill-luck can any rider have, or – if you believe in such tides of karma – how much ill-luck can he attract? Like Ron Clarke, the great Australian distance runner who smashed world records at will yet never won the Olympic prize which no one could have robbed him of, Poulidor seemed so often to fall at the last.

I could have won . . . should have won – this race, that race, so frequently pipped at the last – it is a sort of leitmotif in his career; even now as he looks back.

They've named a road after him nearby but the house where he was born, is that still standing?

'I don't know' he said, with a smile – and 'with a smile' might sound like a cliché, except that with Poulidor it is part of him, a window into a luminous sweet temper. But how come he didn't know whether the house he was born in still existed? Isn't that something *all* Frenchmen of the soil know? *La maison familiale d'origine.*

'My parents were *métayeurs*, they lived in rented houses and worked the land for the owners. Then they moved on, so it wasn't till I was about seven that we found a permanent home.' It wasn't a home they owned, however. Poulidor rode a bike because that was the only way of getting around from village to village, visiting pals, going to local fêtes, going shopping or to school. Many of the roads were no more than cart-tracks so it was, he said, 'a bit cyclo-cross'. The bike, though, gave him freedom and independence, the cornerstones of ambition. Helping on the farm gave him a natural fitness, heaving weighty stuff nourished a deep and enduring strength and boyish exuberance prompted him to go racing. They raced for the prize of a ham, a large cheese or other items of food, the local kids all in the mêlée. No thought yet of where it might lead, until he came home after his military service.

He started training more seriously, generally at night. There was no time during the day with its long hours, dawn to dusk, working for his father on the farm: family obligation. So, by the light of the moon, with *sangliers* (wild boar), wild deer and rabbits for company, he put the miles into his legs. There were only three cars in the vicinity – those of a doctor, priest and mayor – so there was small chance of running into traffic. He was soon racing in criteriums as an amateur; jobbed in to fill out the field against the heroes of the Tour, and soon beating them; Louison Bobet, no less, among them. Telling me that, he said: 'So, I knew I was talented.'

That, surely, is the lode of the mine where the seams of self-confidence are buried. *I knew I was talented*; yet what a miser Fate proved in rewarding that talent.

He turned professional in 1960 and, of course, given the pinched family finances, it was a large decision. His absence meant the loss of help for his parents – and success on the criterium circuit for pick-up prizes was one thing; the rough-house of the pro ranks, where every rider fought to make a living was quite another. But, four months after signing as a professional, Poulidor was picked for the French team in the 1960 World's Road Race at Sachsenring. With two laps to go he was in the lead, on the verge of taking the rainbow jersey. It would have sealed an incredible début, but he punctured, a trio of grands of the *peloton* swallowed him up – Rik Van Looy and Pino Cerami of Belgium and André Darrigade of France – and he came fourth. He had announced himself emphatically yet he sensed that he had been robbed. And however rich the final *palmarès* overall, in default of the most prized victories, it is the disappointment which colours the career.

For the moment, though, he was bursting with confidence. French cycling was at a peak; five French teams – one national, four regional –

raced in the Tour de France and though foreign riders had taken the last three Tours, Anquetil was riding into new authority supported by a galaxy of champions. Poulidor, a late starter at 23, clearly had the maturity and strength to join them.

The founder of the Tour, Henri Desgrange, had replaced trade teams with national selections in 1930 to check the malign influence of the large bike manufacturers whose interests were blatantly meretricious, scarcely in the least way idealistic or sportive. '*Any winner so long as he's riding our bike.*' This offended Desgrange's maverick spirit. But there were demerits in the system and, by the time Poulidor joined the pro ranks, the pressure on the Tour organisation to revert to commercial sponsorship had become intense. When a team had two potential leaders, both of them Tour winners, in its ranks (Fausto Coppi and Gino Bartali for Italy in the late '40s, Jean Robic and Louison Bobet for France in the early '50s) internal tensions eroded collectivity and, as it did in 1959, led to disloyalty if not treachery. (Raphaël Géminiani in yellow, betrayed by a spoiling coalition in his own team. 'You are all Judases' he sobbed through his tears.) The same discord can thrive under any format, of course: as witness the internecine rivalry between Bernard Hinault and Greg Lemond in 1985.

In 1953, the year of Bobet's first victory, the French Ouest team (all Bretons like Bobet himself) were intent on giving the national team and the uppity defector Bobet a pasting. They taunted *Monsieur* Bobet, swapping the yellow jersey back and forth – Robic, Jean Malléjac, François Mahé – with a vicious glee so he couldn't get his hands on it. Counselled to patience by his *soigneur*, Bobet saw them off in the end and after that first victory, he asserted himself with imperious riding *and* manners. Indeed, in 1955 Marcel Bidot, the French team director, produced a contract binding every member of the French team to cooperation in its service: all prize money was to be shared on a pro rata basis, and if a '*tricolore*' won overall, he would surrender all his winnings to the team, except for 200,000 francs for his own expenses. Bobet *did* win and the whole team profited.

National teams also put men like the Luxemburger Charly Gaul at a disadvantage: he simply could not raise a full team of native riders strong enough to support him and had to import riders from other countries. It was never more than a make-do solution. Moreover, the regional teams which filled out the Tour field lacked homogeneity and compromised the principle of composite as opposed to individual victory which is the hallmark of every Tour win.

In spring 1961, Poulidor made a glorious start to the season, further proof of his exceptional gifts: he won his first Classic victory in the Milan–San Remo (La Primavera) beating the finest one-day rider of the time, Rik 'the Emperor' Van Loy. In June he beat Anquetil's lieutenant, Jean Stablinski, to don the tricolour jersey as French champion and was invited to ride the Tour de France with the French team headed by Jacques Anquetil (who was winner in 1957, absent in 1960, but was in rampant form, and had already won the Paris–Nice and the National Criterium ahead of a *peloton* united against him). The implications were plain: Poulidor would be required to ride as Anquetil's *domestique*. Such a menial role offended his own thus far unshaken sense of his abilities and the status they deserved. His team boss also advised him against it and so he declined. This was an unambiguous declaration of intent. Henri Anglade, a robust and devoted rider, bowed to pressure and accepted.

Anquetil made no bones about his plans: 'I want the yellow jersey as soon as possible and *we* will defend it.' He may even have laid a bet that he would wear it throughout the entire race. Whatever the truth, he did take it on stage one and kept it to the finish, but despite this amazing tour de force, he alienated both press and public. Anquetil never wooed opinion; he always expected his considerable achievements to speak eloquently for him. His aristocratic 'take it or leave it' attitude did not endear him to a people who rejoiced in the extinction of the nobility. Why, even the haughty Bobet could raise a smile occasionally. Anquetil almost never did. And perverse it may be, but French bike fans have always favoured the dark-haired film star types: Leducq, Bobet, Poulidor. Anquetil was tricky, fair haired and his nose was too sharp.

The French team, dedicated to riding for Anquetil, squashed the race in the Pyrenees; Anquetil was a limited climber and needed the shelter. Jacques Goddet denounced them all as a bunch of 'frightful yellow dwarfs, feeble, gutless and self-satisfied in their mediocrity'. They were, let us say, the first truly homogenised team of the modern era – like the French *tricoleurs* and the Belgian black squadron of the 1930s – devoted to the victory of their leader. Such totalitarian unity of purpose to the detriment of individual ambition challenged the original code of the Tour. Desgrange's dictum summed this up: the ideal Tour would be one which only a single rider had the power to finish.

Protecting the yellow jersey end-to-end did allow some extraneous tactical sallies. Anglade was released from team duties one day to attack and climb up the general classification. This he did but the next morning when the race exploded at the front he got caught at the tail of the *peloton* and lost 20 minutes on the stage; proof enough that riding the Tour at any level of ambition requires constant vigilance.

On the final day, Tours to Paris, Anquetil launched a searing attack along the valleys, expressly to shape a victory for Robert Cazala to reward his hard work, but when *he* arrived at the Parc des Princes, the partisan crowd whistled and booed him. He had won the Tour by over 12 minutes, the strain of defending the yellow jersey throughout the race had reduced him to physical and nervous exhaustion and this inexplicably savage public reaction cut him to the heart. He went home and christened a new motorboat 'Whistles', but the joke was a bitter one. The spite of the French public, indifferent to the travails he had endured to win 'their' race, soured him from then on. He repaid it with contempt. An inflexible disdain overrode his good humour and it was Poulidor who, perhaps, suffered its worst effects. Though Anquetil's prodigious talents were highly esteemed by the cognoscenti (Bidot said that 'He was the most courageous of them all on a bike. Pride drove him and he had an exceptional *résistance*; he did things no one else matched.') he soon came to see the bike as no more than the machine of his supremacy, the instrument of his revenge for shabby treatment. He didn't *like* the bike. ('No miner loves his pick,' he said.) Indeed, he hated the agonies it put him through, the stress it loaded on his mind and body. Poulidor loved it and still does. That ingenuous delight shone out of him, even at the end of the 1962 Tour, when he stands in third place on the podium in Paris, bouquet flourished, relaxed, content – whilst alongside him, drawn, haggard, hollow-eyed, a picture of lonely dejection, stands the winner, Anquetil. The prickly, brilliant, winner Anquetil was never *popular*. Poulidor was, from start to finish, popular. Tall, dark and handsome, nicknamed 'Poupou' with its echo of '*poupoulé*'. 'Darling'.

It's easy to see why. He is a man of great warmth. He smiles much; broad smiles generated out of a sunny disposition. His manner is slightly reserved but from a natural courtesy, even a small shyness; there is no want of goodwill. He is a man at ease with himself and his life. The hurts were real, the wounds inflicted on him too often calculated and the disappointments terribly sharp, but he did not give in to them. He overcame the trials of his patience and decency, his essential generosity intact. There was much he had to learn to bear.

He was born in April 1936. A few months later the man who became his first *directeur sportif*, Antonin Magne, put on the rainbow jersey as World champion.

'Raymond' Magne said once in exasperation 'vous êtes insaisissable,' ('Raymond, you are a *mystery.*')

Going to see him that day, I hoped to get some faint understanding of that mystery. I had concluded from long musing on the subject that Anquetil at root despised Poulidor's lack of killer instinct; the instinct that electrified his own riding. This accorded with Poulidor's country upbringing: the stolidity of the farmer, prey to vicissitudes of weather, blight, poverty. Poulidor actually singles out for praise his father's *opiniâtreté* (stubbornness) as the cardinal quality he most admired in him. A peasant's fortitude certainly breeds an enduring acceptance of Fate's nastier machinations but if fortitude inures you to suffering, on and off the bike, its sister virtue patience doesn't sit well with the rage to win. Yet, here was Poulidor – solid, patient Poulidor – talking to me of the profound confidence he had felt, the self-esteem. He had beaten Bobet, triple winner of the Tour. He *knew* he was gifted. He was aglow with self-belief. He refused to ride *for* Anquetil and later probably came near to breaking his heart riding *against* him. I began to comprehend. Throw into the calculus his telling Bidot that he would ride for Anquetil in the World's Road Race one year. Bidot reported this generosity to Anquetil whose surly response – 'He's more stupid than I thought' – prompted Bidot to walk out and slam the door behind him. There is no room for sentiment in bike racing, said Bidot. Anquetil had not an iota in his make-up; Poulidor could never quite expunge from his make-up what he saw as an indelible facet of decency: genuine *feeling.*

The rivalry between Anquetil and Poulidor – encapsulated in that slogging match up the volcanic pillar in the Massif Central, 1964 – was certainly worked up by the press. It made good copy and sold newspapers. (*Any story, true or not, so long as we get it first.*) But journalism somehow cheapened the duel with its glib prosings. 'Eternal second' is a neat but empty phrase even if Poulidor latches onto it as a sort of cipher to mark the trend of much of his riding career. The press, as it will, turned the face-off into a sensational clash of personalities, a combat of champions: the black knight (cynic, ruthless, inhuman) versus white knight (brave, big-hearted, the people's favourite). Placard heroes. 'Poulidor' wrote Antoine Blondin 'wears the curse of his ill-luck like a suit of shining armour.' Poulidor: the man of the people, the honest labourer who proved Napoleon's claim that every soldier of France carried a field marshal's baton in his knapsack.

The truth was simpler and more direct.

'The rivalry between us was real, venomous and we were proud that it *was* real. There was nothing false in it' he said. They were, each in his own way, true to themselves despite the publicity. It was Poulidor's popularity – the '*Poupoularité*' of popular coinage – which stung Anquetil. At post-Tour criteriums the organisers frequently paid Poulidor more appearance money, because people wanted to see him. Anquetil was no crowd-pleaser, nor did he look as if he enjoyed hammering himself round provincial small-town circuits in the yellow jersey, so why pay him over the odds? Only, Anquetil had to be there as Tour winner. Poulidor, though, gave them all their money's worth. This was, said Poulidor, deeply embarrassing. And wounding for Anquetil, too, surely? 'Oh yes. It hurt him a lot. He could never understand why people didn't at least applaud him. But he didn't know why I was so popular.'

Anquetil admitted once that of course he would like to see Poulidor win the Tour: '. . . in my absence. It would only enhance my reputation.'

His campaign to cheat Poulidor of victory in 1966, his last Tour, had the look of a vendetta, an act of pure spite calculated to rob a worthy rival. The *peloton* hated Anquetil for it, but for Poulidor there was no redress worth anything except the yellow jersey and Anquetil made sure that was not on offer. Poulidor was in superb form and on one day in the Alps dominated Anquetil with a withering show of force. The Norman, always a reckless descender, had to chase hard down the col d'Ornon to contain his losses to a minute. He explained: 'I missed the first corner in the fog and I didn't feel secure enough to take risks after that. My frame had too much whip in it and the brake blocks were slipping.' His *directeur sportif*, a former team-mate, Géminiani, scoffed: '*Please*, Jacques, don't blame your brake blocks. You funked and froze up, that's all.'

'How much time did I lose on the descent? A minute?'

Gém nodded.

'My life's worth more than that.'

When the story was relayed to Poulidor, he remarked, wryly: 'Anquetil's right – his life *is* worth more than a minute, but I knew a time when it seemed to be worth a lot less to him.'

Anquetil towed his protégé Aimar into yellow and climbed off, the spoiling job done. Poulidor rode on, managing to cope with yet another bitter reversal.

Some commentators accuse Poulidor of unwonted caution in his later career. I don't buy that. He was second to Merckx in 1974. He thrashed him in the Alps and, suddenly, an overall win seemed possible at last.

Alas, the physical reserves were no longer there; desire had outlasted his strength. Of course he was haunted by the sense of ill luck, a lot of it served out by rivals, but in the years of his greatest potential he found himself opposed by a rider who could, when necessary, always beat him, it seemed. Against that fact of superiority there is no arguing. As Wellington said: however many battles you lose, you must win the last one – and Anquetil had the icy nerve always to claim that trump.

In 1965 a young Italian, Felice Gimondi, not Anquetil, fought him all the way before assuring victory in the mountain time-trial. In 1967, when he was hotly favoured to win the Tour, he inexplicably slumped on the Ballon d'Alsace and, hope of victory once more lost, rode the rest of the race as support for the eventual winner, his team-mate Pingeon. Anquetil would have abandoned. Real winners do not work for others: they regard victory as their private property, not to be shared. Poulidor came ninth. He rode away from the stadium with resignation. He even considered a return to the amateur ranks.

In 1968 he again looked impregnable but, on Bastille Day of all days, he fell heavily in the Pyrenees, smashed his face for only the second time and was forced to abandon. Jan Janssen that year became the first Dutchman to win. Yet, like the gallant Eugène Christophe in 1919 (third but so acclaimed and so adored that, by public request, he received the same prize money as the winner) Poulidor – brilliant, unlucky, accident-prone, loveable – was perceived as the moral victor. He was fêted at every post-Tour criterium, whereas Janssen was all but ignored. And in 1969, like a revenant Fury, came Merckx.

Poulidor was not revered merely because the public *liked* him. He was unquestionably of top rank. In 1964 he won the Super Prestige Pernod Trophy for the best all-rounder of the season. Janssen came second; Anquetil, despite his Tour win, third. This was a much more accurate indicator of a rider's standing vis à vis the rest of the *peloton*, and the fact that Poulidor came second to Merckx, in 1972, after 12 years as a professional, is testimony to his lasting powers.

There is no doubt that the antagonism between him and Anquetil was not of his choosing. He never thought of rivals as enemies, merely as competitors for the same prize. What stirred Anquetil's implacable detestation of Poulidor as a rider, I believe, was not only a sense that he had not, or at least did not evince, the kind of deadly will to win of which any true champion was possessed almost by definition – but that Poulidor was simply impervious, *insaisissable*, somehow beyond psychological damage. He never cracked. Anquetil never got to him, despite all the attacks, the jibes, the vicious words, the suffering on the bike. He got buried beneath avalanches of ill-luck and crawled out each time, smiling and ready to plough on, in someone else's service. This hint at humility was, to a man of Anquetil's imperious temper, demeaning. Poulidor had too much class. He had all the physical attributes of Tour aristocracy and remained, for all that superiority, a rider without authority; stuck, as they say, in his own stereotype, his own legend . . . the eternal second. He was incapable of exerting his own will over all the rest – something Bobet and Anquetil could do without compunction. Poulidor always thought about the team. If he couldn't win (and he confessed that he never nursed the ambition of winning everything) it was a personal disappointment aggravated by the sense that he had thereby let the team down, too. First prize meant big winnings for them all; second prize meant small pay day.

He compared his Tours to thin cows with scant milk in them, not like the fat kine of Normandy, Anquetil's homeland. There was no beating records (in milk production *or* racing results) in his native Limousin whereas in rich, fertile Normandy . . .

'At root, my Tours resemble my life. Whatever I do I am the smallholder whose heart fills with hope each spring when the grain promises a bumper harvest, and then the late frosts come, the storms chop off the ears, rains lay the long stalks flat, and still we have to reap them. Is that more or less worthy? It's not for me to say.'

At the beginning, he marvelled at the luck of being able to ride a bike without having to go to work on the farm. He went training with one friend in the mornings and another friend that evening. Neither had the stamina for the double ration that Poulidor thrived on. As his career progressed, he blessed his good fortune that, as leader of the team, he enjoyed the privilege of never having to give up his wheel but was always reliant on the back-up of the rest of his *co-equipiers*. He is awkward, reticent about certain aspects of racing – 'the hypocrisy', he calls it; the pretence of impassivity, like poker players before an attack, masking the true intent. The kidology which comes effortlessly to most of the best riders in the *peloton* unsettled him. He would prefer the straight fight, the elbow-to-elbow to see who is really the strongest, without sleights of mental trickery or reference to a rather gauche, rustic virtue. Serenity, strength, health, confidence, fullness of life – in the upshot these are what counted before any success, albeit that success you strive for with every thrust of the pedals, that success that your innate gifts ought to bring you in hamperfuls.

It was this forbearance, I think, which made him appear at once so vulnerable to Anquetil, a man who guarded his own vulnerability close beneath an adamant carapace of pride and will, a demonic desire to be best. But what Anquetil dreaded in Poulidor was his control. He who seemed to have everything under control – the power to strike the coup de grâce even when he was on his last legs – knew that it was in fact the rage to win that controlled *him*. He could not help fighting back out of the depths of physical and mental distress. The intensity wore him out. The pictures show it: on many occasions, Anquetil is shown sunk in a near catatonic state on the bike, generally from over-indulgence. He was a gourmand of gargantuan appetite; no monkish austerities for him. He was encouraged, cajoled, hustled by team-mates but most fiercely by the sulphurous fuse of his own need never, never, *never* to give best to Poulidor, the man who could accommodate defeat. Poulidor, the one rider he feared above them all, because he knew how good he was. In the 1965 Tour of Lombardy, Anquetil's team-mate Vin Denson told him that he knew Tommy Simpson and could see he was in good shape. All his boss had to do was keep his wheel and he'd be in at the finish. Anquetil and Poulidor were neck-and-neck in the points for the Super Prestige trophy: placings in this race might settle the issue. To Denson, Anquetil replied: 'To hell with Simpson – keep your eye on Poulidor.' Simpson won, Anquetil took the all-rounder's *Trophée* and edged Poulidor out once again.

The surprisingly attractive thing about Poulidor is the acceptance that he *was* unlucky and had to come to terms with it. (First Anquetil, then Merckx.) And yet . . . when I asked him what did he count his best memory (dumb question, maybe, and I admitted as such) he smiled before saying, 'Ah, beating Merckx in the 1972 Paris–Nice' almost without hesitation. It went to the final time-trial up the Turbie climb; his 13th ride in the Race to the Sun. He recalled exchanging smiles – constrained, melancholy glances of mutual sympathy, shared signs of nerves – before the start. Merckx looking at his gearing ratio: 47 x 13 to 17; Poulidor recoiling at the sight of Merckx's huge chainwheel with sprockets up to 21 on the back. They set off at 90-second intervals. Poulidor went second to last, overtook Luis Ocaña and then awaited the arrival of Merckx. The Belgian beat the record he had set on the same course the year before, but Poulidor, ten years older, was faster. Aged 36 he had taken one of Merckx's favourite crowns: he'd won the last three times. And his reaction? Astonishment, delight, the sense that he had 'emerged from his legend' as he put it. However, seeing Merckx so downcast, what did he say?

'If I had known it would make you so downcast, I would never have won.'

He had not an ounce of triumphalism in him – to the expense of his career if not to the magnanimity of his soul. (He won the race in 1973, too.)

After the win, Anquetil came up. His retirement from the *peloton* had left Poulidor adrift. If the rivalry spurred the Norman, it also in a way defined Poulidor. The bike cast away. Anquetil climbed off and never climbed back on. They became friends, close friends. It makes an extraordinary tribute to the power of the camaraderie inside the *peloton* that such an unthinkable alliance was not only possible but seized with unfeigned warmth on both sides. Anquetil came up to him that day in Nice and, typically, making the compliment double-edged in his own praise and Poulidor's he said: 'You see, what pleases me is that at last people will realise that I was not beating a dead man.'

Knowing that Magne had accused him of lack of preparation for the Tour, (something that Magne himself had always done assiduously) I asked him if he had ever gone to the mountains to train, on his own. 'That was my one mistake,' he said. 'But there was no time, we had to ride criteriums before and after the Tour to make up our money. We were only paid a bare minimum and there was no choice.' Nor, one suspects, would he have accepted readily yet more absence from home, his beloved family and dog, those familiar acres.

Was he turning in an excuse? I don't think so. He knows himself; he acknowledges that he found responsibility (the '*rrrrr-responsabilité*' that Guimard stresses is the paramount duty of a leader) difficult to shoulder in the way that would occasionally have undermined the needs of fellow riders. Too gentle, too thoughtful, too accepting. All of that. And, in sum, a paradox too. The Roman historian Tacitus said of the Emperor Tiberius, a man vitiated by supreme power, that he had all the attributes necessary to be emperor except that they were corrupted by his being emperor. Of Poulidor one might say that something in him tugged him away from the crippling demands that winning would plant mercilessly on him, changing his nature, twisting him out of shape. There was that awkward isolation of taking final yellow, being number one, being unassailable for that brief moment, till next time when he would be assailable to everyone, the whole pack ravening for his throat, the *peloton* united to topple him. It wasn't so much that he was afraid of winning but he mistrusted its distorting effect that was visible in Anquetil.

Sitting with him that day in late November, I found a man centred in an enviable calm. Amiable, pensive without being introspective, intelligent. Patience must never be mistaken for not caring. Poulidor cared intensely. He enjoyed his fame and still gets fan mail. He had just returned from a national reception for France's Olympic medallists. He is, after all, one of the nation's best-loved and best-known sons. The face of the garage man who asked how far we were going that early morning lit up when I told him who we were going to see. He was too young to have seen the man racing but Poulidor was, still, the man.

And perhaps that was part of it, at the beginning: that he was, he knew, *Poulidor*. He arrived like a meteor and probably comported himself too much like the star, not enough the tiro who had to pay his dues, put the time in, defer to the reigning nobility. Is that what provoked Anquetil at the outset: the need to cut the bumptious youngster to size? Bumptious, only, never arrogant. He was rather like a Perceval in the Arthur legend, a Nevada Smith in the western retelling of that story: a bit of a bumpkin in manner but stronger, quicker, more determined than any of them could believe. The farm-boy with sporting blue blood in his veins. The innocent smile, the effortless power. The newcomer who had already won enough to refuse the offer of a place in the national team. The Dauphin snubbing the King. He may be a mite vain; it's hard to think how he could turn aside from the amazing celebrity which goes on and on. I recall one day in the summer of 1975, cycling through a small French town, and a knot of boys at the roadside crouching over, clapping and shouting encouragement: 'Vas-y Poupou.' Ha, if only.

Merckx calls him on the phone regularly; he still rides with old-fashioned toe-clips – as we saw on the bike in the garage – and his parting words were: '*A bientôt, peut-être?*'

He smiled.

Curiously, the one photo I have of him where he ought, surely, to be smiling but isn't – is of him crossing the line in Milan–San Remo in 1961, the *peloton* bearing down on him 30 metres back. His eyes are closed, he is exhausted from the effort of keeping them at bay.

Ah, what a winner he had inside him.

6. BARRY HOBAN

Late summer 1963, northern France. The great French rider, André Darrigade, an exceptional all-rounder with an electric turn of speed, was sitting at the dinner table with the first Englishman ever to wear the yellow jersey (for one day in July 1962), Tom Simpson. Darrigade was also several times holder of the yellow jersey, winner of 22 stages of the Tour de France (five times the opening stage – a record) and favoured team-mate of Louison Bobet and Jacques Anquetil. He and Simpson had just ridden a post-Tour criterium. A few days before, Darrigade ('Dédé') had ridden another criterium in Solesmes: he and a handful of star professionals in a field largely composed of semi-pros in the hunt for a contract in a pro team. The big men rode for fat appearance fees; the rabble for 100 francs, which they were obliged to return to the organisers if they won any prizes. Dédé told Simpson that there'd been a young Belgian rider attacking the whole race, no holding him. 'I tell you, he was annihilating us.' Simpson asked who the young Belgian was.

'Oh-banne.'

Simpson laughed. 'He's not Belgian, he's English.'

Simpson knew him well: they were both from Yorkshire, members of the celebrated Huddersfield Road Club, the English home of Brian Robinson and many more of the best riders around at the time. Hoban, two and a half years younger than Simpson, had started off riding grass-track pursuit races and time-trials on a fixed-wheel bike – the cheapest machine available – in an era in Britain when road races were very rare. They cycled to races within the radius their bikes could take them. Hoban, an apprentice electrician, was a natural competitor: he loved the racing, found he had a sharp turn of speed. He saved up to buy a road machine and, when he was about 20, considered his future. Simpson was already on the continent, had ridden his début Tour de France in the Great Britain team alongside Brian Robinson and six others who had crossed the Channel to join the professional *peloton*.

The continent seemed so far away it might have been the far side of the moon – and at least you could *see* the moon from Yorkshire. Hoban didn't even go to London till he was 19, but with that bluntness of purpose and clarity of reasoning which characterises so many of the riders I have spoken to, he decided that however far away that foreign world of professional bike racing might *seem*, it was not beyond him. 'I'd raced against Simpson – my first race was his last before he went to France; I could pursuit, time-trial, ride the track, everything he was known for *and* I was a better sprinter than him. I looked at him and thought *I'm like that.* If he could make it over there, *I* could.' It's an agreeably uncomplicated approach to high risk; the brisk audacity of youth: nerveless, straightforward, logical. Mithridates, King of Pontus, knowing that a rival would certainly try to poison him, as all kings of Pontus before him had been poisoned, took a small dose of poison – a mithridate – each day to build up his immune system. He died old. For a pro bike rider, the daily dose to combat failure is nerve, the essential truism on which the whole complex of self-confidence is based: *I know my worth and if he can do it, I can.*

The *campionissimo* Fausto Coppi famously once said: 'We all have only two legs.' It is, of course, what's between the ears that makes the difference ultimately.

Hoban sought help from the man who had been supplying him with equipment, Ron Kitching, boss of *the* bike shop of the day. Kitching talked to a contact he had at a club in northern France and in 1962 Hoban rode his first season of races on the continent as an independent and had a whale of a time. He had 16 wins, 50 places in the top 5. His second year brought 20 victories. He came 16th in the amateur Tour de l'Avenir, which, as its name suggests, is the testing ground for future hopefuls. He even rode three pro races, one of them a much-bruited criterium, where it took 'a mafia of pros' (as he put it) led by the man they called the Emperor – the Belgian star Rik van Looy (World Champion 1960 and '61) – to check him on the line by half a wheel. And then there was that criterium against Dédé.

These men were, in the slang of the *peloton*, *les gros bras*, 'the strong arms'; the hard hitters, or less kindly 'the bullies'. Yet, for the young upstart, taking them on was a mark of the same aggression any rider needed to cut it in the *peloton*; the racing was hard, no one gave or asked quarter. But, they were gentlemen, too: correct, if aloof. The *gros bras* mixed together, the lesser men had their own alliances; it was very feudal. There was a sharply-defined pecking order and those at the top were very grand: at high table, on a pedestal. Hoban remembers writing home to his mother in awe: 'Jacques Anquetil spoke to me today.' These aces were the royalty. However for all their grandness of manner, they also displayed that particular quality of social duty, *noblesse oblige*, the essential *politesse* between old-style nobility and their dependent retainers.

> I never once saw Anquetil or Van Looy ranting and raving; that kind of behaviour was beneath their dignity. They had a rank in the *peloton* and they acted accordingly. It may have been a status thing, but they'd earned their privilege and upheld the code, an honourable code. Always calm and collected and, actually, not unapproachable. Once, on the way between criteriums in Epernay and Armentières (home of the legendary mademoiselle who cut up her skirt for souvenirs), I pulled into a restaurant on the motorway for a meal and there were Anquetil and Janine. Of course I would never have thought of even saying hello, I was so overawed. Those guys were a generation apart from me, but Anquetil saw me and waved me over. 'Barry' he said 'come and sit with us.' That kind of decency was really the foundation of the camaraderie I have with many of the men who were my fiercest rivals on the road; strong friendships that have lasted till now – Jacques Esclassan, Gerben Karstens, Rik Van Linden, Walter Godefroot . . .

These were the sprinters who dominated the bunch during the late '60s and early '70s, an élite of which Hoban was one, racing towards the finish so close together that it was, as Van Linden put it, 'as if we were riding a bike made for four, going round the bends so tight'. Hoban avoided kamikaze alley (down the side of the barriers, from where there was no escape) in favour of the windswept central reaches of the *arrivée*: harder on the legs but safer. Moreover, they all abided by an unwritten rule of behaviour: if a rider got into the gap first, the gap was his. The other man braked, there was no question of rough-housing him. They barged shoulders, for sure, going for the narrow gaps, the way through the tight press, but that was never a problem. Any rider worth his salt was strong enough to stay on. Bumping handlebars, on the other hand, could unseat you and that was out of order. They were, besides, all earning a living; there was no point in bad practice, in unruly shoving. Nor disputes after the race. They rode hard and clean.

There are pictures of riders fighting though: one here of the Italian Vito Taccone clubbing the Spaniard Jesus Manzaneque – a roadside fracas in broiling heat over the climb of the Beauvallon; bike upended, an overflow of frustration: Latin passion, probably over nothing.

The Italians, of course, were and remain the Italians; their code a very personal and – well – Italian version. Franco Bitossi, like the current king of the sprinters Mario Cipollini, a Tuscan, relied on his team-mates to lead him out in the sprints. Bitossi's *super-domestique* Flaviano Vicentini would hurtle to the front, his boss tucked onto his wheel. Then, when the moment came, he'd drop his hand, catapult Bitossi ahead with the hand-sling used in madison races. But as he propelled Bitossi into the lead, Vicentini came to a dead halt and any rider behind had to slam the brakes on and was, of course, blocked. Hoban and the others got fed up with this and took Bitossi to one side: 'If you do that again, we're going to ride you off the road into the ditch and you will be in the ditch every time till you do stop it.' The old cliché 'man to man' applies here, there was no snivelling to the Organisation. Bitossi, incidentally, had an irregular heart rhythm and, doing a Vicentini, would occasionally succumb to a brief syncope and come to a dead halt for a few seconds during a race. He was, though, much more than a sprinter. He was winner of the mountains prize three years running in the Giro d'Italia and second in the King of the Mountains in the 1968 Tour de France.

I always thought of Hoban himself as a specialist sprinter, with a particular attachment to Bordeaux, where he took two of his eight stage victories in the Tour de France, but like Bitossi, he was a fine all-rounder, able in his day to climb with the best. However he always paid for it next day: he simply did not have that exceptional recovery rate vital to any Tour winner. There is no doubt that willpower can override many obstacles; it cannot though, ultimately, change physiology. As he put it: 'If you can climb, you can climb; if you can't, you can't and there are plenty who can't.'

Hoban's first stage win was a melancholy affair. In the 1967 Tour, the day after his friend Simpson collapsed and died in the terrible heat of Mont Ventoux, the whole Great Britain team came to the start wearing black armbands, and his particular mucker Hoban was elected to ride ahead to take the stage as a memorial to him. I did not discuss this with Hoban; enough has been said about that tragic day and it is of little relevance here. I do believe, though, that Hoban's career was deeply marked by Simpson: both its instigation and its lingering inspiration as he grew in stature as a rider.

On stage 18 in 1969, he joined a break of five riders and took the stage into Bordeaux. The next day, he joined another break of five riders and nearing the finish his legs were exploding, he could do no work to help the escape; he could barely hang on at the back. In the break was one of Merckx's team men, Jos Spruyt, a former team-mate of Hoban's.

Spruyt kept motioning him through. 'Eh, Brit, come on.'

Hoban demurred: 'My legs are killing me.'

'Listen,' said the Belgian 'if you're not coming through I'm not doing any more work.'

This was eminently reasonable but Hoban countered with a bit of Yorkshire nous, race cunning and irrefutable logic. The reigning champion Roger Pingeon, riding for the Peugeot team, was smarting at the cocky dominance of the neophyte Merckx – already winner of five stages and attacking the rest like a berserker. There were no Peugeots in the break; Pingeon was too busy trying to limit Merckx's depredations. This being the case, they had a real chance of staying away and, therefore, Spruyt had a chance of taking the stage win. Hoban pointed this out and urged Spruyt to keep going, even without help. At the finish, Hoban, the better sprinter, took the stage. That was a case of physical emptiness eked out with intelligence.

There is no doubt that racing on the track added a certain shrewdness to Hoban's racing as it did to that of his friend Tommy Simpson. For example in 1961, Simpson and the Italian Nino de Filippis were away in the Tour des Flandres. Filippis was the faster sprinter. Simpson started winding up the pace with a kilometre to go, Filippis took his wheel then came through at full acceleration as Simpson appeared to fade. But it was a ploy: the Englishman simply switched behind the Italian and, when Filippis turned to his left – no one there – Simpson grabbed the moment and swept past. On such minor hesitations can races be lost; hesitations prompted by a rider with nerve, self-confidence and the cat-and-mouse cunning bred on the track.

Like any other rider who couldn't always climb at optimum power, Hoban relied on descending skills to make up time. He was from the start a fearless and accomplished downhill man: standing on the pedals, saddle gripped between his legs, crouched in the tuck position like a skier, at upwards of 100 kph, the extreme G-forces kneading his face out of shape like a distorting mirror. One such day on the Tourmalet, dropped by the leading group, he made up ten minutes on the descent and rejoined. Descending at such speed takes instant reactions, an absolute minimum of braking and no truck with fear.

'Well,' he said, 'when you're young you don't think of that. And there were guys who were fearless in the sprints – men like Eric Leman and

Willy Planckaert – but were useless descenders. Sure, I had blow-outs and pranged, but you couldn't dwell on that: you blanked it out, till next time. It's part of a natural amnesia in what's a pretty dangerous occupation, all round.'

On one occasion, again down the Tourmalet, the field was split to smithereens, the chase to rejoin was frantic. Coming into a wide corner, his back tyre blew. The extreme heat generated by friction of brake blocks on metal rims caused the air in the tyres to explode. Hoban applied the brakes, fanning the front wheel to reduce the heat somehow and lurched to a halt. Had the puncture occurred on a hairpin, he would have had no chance of stopping. There was no team car in view, but the Flandria car (a rival team) came round the corner, stopped and threw him a spare back wheel. Those small acts of chivalry . . .

Hoban began his career with the French team Mercier BP, under the leadership of Raymond Poulidor, and rode with him all-told for 13 years. He left, briefly, to ride for a rival team, but came back and Poulidor said of him: 'I'm delighted that he's returned because this Englishman is very *continentalisé* – he knows what's what over here, and he's good company: a dependable racer with a clear head, exceptional speed and utterly loyal.' A job description for the ideal team-mate.

His 'continentalisation' lies at the heart of his success and involves no more nor less than learning how they do things over there. To begin with, he lived for four years in the Pas de Calais, in Béthune, then moved to near Ghent in Belgium. Fluent in idiomatic basic French and Flemish, he was largely self-taught from within the *peloton*. His style in both tongues was not always either polished or diplomatic. After one stage in the Tour de France, his first *directeur sportif* Antonin Magne was belabouring the team about their poor showing (such lectures were routine) and Hoban, seeing through a certain amount of empty hectoring, said: '*Arrêtez vos conneries*' – which might be translated into a blunt Yorkshire 'shut it, you're talking twaddle'.

The other riders cracked up. Magne turned to Hoban and said: 'Your grasp of French is improving dramatically.'

Magne, winner of the Tour in 1931 and '34, was a difficult man; always correct but frosty, distant, very much the boss. His attitude to the team makes a sharp contrast with that of the newer breed of managers who revolutionised the job in the '70s. Magne was stuck in the mentality of the '30s, where only one man counted – the star who could win the Tour. The rest of the team were interesting only in the totally selfless help they could give the leader. Magne's own win in 1934 was built on such abject sacrifice. Two days running, René Vietto, his brilliant young team-mate, who might easily have won the Tour ahead of Magne, gave up a wheel to him and lost irrecoverable time waiting for mechanical assistance.

Magne was not exceptional in his manner; few *directeurs sportifs* saw it as either necessary or even desirable to pay heed to their young riders. If they couldn't hack it, there were plenty of others ready to take their place. Thus, a new man like Hoban would be expected to drop back to hand over a wheel to a senior team-mate who had punctured; to put up and shut up. Then, by the terms of the unwritten contract, deserving no special treatment he had to fend for himself to get back up to the front in time to do his own job and contest the finishing sprint. If he was too worn and *didn't* make it to the *arrivée*, harsh words from the boss: 'So, where were *you*?'

Nor did outstanding results project him out of the menial role. In his first season as a pro, Hoban beat Anquetil – the arch specialist against the clock – in the Paris–Nice time-trial; then won two stages in the Vuelta a España. Nowadays, the management would have been screaming about him and he'd have had a lever for more money. Not then. He had a job – a very lowly, proletarian job – to do; glittering victories did not alter its specifications. In 1966 for example, Magne did not select him for the Tour de France. This effectively reduced his earning potential by up to half for the season. Without a ride in the Grande Boucle, there would be no lucrative post-Tour contracts. He had had a superb year, including victory in the Grand Prix de Frankfort and stage wins in the Four Days of Dunkirk. Magne's reason for excluding him was arcane but entirely typical of his *ancien régime* thinking. Hoban was very good friends with his room-mate, Rolf Wolfshohl, a considerable rider possessed of what Magne plainly saw as dangerous, even subversive, personal ambitions. 'If I put you in the Tour,' he explained to Hoban, 'you'll ride for Wolfshohl and do the dirty on Poulidor.'

Hoban protested: 'What are you talking about? I ride for the leader' but to no avail. It was an enormous frustration. He went home to Belgium and spent the summer riding local *kermesses*, as criteriums were known there.

In 1967 the team had an abysmal year; Poulidor in particular, and Hoban received a letter from Magne informing him that his contract money would be cut by 30 per cent for the following year. Hoban felt justifiably aggrieved. He'd won all the primes in that spring's Tour des Flandres and come fifth overall. Away, with 17 riders after only 12 km, he tucked in at the back of the break and let rip on every climb. With 20 km of the 245 km to go, the break had been reduced to three riders. However Merckx came up with Gimondi and a tiring Hoban missed out in the sprint. Still, *he* had something to show for the year at least.

He got out the dictionary and constructed a formal reply to the boss of Mercier himself, suggesting that if they were going to cut back on contract money, they should perhaps start with Poulidor himself. Shortly afterwards, Magne called him into the office and said: 'Following your letter, we have decided to retain your contract as it stands.' The response was as always, correct, yet devoid of feeling; a chilliness which compelled diplomacy but no affection.

If Magne did not give a hoot about the lesser riders (they were horseflesh, canon fodder) the opposite was true of Hoban's second boss at Mercier, Louis Caput, who rode the Tour de France in 1947, '48, '49 (stage victory) and '54. Caput was as considerate as Magne was indifferent. In a Flèche–Wallonne marred by driving sleet and snow, Caput made sure that both team cars were on hand at the finish so that the riders could get into the dry, to obviate risk of cold or flu and therefore a broken season. A man of immense charm, long experience, sense and, in such a hard trade, unlikely sensibilities, Caput drew a confidence out of riders to match his own. This is a rare gift and Hoban is convinced that had he been linked with Caput from the beginning his career would have been very different.

Hoban became a senior of the *peloton*, a rider greatly respected as much for his pugnacious racing style as for his sagacity. Italian and Belgian riders to whom the terrain of the stage ahead was unknown would come to him and ask what they were in for. The race profile might show the *averaged* gradients of all the climbs, but some of the cols included unmarked stretches of one in three, and without foreknowledge of that level of severity they'd be in for a whipping on too-high gears. Hoban knew the country.

He would also repay the small chivalries. A young rider Bernard Bourreau, of whom much (probably too much) was expected, found himself in difficulties one day on his first Tour in 1974. Merckx had launched a violent assault on the entire *peloton*, the race had exploded and the leaders were off in hectic pursuit, the team cars driving after them. Bourreau was riding alongside Hoban and, as his team car drove by, the *directeur sportif* Maurice de Muer called out: '*Bernard, reste avec l'eenglish!*'

It was timely advice. Bourreau survived and rode nine more Tours, a solid *coureur*.

For Bill Nickson, riding his only Tour in 1977, 'staying with the eenglish' proved impossible. Heading towards the col du Glandon with l'Alpe d'Huez in prospect at the day's finish, the autobus at the rear of the field, the riders who cooperated to get in under the time guillotine numbered about 50. But their pace was slowing. Gerben Karstens, knowing they were in trouble, told Hoban: 'This lot is going home tonight – I'm off' and he rode away. *Sauve qui peut.* Hoban rode up to Nickson and repeated the warning; if Nickson stuck with him he might have a chance. But Nickson was spent, and Hoban joined Karstens. They got a small group together and survived. Forty-three riders didn't. That was and still is what the Tour's about: mutual help *can* save the day and even going downhill it's better to have a good wheel to follow. Some days, some men simply cannot raise the strength to take it, even though they know it is their only chance.

Hoban himself was dropped one horrible day in the Pyrenees in his first Tour de France in 1964: 197 km, Luchon–Pau, five cols: Peyresourde, Aspin, Tourmalet, Soulor, Aubisque. Federico Bahamontes and Julio Jimenez, two Spanish climbers locked in a real ding-dong for the mountains prize, attacked on the Peyresourde, a mere 13 km from the start, one to either side of the road and weren't seen again. Hoban was dropped. The day before, he had clawed his way up the final climb, over the Portillon and says he got to the finish 'smashed out of my mind'. Scarcely recuperated, he had to ride most of the way on his own. He reached the top of the Aubisque – where Bahamontes had finally crushed Jimenez and ridden on to a solo victory by some ten minutes – and was told by someone in the crowd that there was a small group ahead of him. He dug in, knowing that they were his only hope of salvation. He reached them, the *gruppetto* of non-climbers, and the Dutchman Joop de Roo said: 'Barry, you gotta ride. Bahamontes is already tucked up in bed.'

'We rode bit and bit the last 25 km or so', he said, 'hurting ourselves every bit of the way and scraped in by a minute.' With 3 km to go, a strong Belgian rider, Arthur de Cabooter, winner of the Het Volk in 1961, was so tired he fell at a touch of wheels and was done for. He did make it to the finish but was eliminated on time. These are the minor dramas that are never seen on television: the last-ditch fights for safety, the heartbreak of missing out. In 2000, Stuart O'Grady was knocked off his bike in a clash with another rider some 80 km from the finish of stage five. He was badly hurt but rode on (x-rays later showed that he had broken his shoulder in three places) and managed to hook back onto the autobus. Slumping off the back on every small climb, his useless arm

draped over the handlebars, he was pushed up by the *lanterne rouge* –
Jean-Patrick Nazon, riding his first Tour. (The idiot who had decked him
complained that O'Grady was doing no work to help the rest of them.)
It was a bitter ordeal but testimony to the passion simply to stay on the
bike in the hopes of surviving the bad patch for a better day.

Another famous day, 42 riders came in outside the time limit but were
reinstated. It was that time into Marseille, after Merckx had been heavily
trounced by Ocaña (see my book *Tour de France: the History, the Legend,
the Riders*). He launched an attack from the start and kept it up, at a
merciless pace, all day and the entire stage turned into a pursuit match.
All hell broke behind him, Ocaña's team leading the chase. New tyres,
fitted during the rest day, were rolling off in the heat and any rider who
punctured or had a wheel change was doomed. In fact Hoban was the
only rider to survive a puncture; hanging on at the back in torrid heat,
gasping with thirst but with no time to risk a stop to dash into a café or
a fountain for a drink. At the finish, nearly a third of the field missed the
cut (based on a percentage of the winner's time) and were, in theory, out
of the race. However, because they had been riding at an average of some
41 k.p.h. they were reinstated, among them some of the hardest men in
the *peloton* – blown to bits, to use the slang.

Riders dashing into cafés or pulling up at fountains is a thing of the
past, when there was no constant supply of drinks from the team cars and
Tour vehicles as there is now. When Hoban rode his first Tour, he was
given this advice by an old pro: 'Make sure you carry a five franc piece
and a bottle opener in your shorts pocket.' The point was that grabbing
a bottle of lemonade in a café was frowned on by the authorities but
tolerated by most café owners (there was the honour of giving a Tour
rider sustenance). However if a policeman challenged a rider and found
that he had no money on him, he could arrest him for vagrancy under
French law. And the bottle opener? Spanish riders were demons for
raiding drinks shelves but never thought to carry an opener. (One of Rik
Van Looy's pals was famous for opening bottles with his teeth.) Thus,
when Hoban rolled up to the closed-top Spanish gang with an opener,
he could guarantee himself a free bottle in exchange.

Hoban rode his last Tour in 1978 and, perhaps inevitably, regrets the
changes which have in some ways diminished cycle sport. The charge of
'complaint from the grumpy old pro' is too slick. Old men in ancient
Rome disparaging the youth of their day would moan: '*O tempora, o
mores*' ('the times we live in, the way they behave nowadays'). Voltaire,
who knew a fair bit about the turning of the wheel, put it more

reasonably: 'The more things change,' he said, 'the more they stay the same.' And Max Beerbohm (too rotund, surely, ever to have pedalled a bike) insisted that using the past as a stick with which to beat the present is lazy and unprofitable. We must search for the grace in our own age, not hanker after the grace of a lost time. There are other times, and other ways of doing things. Times *do* change and *will* change and if there are things to deplore in modern cycle racing then there is still much to admire. It has always been so and will always be so. Change does not equal improvement, but cynicism clouds the issues on both sides.

There *are* changes to lament though. In the 2000 Vuelta a España, Jan Ullrich, wearing the leader's jersey, pulled out a week before the finish in Madrid, giving as his excuse the fact that the three-week Tour of Spain was not ideal preparation for his preferred event, the Olympic time-trial. This was crass and unprofessional. He was blatantly using the stage race as a toughening exercise and plainly had no intention of seeing it through. This cheats the organisers of the race, the spectators, the rest of his team and the sport. Ullrich is a rider of undoubted class but he is also one of that breed (Greg Lemond was the progenitor) who pick and choose races to suit their own specific ambitions without regard to the more abstract demands of the sport. Even Jacques Anquetil, who concentrated on the Tour de France *and* the Giro d'Italia, deigned to win the Paris–Nice and various other classic races. Paid handsomely all season round, modern stars *can* pick and choose; they *can* neglect off-season training; they *can* pull out of races which prove not to suit them halfway.

In Hoban's era such a cavalier attitude was unthinkable and, given the more straitened circumstances of the true freelance, undesirable anyway. Merckx won plenty because he trained plenty. Regardless of weather, every Monday, Wednesday and Friday throughout January, the team met at his house and rode 200 km. 'If the training is hard, the racing is easy' he said. The apparent loss of that ethic is sad because it is part of a slacker dedication to the sport as 'sport', even if riders of the past also regarded it candidly – necessarily – as a *job*. In his first season, Hoban rode all the spring classics: the Vuelta (held in April/May in those days), the Midi–Libre, the marathon Bordeaux–Paris immediately after it, the Tour de France, all the post-Tour criteriums *and* the Tour of Lombardy (the so-called 'Race of the Falling Leaves'). It was the epoch of woollen jerseys and shorts, gear shifts on the down tube, leather shoes with sole plates and toe clips. Lycra, aerodynamics and technology have transformed the sport, but if swamping it with money has shifted the balance of interest from sponsors who backed it because they loved cycle racing to more cynical commercial operators who don't care one way or another about the *sport* in contrast with advertising opportunity, the characteristics of the real champions – past and present – remain unaffected. These are the men who love the bike and love racing, whose idea of burn-out is physical exhaustion which only a natural exuberance can remedy. How old-fashioned it sounds.

Hoban's *palmarès* include eight stage wins in the Tour de France, two in the Vuelta, third place in the 1974 Points competition, second in the 1967 Paris-Tours autumn classic (by half a wheel to the great Rik Van Looy), and a mighty triumph in the 1974 Ghent–Wevelgem when he outsprinted Merckx and Roger de Vlaeminck, two of the finest one-day riders around. He rode 12 Tours de France altogether, abandoned once (in 1970) and speaks, still, with passion about bike racing. Fair tribute to the passion he showed on the bike.

7. CYRILLE GUIMARD

In 1972, Cyrille Guimard rode his third Tour de France. He was winner of the first stage in 1970 (seventh overall), second in the green jersey Points competition and fifth in the Mountains prize in 1971 (a year when he came third in both the Tour des Flandres and the World's Road Race) – he was clearly a rider of huge promise. His team leader, Poulidor, had beaten Merckx in the Paris–Nice and the French combine were in threatening mood. Guimard zipped into the first stage with the ferocity of the Cannibal himself: he took points on every small climb, contested all the Hot Spot sprints, won the stage and took the yellow jersey. Merckx's Moltenis won the team time on stage three and with it the yellow, but Guimard was in rampant form. On stage four a violent crosswind split the field and an élite bunch of 20 riders went clear, Guimard with them. Poulidor and several other fancied riders were dropped. Guimard took the sprint and regained the overall lead; Poulidor went down by three minutes. Guimard surrendered the yellow to Merckx in the Pyrenees but was still hard on his wheel when the race entered the Alps; Guimard was now in green. This was astonishing. Merckx had never yet been so hotly chased in the Tour. Guimard, a former champion of France on the track, cyclo-cross and road race, was demonstrating a versatility which matched that of the merciless Belgian – to whom the very notion of letting anyone else win, if he could help it, was anathema. All the illustrious names fell away in the stage over the Izoard, but Guimard stayed with Merckx until almost the last. The next day, in a split stage over the Galibier, Merckx took the morning and Guimard the afternoon.

Jacques Goddet said of the young rider from Nantes: 'I have the impression that we are witnessing the blossoming of a very modern champion, capable of applying a consummate intelligence in adapting his powers and his technique to the varying requirements of the race as it unfolds. He wears both the white jersey (as best young rider) and the yellow. He stayed with the flat-stage riders after the Prologue, took the

Hot Spot points for the day and the six seconds bonus with it; he was second and first over the two climbs of the day and won the combativity prize.'

On the stage up to Mont Ventoux came the first warning: Guimard's knee began to hurt badly and he could not hold the pace. In the mountains he had fitted extra-long pedal cranks so as to match Merckx's furious accelerations, and the added torque had put his muscles and ligaments under crucial stress. The doctors diagnosed tendinitis, a common ailment with professional cyclists. But Guimard was disinclined to be put off. He won the next stage, a flat-out race up the steep, twisting ascent to Le Revard, (28 km and over 1,300 m climbing to 1,537 m). Nearing the line, Merckx lifted his right arm in triumph, but Guimard was still coming and took the win by a centimetre. Behind them, his face creased with the effort of leading most of the way, came a man who was to figure largely in Guimard's career: Lucien Van Impe.

But Guimard had taken his last stage win in the Tour de France.

Both knees were now so painful he could hardly walk. He spent the rest day in bed, could not even get up for meals, and had to be carried down to the next start in a chair. Both the team masseur and the *soigneur*, a former amateur track rider, known as a bit of a witch doctor, were in constant attendance. Guimard's tendinitis was now reckoned to be hydroarthrosis, what used to be called the dropsy, a morbid accumulation of fluid in the serous cavities of the connective tissues; otherwise known as 'fluid on the knee'. His *soigneur* administered injections of xylocaine and novocaine, anaesthetics which would give him up to around 90 minutes pain relief. He climbed into the saddle and rode on.

The chemist who gave me the low-down on these two brand-name drugs remarked: 'Enough to keep a cheating cyclist going.' The day before, he had sold me extra-strength Ibruprofen tablets to mask the extreme pain in my right elbow so I could resume work at the computer. Is there a difference? I don't think so.

Guimard lasted two more days: he was in green still, Paris wasn't far — if only he could hang on. But 10 km from the start on stage 18, the agony was unbearable. He collapsed in tears; his Tour was over. He came to the start of the last run into Paris and, marking the extraordinary courage and brilliance of his ride, Merckx made him a present of the green jersey he had so narrowly failed to win overall.

He came back later that year to take bronze in the World's Road Race and second in the Tour of Lombardy. In 1973, he finished second in the marathon Bordeaux–Paris and started the Tour but did not finish. He was increasingly hampered by the troublesome knee, though his drive was unchecked. He rode his last races, in cyclo-cross, in January 1976, taking the French championship and, two weeks later, fourth in the World's Cyclo-Cross. It was not a bad way to go out as a rider, but he had already signed a contract as *directeur sportif* of the French Gitane–Campagnolo team.

Guimard's quandary had been a common one: if he could keep going by temporary cure, he might squeeze what he could out of an anyway necessarily limited career. An operation would cost invaluable time and, besides, might prove no more satisfactory. However he decided (or his body decided for him) that he could not continue and, in 1975, underwent extensive tests which showed that for six years he had been unwittingly riding with a broken knee cap.

A car had knocked him off his bike on a training ride in 1969; he had sustained severe injuries to his face and head and had been in a coma for ten days. Perhaps unsurprisingly, no one had thought to check his knees. Nor had he considered the possibility of lasting injury there; the pain only ever affected the inflamed cartilages, a pain which transferred to the tendons but never into the joint itself.

The hidden damage had been exacerbated by neglect and his riding career, a career bursting with promise from the start, had survived by sheer force of will, but was now over. But another dazzling career was about to begin. The leader of his team (to whose ranks had also been recruited the second-year pro Bernard Hinault) was Lucien Van Impe.

What followed is up there, in my view, with the best examples of the trade of a superior *directeur sportif.* It is never easy to understand why a richly-talented athlete who can drive himself to extremes in one sphere of his sport holds off from pursuit of the ultimate prize. Van Impe was one such. As Guimard put it, Van Impe slept through all the early flat stages of the Tour and woke up only when he saw a sign reading GPM (Grand Prix des Montagnes). If another rider escaped, who cared? So long as the polka-dot jersey was safe, placing on the overall classification didn't matter. It's odd to think of racing up mountains as constituting a cushy ride in the Tour de France, but given Van Impe's capabilities, that's what it was. Other climbers nursed a similar disinclination. Charly Gaul, the 'Angel of the Mountains', a climber of peerless ability, might well have won the 1956 Tour de France but, in the words of Brian Robinson, rode the first part of the race 'like a novice' and settled for the Mountains prize. There was also Federico Bahamontes, the 'Eagle of Toledo', successor to his great rival (sworn enemy) in Spain, Jesús Loroño, winner of the GPM in 1953. Bahamontes won the Mountains prize six times between 1954 and 1964, but in his first Tour, aged 26, he raced to the cols so far out of reach of the rest none could follow him, but then freewheeled down the other side, because descending terrified him. On the summit of the Romeyre, in the Dauphiné, he dismounted, bought an ice cream from a roadside stall, sat with his legs drawn up in a drainage ditch and ate it – *tranquilo* – till the rest toiled up. This cavalier attitude was imbued with the kind of hauteur and showmanship the Spanish admire in their toreros. When the others did arrive, Bahamontes sprayed them with water, ribbed them in colloquial Spanish and hopped back onto his bike.

Stan Ockers said of him: 'He's a phenomenon in the mountains, he drops us as he chooses'. Loroño agreed: 'Yes, he's a fine climber but he's completely crazy, *loco para atar*' (crazy enough to be tied up).

The Spanish actually esteemed the Mountains Prize more highly than the overall win. It was the seal of real courage, the mark of a rider with superior passion, flair, strength and daring in the arena that all riders fear most. Bahamontes was extravagantly fêted. He did take overall yellow in 1959, largely because the French riders were in disarray. The year before, Bobet, winner 1953–55, declared that he would ride for Raphaël Géminiani, the Big Gun, for a rival team, but the alliance came to grief in what Géminiani saw as treachery ('You are all Judases') and he lost the Tour to Charly Gaul. Once more, despite a so-called *entente cordiale* amongst Bobet, Géminiani, Anquetil and the brilliant newcomer Roger Rivière, the alliance was brittle. Conflicting loyalties reduced the French attack and Bahamontes almost had no choice but to win.

Such was not the case with Van Impe in 1976.

Guimard had only four months to prepare his team for the Tour. He was, however, convinced that the diminutive Belgian climber, a timid, percentage rider, had the necessary physical qualities to win overall. Whether he could be convinced of this himself was another matter. His approach had always been pragmatic. He based his entire season on winning the GPM to ensure a lucrative round of post-Tour criteriums, with big start money for a star of the Grande Boucle. To try for the overall win would jeopardise his success in the second competition. If he lost both, his season would effectively be squandered. Guimard put it to him bluntly: 'Sometimes in your life you have to take risks.' And it was a *large* risk. Van Impe was no time-trialler; his strategy for the race would have to be radically changed. Indeed, there was a certain restraint in his character, a lack of self-belief, of imagination – which galled Merckx for instance. In the Pyrenees during the 1972 Tour, Van Impe, supported by his *directeur sportif* of the time, attacked Merckx. Merckx quashed the attempt and reproached him: 'You never work with me, or anyone, but you sneak off. From now on, I'm going to stay on your wheel and you won't shake me off.'

What Guimard had to do, then, was steel Van Impe's nerve for the merciless exposure he would have to endure and surmount as leader. The first man to claim to have worn the yellow jersey, Philippe Thys in 1913, at first refused this 'gimmick' because it would make him a target for every other rider – and he was right. In 1924, everyone thought Bottechia, the leader, had gone missing one day in the Alps because there was no sign of that yellow jersey. But he'd changed jerseys, knowing that the Italian fans would mob him and cost him the race.

A leader has to be attentive every single day of the race; the weight of expectation on the leader is enormous, he must support a huge responsibility to and for his team. Guimard rolled the 'r' of *responsabilité* with the force of a flamenco dancer's heel drumming the wooden floor. It's easy, for instance, to be a worker, a *domestique*. You have a job, and that is to work hard. Simple. You work hard and you get results. But to take decisions for the workers is very different. That is the added burden of responsibility and it requires great mental strength, a transcendent self-belief. To men like Merckx, Hinault, Fignon, this came naturally. They were, from earliest years, *chefs chez eux*. Even in the playground at school, they were men who knew what they wanted to do. Others prefer to be told, to take orders; to be unaccountable. Such men lack natural authority and the pressure of being required to assume it can have a perverse effect. Guimard quoted the case of Charly Mottet: a wonderful talent paralysed by the weight of leadership. There are plenty of other examples around.

Guimard shares with Eric Cantona a penchant for queer analogy. 'When you are free,' he said, (meaning free of responsibility) 'the river runs and you can pick out a fish whenever you choose. Responsibility demands that you master both the river and the fish in it.' That was something Van Impe shied away from. 'He did not want it but I won, as Manager, the moment he accepted the responsibility of going for the overall win.'

It was, however, no easy task. He had to force Van Impe's nature. 'I don't choose to say that it was *amicale* (friendly) because when you force someone's nature you force him into a different system and in doing that you violate some deep part in him and that violence on the psychological plane is difficult to support or be friendly about. I got him to win the Tour but any more would probably have been impossible. He didn't have the mental structure. His nature was to keep out of trouble, to avoid cares or responsibility.' There is, in that last sentence, the unspoken word 'shirk'. And indeed, after the first win Van Impe relaxed again; he had his marshal's baton. That is how the French put it: ambition's supreme goal achieved.

The conditioning of Van Impe's psychology began in the season's early racing where Guimard persuaded him to ride with an unwonted self-assurance to establish his authority – an authority which was limited by his personality but which was aimed at building an ambition to get more out of himself. The encouragement was already there: he had, against all expectation, won the individual mountain time-trial Morzine–Chatel in the 1975 Tour. The race against the clock had never suited him: too exposed, too hard on mind and body. Third place on the podium in Paris behind Thévenet and Merckx showed what he might do if he cared to listen to the uncompromising insistence of Guimard: that he was ducking his real potential. With a bit more aggression and the ruthlessness with oneself which overrides doubt and renders fear irrelevant, he could win the big prize, to hell with the risk. Alongside him in Gitane colours rode a man to whom the very idea of shirking risk was laughable – Hinault, who had been clocking up a flow of victories: Grand Prix de Chardonnay, Circuit de la Sarthe, Paris–Camembert, Tour d'Indre-et-Loire . . . who knows what subliminal aid that gave to Guimard's hardening of Van Impe's soul? Van Impe certainly began to reveal a new self. He stole victory in the Polymultipliée (significantly, a race against the clock), fifth in the Dauphiné Libéré (a traditional warm-up for the Tour), second in the Trophée des Grimpeurs à Sérénac; in each race behind Thévenet, the '75 Tour winner. Was this a true metamorphosis?

As Guimard told me: 'Van Impe was practically impossible to beat in the mountains. He was a pocket dynamo. But the time-trials were a problem. However, if he had an objective firmly planted in his head, he might succeed.' This had to be a transformation worthy of Svengali: to convince the reticent climbing specialist of the possibility – no more, the *possibility* – of extending his power in the mountains to the rest of the race; to establish his power on terrain where, on past showing, he could not depend on control, to make him *impose* himself. For a man who looked like a schoolboy and stood about as tall as one, imposing himself on the Tour de France was going to be monumentally difficult. It's fair to say that many of the big men in the *peloton* shrank from the 'all-or-nothing' attitude to sacrifice which is the hallmark of the champion. Ambition comes in all weights. Failure lives on excuses and men who too often pursue small things generally become incapable of great things.

But although he was mostly written off as an outsider and no real contender for final yellow, there were signs that Guimard had indeed shifted his attitude. For a month before the race, he did everything – eat, train, go to bed – an hour later than usual, so that when he crossed into France, an hour ahead, his body rhythms would be perfectly adjusted.

Guimard is one of those exceptional readers of strategy and mental state who thinks of everything. It is not difficult though, to see how Van Impe must have flinched. Guimard was three months younger; of an explosive, ebullient temperament; a hard-headed, stubborn Breton who thought a lot of himself and made excessive demands in proportion. He was a superlative competitor, a racer by instinct. Van Impe had none of that. Questioned about him, Guimard replied: 'Let's say that he's rather cautious, he won't take tactical initiative, he doesn't really understand racing.' And this was the rider he was pushing to win the Tour de France. Initiative, responsibility, obligation were the key. If the team were prepared to ride with total commitment to Van Impe, he must be equally prepared to answer an absolute obligation to them. The big prize they could all share in; the lesser prize would be his alone. That was the choice. Therein lay the mutual contract and the individual onus of leadership.

The decisive stage, 14, took the riders over four climbs between St Gaudens and St-Lary Soulan in the Pyrenees. Van Impe lay second, closely challenged by the Dutchman Zoetemelk. Thévenet was suffering and had little left. In yellow, the Frenchman Raymond Delisle (at 33 very experienced but no serious contender for the victory) was making the most of a fairly tame resistance to his lead.

Col de Mente, 35 km. Van Impe dithering, seeking shelter with his team-mates, apparently waiting for someone else to make a move. Zoetemelk and his team-mate the veteran ace Poulidor start talking: the Belgian is looking uncomfortable. Nevertheless, he takes the prime at the col and then settles back into the bunch. Let the others attack and wear themselves out: he'll spring his effort on the last climb of the day to the ski station at Pla-d'Adet. Guimard wants more out of him. This is going to be the turning point – to push Van Impe beyond his fear of making an effort he cannot sustain, of expending so much energy and strength that he has none left and blows everything. Fear is the crucial obstacle.

On the second climb, the col du Portillon which takes the race on a brief excursion into Spain, the Spaniard Luis Ocaña (winner in 1973) attacked and, with four others, built a lead of around three minutes. Behind him, Van Impe's Belgian team-mate René Dillen, was ferrying water and a message from Guimard in the team car for his leader: 'Guimard says attack.'

Seventy-five km to go over two first category climbs? 'He's crazy.'

Raymond Martin arrives with another message: 'Guimard says attack now.'

'If he wants me to attack he can tell me himself.'

When Guimard arrived in the car, racing up the side of the road, car horn blaring, to spit the ultimatum in Van Impe's face, it was a moment of total shock but there was no escape. Van Impe attacked, riding into a state of mind which he had never explored. He was, surely for the first time, experiencing the will to win at a level beyond the calculations of reason to which he had always deferred. His strength did not fail him after all. He reeled in all the breakaways and with Ocaña and the Italian Walter Riccomi, Van Impe embarked on a new rôle: that of a man controlling the race. Zoetemelk had in fact refused an order to attack from his own manager and, by that refusal, lost the Tour. His attack, when it came, clawed back three minutes on his deficit of six minutes – but it was too late. Van Impe launched his intended attack on the final climb, crushed his two companions and pulled on the yellow jersey. He held an overall lead of 3 minutes, 18 seconds; a margin he increased by nearly a minute into Paris. Who can gainsay that it was Guimard's win as much as Van Impe's?

'I got him to win the Tour,' he said, matter of fact. And it was true: a marvel of inculcating self-belief, of overcoming a formidable resistance to the challenge of possibility against impossibility; of the stirring of a majestic leap of imagination – daring to ask 'what if?' and pursue that question with careless energy.

To crown a phenomenally successful début as *directeur sportif,* Guimard saw Hinault win the 1976 Prestige Pernod title, awarded to the French rider who, over the whole season, gained most points in qualifying races.

As a rider, Guimard became a leader quite early on and habitually analysed every race afterwards; from strategy to tactics. It was perfect grounding for his work as a *directeur sportif,* whose reading of the many and varied elements which bear on a team's success is crucial: the character, capability, and mental state of his own riders and their rivals;

the nature of a course; the overall plan for the season; objectives and tolerances; technical matters – all the fundamentals, nothing overlooked. One thing Guimard discounts totally from his responsibility is motivation – which, given the Van Impe story, might seem odd. However what Guimard did there was more to root out what might be seen as a fairly complacent rider's innate *demotivation*. A professional who has to worry about motivation is no professional. Motivation comes with the job. As Noel Coward said irritably to the fumbling actor who couldn't identify his motivation for a particular move on stage: 'Your motivation is the cheque at the end of the week, now get on with it.'

Brian Robinson recalled how his first *directeur sportif*, Raymond Louviot (Tours in '34 and '39, two stage wins) would drive up in the car, lean out and say: 'Come on, what are you doing?' and drive off. Do nothing and you lose. No win, no money.

Demotivation, though, is another matter. It is a nagging illness caused by failed confidence, nagging injury, lost form or perceived neglect within the team . . . it is on these things a manager has to concentrate. His total concern must be to do nothing that can fracture morale; one misplaced word can break someone. Each rider must discover in himself why he is a racing cyclist and what drives him. Motivation cannot be learnt, inculcated, fudged or pretended. It is the radical core, the basic famine of any true professional in any field.

Guimard concluded quite soon that the most important factor in establishing a strong team was not the riders themselves but the structure within which they had to work. Moreover, one had to mould a team in which each rider could exploit the highest of his own potential. He never bought a star; his philosophy was to recruit young riders from the amateur ranks and to form, educate and then train them. Some of his riders may not have been as individually strong as others but the system in which they rode realised more of their potential; the dynamic of the group drew more out of the individuals. When he was interested in a young rider, he visited him at home to spend a few days with him, meet his parents and the president of the cycling club. If the lad lived on a farm he'd talk about cows. They could talk about cycling later. Above all he wanted to *sentir* the man; get a sense of him, sniff out what made him tick – his environment, his culture; his personality, mentality and background. This was at the time a revolutionary approach; based in human management. 'I won races through human management of men' he said, 'not by telling them "You're strong, just roll".'

Perhaps his most famous recruit was Greg Lemond. (As scout for

Cofidis, he spotted Lance Armstrong, before his cancer, and latterly, David Millar.) In 1980, Lemond – an amateur, world junior champion at the time – won the Circuit de la Sarthe, racing against pros and Guimard, now managing the Renault team, had come to watch him in the Ruban de Granatier Breton, an open stage race in Britanny. He'd finished second in two stages and was within easy strike of the lead overall. Two Russians had attacked. Lemond gave chase, gained five minutes on the chasing pack, and was about to rejoin the breakaways when he punctured. The French mechanic looking after his team had pulled off the road for a nap. Lemond continued on the flat tyre and rode 10 km before the mechanic arrived. The race radio kept calling for Lemond's car so Guimard, who was following the race with one of the officials, decided to drive up and see what was going on. The break was out of reach down the road, the bunch were about 30 seconds away, there was no chance of Lemond getting back. The mechanic insisted he could still get third, at which point Lemond threw his bike at the team car; then he threw it on the grass at the side of the road. When he might have won, third was *nowhere*. Guimard observed this and decided to approach the American after the race. Someone asked him: 'You want a racer like that?'

'No; I want him – he's got character,' Guimard replied.

Guimard saw in Lemond that violent need to win; an aggression, an edge that is logical and normal in a champion. He was, simply, *un tueur*: a rider with a killer instinct.

'If someone tells me they've found a marvellous rider, no temperament, I say: "Is he *un tueur?*" And if they say "No, never any problem with him, he's so easy to direct." I tell them to forget it. I want a rider whom I can work on, someone who agrees with me and then says ". . . but . . ." Just "yes" makes me laugh.'

Guimard approached Lemond after the race and told him he was interested in him – only there'd be no more hurling bikes around.

Guimard went out to America to see where Lemond lived, to meet his family, go to the school he attended – everything to understand what was normal for him at home, because transplanting him to Europe would inevitably pose all kinds of challenges. Homesickness, a completely alien culture, and the shock of entering the pro ranks: all of these might hamper his ability to acquit himself well in the rigours of the job.

Speaking of his first season as team director at Gitane, Guimard said at the time:

There has been a lot of envy, a lot of criticism, much of it from certain *directeurs sportifs*. I think what upset them most is that we have refused to do things their way. In my opinion, their system is the reason why French pro cycling is in such a sorry state, the reason why we are not winning anything at international level. When you refuse to join a system it's obvious you're going to run into a number of barriers, and offend a certain number of people who don't want things to change. That's exactly what I do want, to change things. At the same time, it was inevitable that, as soon as we started to win races with a 'little team', people would be jealous. That's entirely in the logic of things.

The old system to which Guimard refers was of the strict hierarchical style. The Manager would say to the rider: 'Just race and we'll talk about things later . . . ' No decisions shared or explained, orders given without reason, every rider lumped in with every other rider. That was not enough for riders of ambition with a drive to set objectives, to plan a season and a career. Bernard Hinault, for example. Guimard had watched him race as an amateur at the curtain-raiser race before a pro criterium in St-Brieuc. He attacked from the start, lapped the field and effectively stunned the opposition. Guimard was impressed at his fellow Breton's *fougue* – his fire, aggression and energy. He turned pro soon after and Guimard came to see him at a late season race, Blois–Chaville, in October 1975 to persuade him not to leave the Gitane team since the likelihood was that he would be taking it over. (Hinault was contemplating a move to Poulidor's team: it would have been a disaster. Hinault was never a rider to play second fiddle to anyone, however grand.)

Hinault was temperamentally unsuited to the old style of management; the approach of a fellow Breton promised a real partnership and he agreed. Guimard contributed a precious ingredient to the career of a rider who might seem to need no advice in the matter of racing: the man was a racer to his core. But it was Guimard's understanding of Hinault's character which helped mould him. 'When we enter the Tour' he told him in 1976, 'it will be to win it' – and he kept his promise. Essentially, though, his concern was not to rush things, not to take too much on in the early phase. As Hinault put it, a career resembles a classic day race: go too hard too early and you blow everything. Guimard's approach promised proper nurture and full liaison, a genuine bond between rider and director.

'All riders are different,' Guimard said. 'They need to be treated in different ways. It's no good telling them all to do the same thing, that's ridiculous. You must make a careful study of each rider and tailor your demands of them to their needs and feelings. One day I was with a *directeur sportif*, (I can't remember which) and – all the riders have earpieces now – he gave his team an order; the whole team, the same order. Then all the other teams got the same order. Nothing can happen from that. If you give an order that doesn't conform to the rest, then you can win . . . so long as it works, of course!' and he laughed.

Guimard had Hinault's backing in the shaping of the team's *collectivité*. He suggested that the riders should swap room-mates in rotation, so that every member of the team got to know the others. This didn't stand in the way of friendships, but it would impede the forming of cliques.

I met Guimard in the bar of the Véloclub de Roubaix where, an hour before, Jan Museeuw rode into the *vélodrome* and, as he crossed the line for victory, held up his knee, symbolically. He had injured it badly two years earlier and nearly succumbed to gangrene and he was signalling his amazing return not only to the bike, but to the top with a win over the *pavé* of 'the Hell of the North' (Paris–Roubaix). It seemed entirely appropriate that I should be talking here to another fine rider whose racing career was so impaired – and finally truncated – by damage to a knee. A small coincidence maybe, but a reminder of what courage many of these riders show in surviving and reversing circumstances which threaten their already necessarily limited life as a professional cyclist.

Frank Bruno once said to his trainer, George Francis: 'George, when you die, will you leave me your experience?'

In Guimard I encountered an extraordinary astuteness about the complexities of bike racing. As a rider he had a reputation far from endearing to the authorities, for his frank speech and forthright opinion. A passionate champion of the riders' cause, his language was vehement and uncompromising in attacking directors and officials more concerned about protecting their own interests than those of cycling and the cyclists. Not a comfortable man to be around maybe, if comfort is what you're after, but that never made a champion – and Guimard had a remarkable way of grooming champions.

8. EDDY MERCKX

'A life without passion is a life empty of meaning.' Eddy Merckx

They called him 'the Tamburlaine of the pedals' (Tamburlaine was an archetypal murderous Tartar), 'Beethoven of the Big Ring', '*Sauvage*' (the Savage), 'Wild Man', 'the Executioner on a Bicycle' and, most notoriously, 'the Cannibal'.

Journalistic self-indulgence. What matters is what you do on the bike, and what *he* did on the bike has never been surpassed, not even matched. He was sphinx-like, impenetrable and yet a man of extreme sensitivity. He was withdrawn, guarded: his one defence against the pressure, the isolation of being number one. He feared and mistrusted journalists because they lacked respect and mostly got it wrong; any exaggeration for the sake of a story. 'Heart of butter' someone said of him – and the French *sauvage* also means 'shy'. That's the Merckx enigma: heartless *on* the bike, soft-boiled off it.

He rarely said much but he knew himself well, the result of forever pushing himself beyond the limits he'd overstepped by risk. When he did speak about himself he spoke with plain direct sense: 'The pressure of popularity often made me retreat within myself. Only on a bicycle did I feel really at ease.'

He started as a boxer and became district junior champion in the suburb of Brussels where he grew up and assimilated an important lesson about *winning*: the spontaneous habit of *le punch*. In the four corners of truth, a boxer who can't punch doesn't win and the attacking spirit runs through Merckx's career like fire down a fuse, an instinct shaped into a compulsion. He even came to describe the natural ferocity of his unflagging readiness to take on the rest of the *peloton* as a 'religion of attack'.

He idolised the local star Stan Ockers; Fausto Coppi was the god, cycling was the sport. He was (and remained) a capable footballer, but cycling it had to be and after the first victory in 1961 the boyish grin cracked wide. Whenever that grin did break, (albeit rarely except on the finishing line, he once remarked that he never really enjoyed the business until the race was over) even after the truckload of professional wins, it seemed always lit with an unspoilt enthusiasm completely at odds with the hard world he dominated. His mother tried to cool his ambition; bike racing was too dangerous, a professional career too chancy. But another win in Hals in 1962 persuaded her at last that, like him, she had no option. He swapped play on the streets where he'd always been happiest for work on the road.

Selected to ride for the Belgian team, Merckx underwent the routine prescribed tests. The doctor's report showed anomalies in his heart rhythm; his selection was blocked. Jenny Merckx, clearly the big puncher in the household and as redoubtable a supporter of her son as she had been his spirit of dissuasion, was having none of that. 'Eddy's heart is as solid as his father's' she told them and, the gold medal later, the Belgian team manager sent her a telegram of congratulations: 'Happily we followed your advice.'

Merckx turned pro with Peugeot and in his first season (1965) came under the sage influence of the man who rode into the rainbow jersey later that year: Tom Simpson. Older pros aren't notably generous to newcomers in the *peloton* – it's a tough *métier*: best the novice should learn how to take a kicking early, or get out and not waste space. But to a newcomer bursting with talent and impatient to cut a swathe, help or advice can be like towing a climber to the foot of the mountain. Merckx always acknowledged the large debt he owed Simpson – a debt Simpson was handing on from what he in turn owed Robinson and Robinson owed Barone, and so on and so on by generation. A camera caught a moving picture of him in his second Tour riding up through the Ventoux furnace and doffing his cap as he passed his old boss's memorial placed above the road where he fell.

Like all débutants, Merckx hit the wall early. In his first major race, the Flèche–Wallonne in '65 he punctured and wasted himself getting back on, sunk by a poisonous cocktail of adrenaline, oxygen debt and lactic acid, and he had to abandon. Inevitably he wondered: 'How am I going to live with this lot?' (Boardman records an identical experience.) However, a year later he took the first of his record seven wins in the Milan–San Remo, the *Primavera*. It was a close thing. He launched his sprint from ruinously far out and had to hang on by his toenails against the challenge of Durante into a photo-finish. This showed his lack of experience; but you learn from mistakes, especially mistakes confused with success, and in the *peloton* you learn fast or you're off the back never to catch up. Besides, caution was never in Merckx's vocabulary; like Nelson his principle was 'Never mind manoeuvres – go at 'em,' but to rely on raw talent without racing intelligence is like riding on an empty stomach. If he never cared much for 'tactics' (the fancy word for caution) Merckx tempered himself into a rider totally immune to the psych and kidology that can unhinge even great riders. No one in the bunch could interpret that famous mask of impassivity. They never knew how Merckx was feeling; only that he was shredding them. Moreover, he never let up – on them or himself. On the sixth stage of the 1972 Giro d'Italia, a journalist mounted a bike, mingled with the riders and conducted a few off-the-cuff interviews. One of them, Tosello, grabbed the microphone, rode up alongside Merckx, already in the leader's pink jersey but still attacking like a fury, irrepressibly, day after day and said:

'You're nearly home and dry, why not give the rest of us a chance?'

Merckx smiled and said – in Italian – as if it were a gentle message of condolence: 'You can say what you like . . . I'm indifferent.'

With him it always was *à l'outrance*: ride to win or don't ride at all.

In the 1967 Paris–Nice, the first stage race of the season, the Race to the Sun, he took an early stage and the leader's white jersey. This was allowable: he could keep it warm for Simpson and take the early burdens of leadership. Simpson duly attacked over the col de la République near Lyon and took over the lead. Two days later, Merckx was off again, and it took a visit from Gaston Plaud in the team car to remind the hothead of team responsibilities. Merckx sat up, waited for the patron and relayed him 25 km to the stage finish and overall victory. If Merckx's apprenticeship was brief it was, nevertheless, part of the professional duty he signed to.

That season, Merckx emerged as a classic one-day rider: he took a second Milan–San Remo then the Belgian classics Gand–Wevelgem and Flèche–Wallonne in front of the home crowd. On the long road to San Remo he attacked, in company with the Italian Gianni Motta, who offered him a sizeable amount of money to help him to win the race. Merckx demurred. Motta went from one million lire up to six million but still Merckx refused. His reaction was always the same: 'When riders made me offers like that, I just pushed harder on the pedals.' The Italian riders were notoriously prone to in-the-saddle bargaining but, as 'the Gipsy' Roger de Vlaeminck, a great one-day rival of his once remarked: 'True champions sometimes buy a victory, they never sell a race.'

This exchange with Motta was perhaps Merckx's first taste of an undoubted fact (then, at least) that there is pro cycling, and there is Italy. He rode his first Giro that summer, as *domestique* to Roger Pingeon, who went on to win that year's Tour de France, and saw how they did things there: riders taking pushes from the *tifosi* like skiers on button lifts, or else hanging onto car doors for kilometres at a time. (Riding in the BigMat team car up a steep short climb during the Tour Down Under, we passed a Belgian riding for the Italian Saeco team: he reached out and grabbed my window post with barely a sideways glance.) Merckx confesses that he took a push on the climb up Mount Etna. The act of a cheat or a 21-year-old-pro wising up? He never took pushes after that . . . unless it was from team men, on the flat while taking a pee.

He won two stages of that Giro and, nearing Milan, was handily placed third. Then, on the big stage over the Paso di Tonale, his strength leaked away; he was seeing all the colours of the rainbow but clung on and reached the finish happy enough, ninth overall. 'I began to think that I had some future in this kind of race' he said – an understatement that rumbles like the faint thunder of an approaching electric storm.

The switch to an Italian team marks the flowering of the mature Merckx. He'd been ready to join Ford and ride with Anquetil and his alter ego Raphaël Géminiani – a twilight dream partnership that must surely have ended in a nightmarish clash of temperament and interest. For Merckx had already emerged as what Henri Desgrange termed a 'first fiddle', a leader unsuited to any subordinate role.

Instead, a Belgian businessman and former six-day rider Jean van Buggenhout persuaded him (encountering little resistance) that it was time for Merckx to be Merckx and assume his own natural authority and power. The new outfit Faema, based in Italy, brought him into contact with Coppi's legacy: the sophisticated training régime, diet and analysis, which had revolutionised cycle racing. Immediately after the War, Coppi introduced scientific method. It was no longer enough just to ride the bike as hard as you could for as long as you could. This was uncouth, a fairground booth slugger's mentality. Coppi elevated cycling by refinement of effort, preparation and strategy. Sadly, as elegant a cycle racer as Coppi was, he was forced – by alimony claims, of all things – to become more of a fairground performer. He signed up for endless contracts to be honoured way after the money he earned from them had been spent.

If Merckx was never what anyone could call an elegant rider, there is no question that he quickly became a racer of ruthless efficiency. His mentor, Adorni, gave him advice which might not go down too well today: 'always leave the dinner table a bit hungry', to ease digestion – but he honed the chubby youngster, always prone to putting on weight, to a lean 72 kg – light for a big-boned six-footer. He also found himself riding alongside Adorni's own mentor, Felice Gimondi, a man whom he described as 'the most exemplary, the most professional rider I've known' and one of the few men in the pro *peloton* whom he came to regard as a friend, or as he himself defined it: 'someone who occupies a small part of your heart.' In the snake-pit of sport there are few enough of them, where caginess if not rivalrous envy is the more usual currency of acquaintance.

The dividends of the Italian job showed at once: he began to climb like a specialist and in the Giro that year, he said, 'I wasn't riding, I was flying.' After only 30 km of the landmark Lavaredo stage, he had ridden all the genuine opposition off his wheel and blasted on to that victory and, unchallenged, the overall one. The Italians must have begun to have serious, *patriotic* doubts about this killer whom they'd unwittingly nurtured and let loose on their roads: a man self-evidently set on a personal mission to crowd-in with the titans of their own mythology: *Campionissimo* Coppi, Gino 'the Pious' Bartali, Learco 'the Locomotive' Guerra, and 'Signor Giro' himself, Alfredo Binda.

In the 1969 spring races, Merckx had shown masterly form, he hardly felt the pedals. He took his first Paris–Nice. In the Milan–San Remo, a gammy knee was giving him bad gyp. At the foot of the famous Poggio hill, so often a launch pad for the decisive break into the fast run down to the finish, he very nearly dropped out, but by the summit the pain had knuckled under to the will-power: a third victory, followed by a staggering clutch of wins – Tour des Flandres, Liège–Bastogne–Liège, Gand–Wevelgem, and the second Paris–Roubaix, all in succession.

A month or so later he went south to Italy as reigning champion of the national tour.

Polidori took stage one and on stage nine surrendered the leader's *maglia rosa* to Merckx, already winner of one road stage and a time-trial. A brief loan of it elsewhere merely delayed the assertion of his full *seigneurial* rights on stage 15: an imperious display of power in the individual 49 km time-trial. There then followed a rest day.

Sunday 1 June, Parma to Savone. Results of the routine dope test, published *16 hours* after the control, revealed traces of a stimulant, Reactivan, in Merckx's urine. The doctor who broke the news to him was embarrassed, apologetic: 'I know you are innocent but there is nothing I can do.' Merckx was out of the race. It was a brutal shock. This was a moral catastrophe of stunning proportion.

'It was the worst injustice of my career' he said, 'the sky had fallen in on my head.' He was inconsolable; he wept. Remonstrations at the highest diplomatic level flew from Brussels to Rome; furious questions were tabled in the Belgian parliament. The affair very nearly drove Merckx to give up what was central to his life.

'The trouble with Eddy is that he has been vaccinated with a cycle spoke' his wife Claudine once said. 'A few days without cycling and nothing works.'

It is an unhappy image in the circumstances yet, if we cannot believe without cynicism in the pure love of the bike and the passion for cycling – even today, even among top riders – what future is there in the sport?

As Mark Twain said: 'A man has no business getting depressed about reversal, he ought to be making up his mind to get even.' To the 7,000 letters of support he received after his elimination from the Giro, Merckx sent picture postcards of thanks, concluding: 'I will do everything in my power to maintain your confidence.'

For all his rage to win *on* the bike, Merckx is a mild-mannered man; he has always comported himself decently, with (perhaps chilly) reserve. He explains that diffidence as a wariness which his maladroitness with words could not dispel. Brought up in a bilingual culture (French and Flemish) he was never wholly sure of himself in either language. He was even pilloried for being a snob, talking French when Flemish would have been expected. Against such moronic criticism no one is immune. The press frequently, if not always mischievously, misinterpreted him. Increasingly he fended off their intrusions and learned to clam up so as to protect himself. (How different from the garrulous disclaiming of the monoglot Americans.) Above all, Merckx conducted himself with dignity. For example, when an irate French fan sprang out of the crowd on the Puy de Dôme in 1975, when he lost his first Tour and charges were pressed by the police, Merckx demanded only a symbolic one franc in damages. Even in the language he used ('this most beautiful race in the world' he called the Tour de France) Merckx clearly saw himself as heir to a *noble* tradition of cycle sport, to use an unashamedly *enthusiastic* expression in these downtrodden, suspicious times. He revered the men he sought to emulate. Overtaking Jacques Anquetil in a time-trial in the 1969 Paris–Nice he perceived that the *Maître* was clearly in all sorts of distress and could not bear to catch his eye: he respected the great rider too much to risk any triumphalism.

To the insults and injuries he himself endured (and there were plenty – *Merckxisme* was no joke in France; the Italians were flagrant about protection fees payable for victory on their roads; and even some Belgian fans were choked by his apparent disdain for their need to drain more from him than he gave: '*Do you think you're God?*' they'd say) Merckx acted impervious, even if he wasn't, and simply masked the wound. He defied convention, living up to his own expectations of himself and not other people's, treating Kipling's two impostors, Triumph and Disaster, just the same. As a man and as an athlete, he placed the highest premium on integrity, being correct, honest, so he could look at himself in the mirror. His wife said: 'He was driven by a very personal inner force. He didn't look for glory. He wanted simply to be at peace with himself.'

It's odd to think of the hardest race of them all as 'beautiful' and only the most dedicated will recognise in it an arena in which to seek out private tranquillity. Yet it's quite common among the men for whom the Tour de France is *the* ultimate challenge, to say that going into it is like entering a monastery: on those who seek to win it, it enforces a total seclusion of mind and body. Antonin Magne actually accused Poulidor of shirking the eremitic sacrifice necessary to harden himself properly. Bad luck was one thing, slack preparation quite another.

I make no apology for what may seem, in the foregoing paragraphs, a rather sepia-tinted view. Not all opinions have to be drug-related and overlaid with cold turkey.

Like all the great champions, notably his friend Kelly, Merckx was never less than 100 per cent motivated, but after the Giro debacle, weeks away from his first Tour de France, we can only guess at the fury of competitive rage he had chewing at him. He had never exteriorised his emotions; his parents had taught him early to put up and shut up. If his bike had to do the talking for him, there was quite an oration on the way.

A doctor informed him before the Tour set out from Roubaix that he had the heart of a cardiac patient: 38 pulses per minute pumping blood out of an oversize tank, and that normal medical advice would be to rest for at least a fortnight. Touching to think of a doctor examining Tour riders and using the homely word *normal.*

Merckx took yellow after the 8 km team time-trial on home turf round Woluwe St Pierre and on the seventh stage he launched the first real show of force, up the Ballon d'Alsace (the first mountain ever crossed by the Tour). He jumped from a group containing, amongst other members of the *peloton*'s aristocracy, the winners of the past four Tours;

Poulidor went off the back with a broken pedal, Gimondi (1965) punctured; Luis Ocaña (who won in Merckx's absence in 1973) fell; Jan Janssen (1968), Pingeon (1967), Lucien Aimar (1966) and de Vlaeminck peeled off one by one. Rudi Altig and Ralf Wagtmans hung on but with two weeks yet to ride, they must, each one, have thought this was crazy stuff. More prudent, in the interests of legs and lungs, to leave the madman to it. After the stage, which Merckx won handsomely, the Frenchman Pingeon was dismissive: Merckx's superiority was more apparent than real. Okay, he'd taken minutes out of them on the Ballon but only because they placed no importance on the stage. The serious contenders weren't exerting themselves. The Belgian had buried himself in futile expenditure of effort, pumping up a minor climb into a major obstacle. The rest of them would wait till the Alps to see what he was *really* made of.

This was the voice of experience but it was fading experience. Merckx said he'd struck hard to probe his rivals' strength and he felt reassured. Indeed, he was simply abiding by the true spirit of Desgrange's original conception of the Tour.

The Tour rode into the Alps where Pingeon set out to show the whippersnapper that the grands of the *peloton* were not windmills he could tilt at with impunity. He slipstreamed him onto the col de la Forclaz – 1,526 m and some piggish gradients – then jumped clear. Every time Merckx caught up, he surged away and he took the stage into Chamonix by a healthy distance and clawed back some time, though not much. He was still five minutes down and the rest of the field was already in rags: Poulidor at nearly 7 minutes, Gimondi and Janssen 7-plus, Altig 10, Hermann Van Springel 12, Aimar 16 . . . but Merckx had looked beatable. He had made a fundamental error in swapping his 175 mm cranks for 177.5 mm. The extra torque was nearly unmanageable and severely limited his capacity to answer Pingeon's sudden accelerations. Then he got stomach cramps. But, as Hinault would say, there was nothing like a bad day to get you back on the bike chafing for action.

Over the cols of High Provence to Aubagne on the coast, only Gimondi could stay with him. Poulidor and the rest ceded a further two minutes. Still Merckx kept piling it on. He widened the gap in the individual time-trial in Revel and the race moved into its last major arena: the Pyrenees. On the col du Portillon, Gimondi finally cracked and Merckx came in clear of Pingeon by eight minutes. The journalists, stumped for any further hyperbole in which to frame such crushing superiority, were as exhausted as the riders. Merckx had squeezed all the dramatic tension out of the race; he was like a gaoler dragging prisoners out of gaol each day to mock and abuse them before kicking them back inside. Barry Hoban put round the joke: 'Did you hear, Gimondi and Poulidor got fined for taking a tow from a lorry. Merckx? Oh, he got fined, too – he was towing the lorry.'

Veterans warned Merckx he was doing far too much; his *directeur sportif* Driessens cautioned him, but Merckx always did what he felt and he was doing exactly what he did best: it wasn't in him to act otherwise.

17TH STAGE: LUCHON–MOURENX

Van den Bossche, Merckx's mountaineer, drove the pace hard over the first climbs of the day, the tiddler cols de Peyresourde and Aspin, and onto the leviathan, the col du Tourmalet. The pace was unforgiving; Gimondi slipped into that purgatory the French call *perdition*. Nearing the col, at 75 km, Janssen and the rest were already cursing their mechanics for not fitting smaller gears, when Merckx changed into 52x17 gears and sprinted for the Mountains points, shouldering past his lead-out man. It was uncharacteristically mean to deny a small rider the gift of a big gesture and Merckx later publicly regretted it. It was prompted by an uncontrollable flash of anger. The night before, Van den Bossche – a rider Merckx valued highly – had told him he'd accepted an offer to join Molteni at the end of the season. Mutual loyalty was crucial not only to Merckx's success but to his code of ethics. Needing the team's absolute confidence – which he repaid with prize money, contracts, equal team pay – Merckx felt let down. Still, no excuse: it was ungenerous, selfish. (He himself later signed for Molteni, an Italian sausage-maker.)

Hitting the descent ahead of the group Merckx went down flat-out. It wasn't a planned attack; prudence, rather, to enjoy a clear line without obstacle. Poulidor shrugged: what was the point in such exertion with 130 km still to ride? Janssen just watched numbly and reported later: 'We couldn't get back to him, we didn't even *want* to any more.'

At the foot of the mountain Merckx, always a reckless descender, had gained three minutes on the chasing bunch – if indeed they were chasing. The air seethed with heat, an angry wasp sting smarted on his wrist; Driessens drove up to tell him to take some food and a breather while the others caught up. A few yards on, the team car broke down and Merckx, eating a slab of rice cake, cruised past alone into the cooler shade of the overhanging gorge of the Gave river. The nobility behind him were probably doing the same; they'd be on him soon. But the road was deserted, nobody came – and then he thought, maybe it was worth trying a long attack to the finish, an exploit to remember 'on such a magnificent mountain stage'.

That incredible solo ride – as much a leap of imagination as of bravado – seemed to spring from a simple exhilaration of riding the bike and having a go, like Bonington swarming up the north face of the Eiger – because he felt ready for it so *why not?*

On over the cols du Soulor and d'Aubisque and the final run home; for the last 20 km that familiar grim sensation – pain everywhere, tongue like a slice of coconut matting, throat dusted with chilli, lungs in a straitjacket – but then the incomparable relief, the bliss of getting off the bloody bike because it was *over*, he'd done it, the crazy challenge . . . *and* he'd pulverised the rest by a further eight minutes.

He rode into the Paris *vélodrome*, his spine tingling, tears in his eyes, to hear the thousands inside chanting his name: he won yellow by 17 minutes 54 seconds *and* green Points jersey *and* the King of the Mountains Prize (a feat never equalled); *plus* the overall team prize. Belgium fêted her first winner in 30 years. King Baudouin sent messages of congratulation and, the day after man's first steps on the moon, the French press were hailing the stupendous victory of this Belgian, this man from the planet Merckx.

After a post-Tour criterium, Anquetil, who treated his own alimentary system as pitilessly as he dealt with Poupou, decided to see *what this boy Merckx has got in his belly*. They started with champagne, proceeded to white wine, red wine and then traded whiskies in a night club. A photographer sneaked in for a few 'Intimate Portraits of the Tour de France' and Anquetil, well cut, went for him. Merckx and friends left for an all-night restaurant where Eddy – who, like Damon Runyon's Nicely Nicely Johnson 'dearly loves to commit eating' – tucked into onion soup with heaps of grated cheese, chicken breast and a large steak. The rest could not keep up with the gourmand's gargantuan pace and, bloated, dropped away – what was new?

That September, on the track at Blois, Merckx's Derny pace-man crashed when avoiding a fallen rider and was killed; Merckx came off heavily too and came to on the operating table. They kept the awful news from him.

The tragedy changed him. The shaky relief, the guilt of surviving; he was profoundly depressed for several months. His pelvis had been displaced and he would never again ride without pain, which was often so excruciating it reduced him to tears. That he achieved so much against such chronic discomfort is truly amazing. It's another clue to his unapproachable superiority: his abnormal resistance to suffering. He had an iron constitution coupled with an unyielding will.

Before the crash, no one was capable of beating him in the mountains; after it, he was vulnerable – just. It didn't stop him taking the polka dots in his second consecutive Tour victory, but though he might seem nerveless in the saddle he was a bundle of nerves out of it: forever adjusting its height to ease the nagging discomfort in his back; tinkering with the machines. He turned up to one Giro with 20 bikes, all set up differently. Thévenet said that for a rider of such strength it was amazing what niggly ticks and indispositions seemed to worry him; as if he had any true right to be bothered by minor problems. His worrying occasionally got on everybody's nerves.

Was he the greatest ever? There can be no cogent argument against the case. Greg Lemond is on record as saying that the *peloton* is full of Merckxs these days; but this is ridiculous. Lemond ushered in an era where riders might not have less of a talent but they were permitted to do less with their talent.

Marcel Bidot, an early *coureur* who finally earned even the Tartar Desgrange's praise, certainly thought Merckx had no peer: 'You have only to look at his *palmarès*. He knew how to lift his arse out of the saddle.' The Belgian, Rik 'the Emperor' Van Looy, a man of erratic temper and rasping tongue, typically disagreed though. 'Merckx will never be the greatest of all time; Anquetil hurt me more when I was at the peak of my career than Merckx did in its autumn.' A meaningless jibe. Some men never retire graciously and Van Looy was one of that prickly, insecure breed who would always rather hand a victory to a rival than to a team-mate.

Merckx's generosity with his talent was exceptional. When many Tour winners of recent times have *ridden* fewer Classic races than he *won* and have built their victories on the small-business principle of limiting their losses, Merckx's all-year-round energy (from winter six-day races to the Giro di Lombardia, the Race of the Falling Leaves) was as much a tribute to his own zest for the sport as to his inflexible sense of obligation as a pro. His uncalculating spontaneity in attack, winning from the front whatever it cost (forget calorie counts, wattage and computer read-outs) is a lasting inspiration to anyone fired more by passion for the bike than for their bank account, public image or pulsometer.

He smashed the World Hour record in a ride that he described as an hour of purgatory: 'No one does that twice. I thought I was dying' he said. He had open wounds on his buttocks and couldn't sit down for four days; yet when Rominger broke his own *warm-up* ride by nearly 1.5 km a week later, Merckx declared: 'Seeing Tony today, I suddenly felt that I was a very minor rider. To achieve such a mark at sea level . . . I take my hat off to him.'

It all ended on 19 April 1978 at an evening kermesse in Belgium. He was mentally empty. As he rode away, he turned to his *soigneur*, the man who had looked after him throughout – fending off the reporters, talking through the stresses of the day, easing the physical discomfort, getting him ready for the conflicts, restoring his mood, taking the hardness out of the over-taut muscles – and said: 'You see, Pierrot, I've just ridden my last race.'

Some time after he had climbed off the bike, he summed up his feelings: 'People often told me that after my career, I'd at last be able to enjoy life. They were wrong. I can say today that I wasn't missing anything when I was riding. I was perfectly happy.'

He still rides the bike. In one open event – amateurs and ex-pros of all ages – a photograph shows him riding up behind an old guy having difficulty on a climb, gently taking hold of his saddle to propel him up the slope.

It is a truism but one that it does no harm to restate, that the difference between pros and amateurs is *preparation*. And between the great pros and the lesser? It's not that they come from Mars; they're just better and they work so much harder . . . all the time.

Merckx's luckless contemporaries in the *peloton* always counted coming second to him like a victory; *beating* him put them on another plane.

9. BERNARD THÉVENET

Only eight men have won a Tour and returned to win a second after losing or abandoning another. Philippe Thys won in 1913, '14 and '20 (he abandoned 1919); Firmin Lambot won in 1919 and '22 but came third in 1920; two great French rivals, André Leducq and Antonin Magne took two victories apiece between 1930 (Leducq) and 1934 (Magne); Fausto Coppi won in 1949 and '52, didn't ride in '50 and came tenth in '51; Jacques Anquetil won the first Tour he entered in 1957 but it took three barren years before he began a sequence of four straight victories, and Bernard Hinault took five victories but had to abandon his third ride and lost on his sixth. Each case is different but Bernard Thévenet's come-back win in 1977 was of particular interest to me, given the nature of his first win.

On 13 July 1975, Thévenet rode into cycling history on the slopes of Pra-Loup. Two kilometres from the summit finish he changed up to the outer chain-wheel (the 'big ring') and overtook a spent and agonising Eddy Merckx, who was scarcely able to stay on his bike. He distanced him by nearly two minutes, caught Gimondi, who had tried to help the ailing Belgian, won the stage and took yellow by 58 seconds. But to Thévenet the history is not so clear cut.

I met him at his hotel in Charles de Gaulle airport, when he was heading for the Cyclo-cross World's in Holland. He's stockier than in his racing days, but the frank smile is the same. He laughs readily, an open, warm personality; an intelligence which clearly underpins everything he does, on a bike and off it. He weighs things up; he is a thinker. When had he known that he might win the Tour? 'Ah . . .' he reflected, gave me a steady look and whistled as if to say 'tough question, who knows?'

He rode his first Tour in 1970 as a new pro with Peugeot. At the start of that season he had taken a sensational victory in the one-day Côte du Mont Faron, beating a whole clutch of big men – Merckx, Roger Pingeon, Felice Gimondi and Rudi Altig on the climbs round Toulon.

When he was not selected for La Grande Boucle, he was expecting to ride a lesser race, La Couronne. However the Wednesday before the Tour, he called to collect a friend for a training ride and was told his mother had phoned: Gaston Plaud wanted to speak to him urgently. 'Ferdinand Bracke and Gerben Karstens are ill – get yourself to Limoges, you're riding the Tour.' He hesitated. An old friend, Victor Ferrari, who'd ridden the Tour in 1929, scoffed: 'You're going to say no? You mad? Get going.'

Rather drôle, he said, to find himself in the *peloton* alongside men like Merckx, Poulidor and Guimard: names to make any 22-year-old newcomer shiver. But the class of the man – physical and moral – was already in clear evidence. He rode onto the Ventoux with the leading group. Feeling good, he accelerated early on. This was probably unwise: instinctual bravado – as Kubler found out (see page 52).

The southern approach, from Bédoin, climbs 1,583 m to the col, 1,909 m; over 21 km at 14 per cent. The road winds up the lower slopes through fragrant pine woods until, at 6 km from the summit, it breaks out onto vicious concrete ramps on bare rock awash in a sea of limestone shale. From a distance, this makes the peak appear to be snow-capped. It rears up out of the horizon in massive grandeur. You can't believe that a road can go up there. It's the very isolation of the massif which renders it so daunting. Ventoux isn't like any other mountain and, as Kubler found out, mountains do have a way of dealing with us. It's not just the extremes of weather peculiar to Ventoux – skies the colour of molten lead dripping such a furnace heat that even the air stifles, or else glacial cold when the mistral blows with a ferocity that can blow you off your bike (it nearly did me) – but the steepness, the thin air which makes breathing tortured, the dominating physical presence that can turn the legs and psyche to water. It also straddles the race route when everyone is already falling over with tiredness. All this makes it a formidable obstacle, one of those cols they call 'judges of peace' – the real arbiters of the race, most feared by all riders. Ventoux tolerates neither weakness nor arrogance.

Thévenet had certainly laid down an audacious challenge. The big men simply upped the pace and dropped the neophyte. Nevertheless, he stuck to his task and came in fourth, behind Merckx, his lieutenant Georges Van den Berghe and the hero of French cycling, Poulidor. Merckx, already suffering from oxygen debt and suffocated by the press of photographers and journalists at the finish, fainted on the winner's podium. That evening, the Solonor–Lejeune rider Lucien Aimar, Anquetil's protégé and winner in 1966, rebuked the young wolf: 'You're committing suicide, you're throwing yourself away, and I'm going to profit by it.' Pingeon had said much the same about Merckx on his début Tour in 1969. In actual fact, Thévenet was making a substantial mark in a field largely cowed by Merckx's superiority. Jan Janssen railed at them:

'Everyone's looking to himself, nobody's racing. Merckx is the strongest, agreed – but Aimar and the rest can't count on me to help them any more. Nor Van Impe – who ever sees him? They're not *coureurs*, they're bloodsuckers.'

Four days later, Thévenet was in the leading group on the slopes of the Tourmalet, 5 km from the *arrivée*, when a motorbike drew up and the press-man, Victor Cosson, (third in the '38 Tour) said:

'You're the freshest – attack.' He rode into La Mongie alone, winner on one of the legendary proving grounds of the Tour.

'There are legendary names in the Tour,' he told me, 'names that I grew up with, that really constitute the myth of the Tour: Izoard, Tourmalet, Galibier, Ventoux. My generation was nourished on that legend; I don't think it is the same for today's riders.'

(The Tourmalet is one of those mountains in what is called the 'Circle of Death'. Climbing it you really *do* feel the weight of geography, myth and history hanging from your saddle. Getting to that col is one of *the* great moments, I should say, of any cyclist's riding career.)

Thévenet came to the '71 Tour as the acknowledged leader of the Peugeot team and took a second-stage victory in Grenoble (near where he now lives) that famous day when Ocaña attacked at the start and left Merckx to a lonely, back-breaking chase. It was a memorable day. Certain images stick in his mind: the moto speeding past, the pillion holding up the slate with the scrawled and rescrawled chalk message which got more and more illegible, Merckx riding up alongside and asking him for a drink. He passed the bidon across, Merckx took a deep swig and handed it back with a nod of thanks, so tired he couldn't speak. That gesture of gratitude from a man he so admired was, he felt, a considerable honour.

He took fourth place in Paris, the first Frenchman on General Classification; greater things seemed possible and it awoke the ambition to win the Tour. That, as he put it, was when he began to 'caress his hope', as you might tickle a trout. He could not say then that victory was in him; almost a superstitious unwillingness to do more than hope. Nonetheless, that hope steadily hardened and became a goal, a desire.

That dream had been there a long time.

Born 10 January 1948, in a tiny hamlet some 5 km from the village of St Julien de Civry, in the pastoral Charolles region famous for its cattle, Thévenet grew up a farmboy. From the age of six he went to school clinging to the luggage rack of his elder sister's bike. At seven he got his own machine and did the daily 10 km round-trip. A Christmas present, a sports encyclopedia, sparked the idea of a sporting career – but what? Tennis? Football? Cycling? No tennis court for miles; no local soccer team; but he *had* a bike. As a reward for passing the certificate of Primary Education at 14, both older sisters asked for a Solex – the famous motor-assisted heavy bicycle. He asked for a racing bike, his parents compromised and bought him a racer-cum-tourist machine. They knew what was afoot. The Tour de France had passed their farmhouse once; it was a race that 'even the land people, who weren't generally interested in sport, followed'. It begins a week before the long summer holiday and all France is (or used to be) gripped. The recent doping scandals have reduced the event rather; transformed it, he said, into less of a *French* thing than just another sporting event. But Papa Thévenet needed the boy for work on the farm; he turned, as they say, a jaundiced eye on cycling.

One of his pals was already racing at the Charolles club, 8 km from home and Thévenet, still a minor, begged a signature for his junior licence from the club president. It was against his nature to deceive his parents but the desire to compete was too strong: he rode his first race on the quiet, the results were published in the local paper and there was a row. The club president came to the house one evening to mollify his mother and father – the boy had promise; why not come and see him race? They did, he won and in the next five years with the Charolles club he made his way upwards, toughened himself on the road, took an international race (the Tour de Roussillon) and after a good showing in the amateur Grand Prix de France against the clock, was invited by the director of the celebrated Boulogne-Billancourt cycle club (ACBB) to join what was, then, the leading such outfit in France, the cradle of many stars including not a few of the foreign legion, the Brits and Aussies. The provincial circuit might be a lot tougher and the provincial riders just as talented, but who noticed? Paris was the reference point: the big races went to and from the capital, the most ambitious riders rode them and the influential cycling journalists worked out of offices round the corner from the ACBB. (The French sports paper *L'Equipe* for example was based here, descendant of *L'Auto* which sponsored the first Tours de France.) Over two years in Paris, Thévenet learnt his trade, became amateur Champion of France and signed his first pro contract.

He spoke of ambition and imbued it with a complexity beyond the mere desire to win. It struck me forcibly how much of a thinker he is and that, surely, is what marks out the great riders from the lesser – the 'robot men' as he called them, content to be dictated to by what other riders do, by circumstances, by the read-out of their computers, even. The real winners decide their own fate; they owe their ascendancy to their capacity to override every obstacle, mental, physical and moral; to ride their own race, to know the moment to make optimum effort by a mysterious combination of experience, instinct, will-power and sheer audacity. He made that very French gesture of rubbing forefinger and thumb together, 'caressing' the *je ne sais quoi* . . . And for him that mysterious combination came vibrantly to life on Bastille Day, 14 July 1975. At the *départ* of the Izoard stage, Louison Bobet approached him; Bobet, the rider he had most admired as a kid. The triple winner congratulated him on the previous day's win but added: 'You know, to be considered a real champion, you have to cross the Izoard alone and in the lead with the yellow jersey on your back.' Coppi had done it and had watched as Bobet did it, seeing a rerun of his own great exploit – the champion alone and untouchable. Thévenet is acutely aware of the Tour's history; like so many riders of his generation his early years were steeped in its myth and legend. Such a long sense of the great race is common and he is modestly conscious of his place in the myth now, even if he wasn't at the time. The race, after all, was far from over.

For this was the last but one day in the mountains, the only terrain where he could hope to take more time out of Merckx and, whatever defeatist talk the 'Cannibal' had voiced the day before, there was never any telling with him. He'd cracked in the mountains on the '74 Giro, lost over eight minutes to Fuente and clawed it back over the last three stages. Some ten minutes adrift, he had ridden like a fury in the '72 Tour to redress Ocaña's supremacy and, though it was a fall which carried the Spanish ace out of the race, Merckx's combativeness had never been less than a very potent threat. Thévenet had an advance of 58 seconds, but against a rider of Merckx's appetite and genius for attack that was, he said, 'a nothing; a speck of soot'. Merckx was so driven; he would accelerate at any time, anywhere. If Merckx was behind you, there was no safety. The tactic had to be to carry the fight to him; and there were, too, those words of the great Bobet, a challenge he could not shirk. There must have been a sense, surely, of destiny accompanying him.

He began the day with no compelling sense that this *was* a big day, however. Indeed, he suffered a temporary loss of confidence on the descent of the col de Vars; thought he might lose too much time. Never even a handy descender, he took it even worse than usual and was perturbed. Merckx, defying all risk, plunged off as he had done the day before, wrenching minutes out of the more timid Frenchman. But it is characteristic of Thévenet never to accede to nerves. In the Pyrenees he had seemed unshakeable. So far, Merckx's fervid attacking had not punctured that composure and, along the valley towards the Izoard, Thévenet rejoined and saw that the moment was on him: this was the ground he must take; he resolved to drop Merckx some distance from the col.

The Izoard is a fiendish climb: the gradients are wicked, the landscape awesome, the Casse Déserte frightening and the scree-strewn slopes of the mountain look like an avalanche on the point of sliding. There is no shade; if there is sun, it is pitiless. The formula must be to ride at such a rhythm calculated to leave you with just enough spare to cross the col and count on recovery on the other side. Expend too much and you blow; too little and you lose the gains.

Thévenet attacked twice, three times; Merckx reeled him back in by force of will. Then, 8 km from the summit, Thévenet went clear at last. Merckx could no longer hold his wheel. His morale soared, Merckx's slumped. The yellow jersey was heading, alone, for the summit of the Izoard. Watching from a following car stood Bobet; just as Coppi had stood by the road in 1953 and watched in admiration as the young Louison rode by alone in yellow, heading for his first victory in his sixth Tour. Thévenet, too, was riding his sixth Tour. He had learned well the lessons of those rides – how to economise effort over a three-week period, to husband strength so as to avoid the bad day when all can be lost, at the same time how to know when to bet everything on a big throw. This was that moment: he seized it.

By the side of the road waited a young woman in a bikini waving a placard: MERCKX IS BEATEN. THE BASTILLE HAS FALLEN. Thévenet knew, though, that as long as Merckx was on the bike he was never, ever beaten. Yet that ride over the Izoard was sweet, his body was prickling with gooseflesh:

'Ah . . . the last 3 km, the crowd pressing in on both sides in front of the motorbike escort. They were going crazy. I hardly noticed that I had crossed the col.'

Despite breaking his jaw in a heavy fall before the start of the Galibier stage, Merckx rode on to Paris, reduced to taking liquid food only. Thévenet could not relax.

'He was much more experienced than me; head-to-head with him I could never feel sure of myself.' He ceded time in a mountain time-trial and even at the beginning of the final stage, which ended on the Champs-Elysées for the first time, Merckx was snapping at the yellow jersey. But Thévenet, wearing what has become almost a magical number in Tour lore – 51, pulled on the final yellow; as Merckx had done in 1969 and Hinault had in 1978 – both in their first Tours.

He seemed to shrug off a winter of strength-sapping post-Tour social engagements, a bout of bronchitis – and a badly reduced programme of training as a result – to win the Dauphiné Libéré and came to the '76 start feeling confident enough. Quite against expectation, he came third in the Prologue (not his speciality), fell on the second stage into Caen and rode on with a bruised shoulder. Nothing untoward. A time-trial left him over four minutes off the pace and the Alpe d'Huez climb cost him over a minute in arrears. His confidence leaked away, doubt afflicted him and it was soon clear that his reserves were finished. A liver complaint had further weakened him. He was riding on the remains of his strength alone. That strength ran out on the 19th stage and he climbed off the bike. He sat in the sag wagon, a picture of misery and dejection.

'It was the worst disappointment of my life' he said. 'I came to the start and thought: I've won the Tour . . . and I abandoned.' He laughed and talked of that dark secret all great sportsmen penetrate: the grim initiation rite of defeat. Such a reverse is very difficult to accept: he rode professionally for 12 years and encountered many setbacks, but this was a catastrophe. Pride, self-belief all in a ruin of doubt: had he prepared badly? Had he failed to eat properly? Had he not been concentrating?

'It is one of the great virtues of sport, learning how to face up to defeat; learning how to admit to the setback, what to do to try to combat the weakness – physical, moral, mental – that lay behind the defeat. You must learn to endure and to rebuild, to fight back against these bad times.' He reflected and asked: 'Why was I beaten? What do I have to do to get back?' Extending this you uncover an underlying principle of a drive to win: 'What powers do I possess? What do I want to achieve? How do I deploy those powers to achieve my ambition?' These are questions which are asked with absolute detachment only by those who are big enough to answer them. The failure is yours and the riposte must come from you. What makes them all special is the power to come back.

In 1977, Thévenet returned to the Tour; stronger than in '75 he faced a newly-inspired Lucien Van Impe, the previous year's winner; the Dutchman Hennie Kuiper, a real fighter; World champion in '75, Joop Zoetemelk and the evergreen Poulidor . . .

I asked him about the Alpe d'Huez stage.

'Ah, most people forget that. It was the most terrible stage of my career. Two days stand out in my memory: the Izoard in 1975 and that day.'

Van Impe attacked 7 km from the col du Glandon – the most vicious climb of them all, said Thévenet. No one responded and Thévenet towed the rest (Kuiper, Zoetemelk, Galdos) to the top on his own. Van Impe was by now leader on the road. Thévenet, thinking he had lost the Tour, had no choice but to risk everything on the chase, unaided. At the foot of the Huez climb, Kuiper suddenly attacked, followed by Zoetemelk. Thévenet, exhausted, had no immediate response. Slowly he regained some flow, hairpin by gruelling hairpin, and caught them. Zoetemelk cracked; Kuiper attacked again and Van Impe was still up ahead. Losing time on Kuiper metre by metre, Thévenet heard voices in the crowd, probably Dutch, shouting:

'You've given up . . . you've lost it,' but the weight of the roar was for him. With only 49" advance over Kuiper on General Classification this ride might cost the yellow jersey. He was, he said, at rock bottom on that climb, riding on automatic, close to toppling off, striving to contain Kuiper and desperate not to disappoint his loyal following of fans.

He overtook Van Impe who'd been capsized by a car. Wheel buckled, no support car at hand, Van Impe knew his chance of winning a second Tour had probably gone but even so he called out to his French rival: 'Go on, he's not far.'

'I found that very fair play' said Thévenet. In sight of the *arrivée*, he went onto the big ring and, with a stupendous effort to save vital seconds, sprinted himself to a dead stop. He was spent, incapable of walking up the steps into the hotel. He had to ask the team driver to help him up. Prostrate on his bed, he couldn't even stagger to the balcony to greet the fans calling for him, nor even to eat. He fell into a stupefied sleep and woke again at about 11 p.m., ravenously hungry. The hotel kitchens were closed; one of the team men rustled up some bread rolls and butter and Thévenet packed in as much as he could swallow. There was tomorrow to face, but his body had started to recover. This capacity to recuperate is one of the central mysteries of the finest Tour riders – a *mélange* of sturdy frame, iron nerve and spiritual pride.

Thévenet had kept the yellow jersey by eight seconds and, in Paris, won overall by 48 seconds, the narrowest margin yet recorded. Merckx finished his last Tour in sixth place. It had been the only time he rode l'Alpe d'Huez and, trounced by over 13 minutes, he'd at first wanted to abandon the race, but after all he *was* Eddy Merckx and he didn't.

That '77 victory is amplest proof of Thévenet's qualities as a rider and as a man. It was a remarkable test of his character, courage and determination. Fulsome with his efforts on the bike, he is generous with his opinion off it. For Merckx he reserves the highest opinion, as a *man*. Chivalrous, he called him. Of the racing scene today, he says that one cannot make judgements about the narrowing of ambitions. Every era has its own fashion of doing things and today's era is one of ultra-specialisation. In his day, if a rider confined himself to one sort of event, even winning it, the response would be: 'So what else has he done?' Nowadays, he believes, no one rider can excel in all the varying disciplines: classics, big tours, track. Sponsors spend much more and expect more from the teams. Twenty-five years ago there would be a *directeur sportif*, a mechanic and the rest would be employed as needed. Compare that to the Mapei contingent now – 20-odd riders and twice as many support people. The preparation is more detailed, too. Results are analysed, time spent correcting weakness. Descending was always his bugbear, but he had to make do. Ullrich, on the other hand, could devote an entire training period to learning how to descend – a learnt skill which saved his Tour in '97.

New technology has made the sport safer. (He mentioned the gear change being on the handlebars instead of by lever mounted on the down-tube of the frame.)

In the past, the transition from amateur to pro was very difficult – a narrow bridge, he called it – whereas today's élite amateurs are mixing it with pros all the time.

> My first professional race was on the Côte d'Azur, in February, the Grand Prix de St Raphaël. I rode the first three-quarters of the race with the leaders and felt fine: 'Hey, this is all right' – then *baf*! They went. I was out. That was the difference. Amateurs would average 45 kph and swing between 42 and 48. The pros would average 45 kph but swing between 37 and 60. The attacks came when the road got hard. Amateurs just try to grind out the weaker riders.

Retirement came when he realised that training was no pleasure, that it had become a duty. The hardest thing was the change of rhythm instead of a year divided into a succession of racing in the *peloton* – two-day periods or several weeks, interspersed with training, alone or with the team – retirement brought the relentless repetition of five weekdays and a weekend. And there was the sudden absence of his friends in the *peloton*; people he had spent so much time with, as a rider. His wife had made friends there too, and suddenly the regular contact had gone. We talked on a while over a beer at the end of our formal interview – a friendly chat about bikes and cyclists and it was, in summary, *that* sentiment I carried away: his deep and lasting affection for the world of cycling and the riders.

'One day you are riding against someone, the next day you're riding with them to make an escape work. It is rivalry, but not hostility.'

Chapeau, Bernard.

10. BERNARD HINAULT

One Wednesday morning in late March last year the phone rang. A man's voice asked me, in French, if he was talking to Graeme Fife.

'*Oui*' I said.

'*C'est Bernard Hinault*' he replied.

Almost instantly most of my French and not a little of my English vanished. I recovered myself, fixed a rendezvous for 10.30 a.m. on 8 April at the offices of the Tour de France organisation in Boulogne-Billancourt, Paris, and put the phone down.

Blimey.

I'd sent him a fax in January asking to meet him. It was the only number I could get out of the Tour organisation; he is very guarded about giving interviews; fair enough. There was no response so I wrote a letter repeating the request and sent it c/o La Société du Tour de France. After the return phone call I sent a note confirming the meeting and reflected on how willing these cyclists are, generally, to field questions from complete strangers, often for no payment, either.

Bernard Hinault is one of the finest racing cyclists of all time. They call him the Badger – prickly, self-contained and at his most dangerous when cornered. A compulsive winner, you might say, with an astonishing list of victories. Arriving for the appointment early, I sat by the Seine for a while to compose myself and then strolled round to the office block. It was locked. Another man arrived and a concierge materialised inside the glass lobby. He opened the door and the two of us went in. I took the lift to whichever floor the Tour offices occupy. There was no one there. I went down to the lobby again. Had I made a mistake? Had Hinault thought better of the idea? Forgotten? Or just not bothered? I stood outside in warm spring sunshine just a mite worried and, on a whim, walked over to the adjacent offices of *L'Equipe*. There, on a large settee in the foyer, sat Bernard Hinault and in an armchair, another man, who turned out to be his driver. Hinault smiled, stood up and we shook hands. I fumbled with my bag, extricated the recording equipment (I am not so confident, yet, of transcribing spoken French in the necessary fast précis) and we talked.

9 April 2000. Paris–Roubaix, doyen of the one-day classic races, first run in 1896, won by Johan Museuuw after a heroic lone break of some 40 km. The prize, apart from money and a place in the hall of fame, is a symbolic cobblestone, a lump of the infamous *pavé* with which the old tracks of this Hell of the North are paved.

Presenting Museeuw with his victor's cobblestone in the Roubaix *vélodrome*, Bernard Hinault congratulated him on his comeback from his private hell – the leg injury which put him out of the Hell of the North two years ago and almost finished his career. Gangrene set in and he very nearly had to have his leg amputated.

In his day, the Badger denounced the race: 'What have we done to deserve being sent to Hell? *C'est une cochonnerie* (it's dirty tricks, a load of cobblers).' Yet when I asked him about this classic test of nerve, stamina, bike-handling and sanity, he replied: 'It really belongs to another time, but it's part of cycling. Some riders adore it. Why stop it? There's no reason.' *And*, it's on the calendar: you can't shirk it and claim to be any good.

'Some riders adore it' – here he means the Belgians. Museuuw is last in a long tradition of swashbuckling Flemish rough-riders who treat the Paris–Roubaix as their preferred duelling ground. Roger de Vlaeminck, 'the Gipsy from Eelko', who could ride a bike along a railway line, won it three times as did Merckx and Van Looy. The Italians like it, too: brittle-boned Coppi risked the fearful battering of the race to win in 1950, and he came second in 1952. The French dominated it in the early years. Maurice Garin (winner 1897 and '98) and Henri Pélissier (winner in 1919 and '21) were the first double winners, but after Pélissier, the list of winners includes very few French names. The vast majority are Belgian with a sprinkling of Italians (Francesco Moser, another gipsy, took all three between 1978 and '80). The French avoided it largely because of the risk of injury which might put them out of their Tour.

Hinault gambled on broken bones and a lost Tour on three occasions and, in 1981, in the rainbow jersey, rode to the first French victory since Bobet's, 25 years earlier. Bobet was in the *vélodrome* that day and it was quite apparent from much that he said to me that Hinault's sense of history, the shaping of his *palmarès*, the calculation of his wins, was central to his ambition – an ambition which he served as devotedly as a mission. He may have reviled the Paris–Roubaix when he was riding it, but he knew, absolutely *knew*, that he had to win it if he was to join the pantheon of the immortals. It was a momentous victory, won in the commanding style which was Hinault's personal stamp. He rode into the stadium with four other riders, including two *pavé* specialists, Moser and de Vlaeminck. Hinault had noted the wind direction from the flags round the track, took the lead at the bell and, the breeze at his back, sprinted in from 400 metres out.

That morning he had told the team he was going to win – he just knew it, and the impression of his formidable self-assurance and containment is still strong. He's amiable, direct and conscious of his standing as perhaps the last true *patron*, the boss of the professional *peloton* to whom other riders defer not only because he is the best or the strongest, but because he's a leader too and a flamboyant winner. Merckx was really too private for that, but Hinault has a very Gallic flair; he's a natural general.

He is notoriously disinclined to harp on the past. His career needs no advocacy from him – yet it is clear from the cursory assessment he made of today's riders that, in general, they do not match up to his own definition of a true champion.

Asked about the difference in the pressures on riders today he replied: 'No. There are no pressures on riders.' This was strange. He continued. 'Everyone has the impression that there are pressures on riders to get results. No.' I began to see which way he was going. 'If there *were* pressures things would be quite different.' And he developed the theme: old-days hard, present-day soft. Given the conditions under which they ride (so much better than in his day) and the fact that it is the norm for them to be guaranteed a salary before they have even turned a pedal, the lack of dominating results is '*bizarre*', which was his very French way of saying 'what's *wrong* with them?' Some Italian teams do pay their riders a portion of their annual income and expect them to earn the rest however they can, as in the past. 'That gives a certain motivation to ride hard, to win races' he said. Winning races is for him the sole purpose of riding as a pro, 'not bike touring'. Cycling is a trade, an honourable calling; as Anquetil put it, riders earn their living by 'millions of turns of the pedals' – a bargain between work and reward which no longer holds in the same way. This is not the fault of the riders: global TV coverage of the sport and the massive cash injections from sponsorships which exploit the opportunities for screen advertising have inflated commercial interests in the sport – every sport – out of all proportion. Instant telly stardom is more attractive than a place in history.

Hinault's approach was, from the start, utterly self controlled: to shape his season around five principal objectives. Analyse his *palmarès*, and you see the pattern matching his own definition of a super-champion; namely a rider who can win one of the spring classics (he won seven) *and* a Tour de France (he won five) *or* a Tour of Italy (he won three) *or* a Dauphiné (he won three) *and*, in the late season, a Grand Prix des Nations (he won five), a World's (he won one), and a Paris-Tours (which he didn't win). It's interesting that he should choose as an example a race he never won. He might have picked the Tour of Lombardy, the 'Race of the Falling Leaves', which he took in 1984 – with a lone break of such bravado, from a few kilometres out, that his manager said he was mad. Hinault just laughed.

In 12 seasons, he said, he achieved a 95 per cent success rate. 'You can never be sure of winning. You might lose for a nothing – a puncture, a bad position at a key moment in a race – but of the five Belgian classics, for instance, a real champion will be able to win at least one.' No one can maintain premium effort through the whole season, there must be 'beaches of rest, real rest' interspersed; but a rider who does not plan each season from start to finish with deliberate care, falls short of professional obligation. For that reason, he finds it odd that some contemporary riders choose to base their year on one race. If they lose that, they lose everything. Moreover, such an approach makes insufficient physical demands on them: they don't do enough. In that respect they don't equal riders of the past 'like us', Hinault says: 'Merckx, Anquetil, me, Moser, Giuseppe Saronni, the Spanish. Today they ride in the best conditions imaginable, the means at their disposal are much better, yet they aren't as good.' He said 'good' meaning, I think, 'prolific'. I asked him about this new era of specialisation and, as with many of my questions, he rebuffed the idea unhesitatingly, with a firm 'Non', but then proceeded to recast the question in his own way and, finally, agreed with it. It was a minor sample of his mind-games: the constant vigilance, reading other riders' intentions and fooling them, the mysterious art of 'psyching out'. One can see the kind of dominating presence he exercised in the *peloton*; the playing of what he called a *morale terrible* – his essential ingredient for winning on the road. Of winning *everything*, at one time or another.

That *morale terrible* amounts to sizeable will-power, ego and self-confidence rolled into one. Take the '86 Tour, for example. The previous year, his fifth win, he beat Lemond, the young pretender, into second place by a slender 1 minute, 42 seconds. Lemond always claimed that he had been forced to give up his own hope of victory to the twilight ambitions of the boss. At any event, Hinault said he would work for Lemond the following year; effectively surrendering his own chance of a record sixth win. He had long since announced that he would retire round his 32nd birthday, that November. The slant on that '86 Tour tilts sharply, according to your affiliation. Certainly the Badger appeared to be interpreting 'work for' in a decidedly eccentric fashion: riding almost everybody off his wheel, making even the specialist climbers gasp on the cols, punishing Lemond psychologically with what the American read as a blatant show of treachery and arrogance. Hinault insists that his promise was good, that he was doing no more than reduce the field for Lemond by weakening the opposition. Despite the celebrated shared win at l'Alpe d'Huez, there was no love lost between them and a riddle posed itself: *did* Hinault go for the win or not?

The Alps nearly finished him. He endured appalling pain in one knee; came close to climbing off on the col de Vars, in tears, he was in such agony. But a motorbike cameraman spotted it and told his driver to stop because the Badger was going to quit. The prospect of that humiliation was enough to keep him going. As a show of brutal determination that was typical. He won the 1980 Liège–Bastogne–Liège in shocking weather, his hands frozen to the bars.

My feeling is that the offer to second Lemond was genuine but a sort of insurance policy. Hinault must have known that the American had become too strong for him; by aiding him he would share in the spoils of victory *and* the esteem of a French public as quick to applaud generosity as they are slow to love the aristocratic hauteur which characterised Hinault's personality, as well as Anquetil's. However, had the sixth win offered itself, I have no doubt he would have grabbed it and made the excuses afterwards (Lemond wasn't strong enough, not ready, he lost his chance). What he said at the time, and subsequently, bears this out. Lemond's victory had to be hard-won, reputable. This clearly would not have been had Hinault simply defended his man, then eased up to let him through without a fight. Instead, as Merckx did with Thévenet, Hinault assured Lemond not only of the final yellow jersey but of a glorious triumph over a quintuple winner. Paradox or just plain tricky? Probably a bit of both. And between the rather gauche American, who never quite settled as a full initiate in the masonry of the *peloton*, and the Frenchman, a *seigneur* in the feudal hierarchy, with all the wiles and guiles of continental pro racing, there was never more than guarded respect. Lemond was, after all, the first rider to change radically what had always been the accepted norm, by limiting his real effort almost exclusively to the Tour de France to the detriment of the old professional obligation to extend talent more broadly, to reach for wider goals, to shape a richer *palmarès*. In Hinault's view, therefore, he was not a true champion. Three yellow jerseys, two rainbow and little else.

The American riders are not greatly liked by French fans. They have tended to be parsimonious with their undoubted talents and for this trend – this narrowing of focus – Lemond is rightly blamed. Lance Armstrong is the latest exponent. Despite living for much of the year in France, he speaks virtually no French and what little he does essay is very basic. This lack of communication, aggravated by his increasing isolation from press and public, has badly frustrated the French press and remarks about the Tour de France being a bike race not a popularity contest not only demeans the myth of the Tour but is evidence of a particular brand of egocentricity which is emphatically American. Hinault's conflict with Lemond typifies the clash of sporting cultures. The Tour de France has its myth. In popular perception (and if perception is not the whole story it is most of it) the Americans see it as the A1 route to big bucks and cycling fame. There is, in cycle sport, so much else.

Of the Tour de France Hinault was adamant that the changes it has undergone – willingly or reluctantly – are part of a necessary process; welcome, and not in the least regrettable. Henri Desgrange's principle for the Tour was constant renewal. The latest doping scandal has made renewal imperative. Can the Tour achieve that? I asked. He dead-batted the question; spoke of better accommodation, better technology, better conditions. I pressed him on the drugs issue: that, he said, is for the International Olympic Committee, a neutral overseer, to address; cycling has a high profile in these murky waters only because it is the one sports federation which has acknowledged the problem and is trying to put its own house in order. Guimard, Hinault's old boss, told me that it was EPO (erythropoetin which increases the level of red corpuscles in the blood) which had radically changed bike racing. After the introduction of EPO, riders were compromised: riders who had not dosed themselves on the miracle dope knew they had to take it if they were to have any hope of competing against those who already were flying on it. In this context, the efforts made by most of the national cycling federations and most of the first-rank pro cycling teams to eradicate the evil is truly laudable. The drug scandal nearly finished the Tour de France and it is a testament to the real magic of the race that it survived and tackled the problem head on.

As to the Tour being just another sporting event rather than, as it always was, uniquely *French* – well, Hinault claimed, the Italians ride it and the Germans and the Brits, maybe tomorrow the Chinese. It's global; 60-odd TV networks beam out images of the Tour. It's on a par with the World Cup and the Olympic Games, except that they change venue each time while the Tour stays in France, that's the sole defining difference. (Of course, you have the World's which changes venue, but that's only for a day event.) This is a telling comment: for him, apparently, the only World's title that counts is the Road Race. And, forced out of the '80 Tour with tendinitis, he devoted himself to proving his superiority by winning the rainbow jersey in it. One objective lost, another – equally illustrious – gained. There is something almost demonic in the way he went for and took some of his wins; much as Muhammad Ali could predict the round he'd hand out the count. ('I am going to win today, don't ask me how I know.') Deaf to Guimard's pleas, he attacked in the '79 Tour of Lombardy with 150 km to go, and rode in fresh as paint.

His formula for the constitution of a winner was fairly routine: physique, above all; the morale, because sometimes it *is* unbelievably hard and you have to surmount overwhelming odds; and the alertness and tactical nous for reading a race. An absentee in the '83 Tour, which was won by his erstwhile lieutenant Fignon, he was soundly beaten by him in '84. Fignon didn't have a bad day and even said publicly that he thought his ex-patron's efforts to contain him on l'Alpe d'Huez were laughable. Even Merckx criticised him for wasting energy. Hinault, riding for the newly-formed La Vie Claire team, lost by over ten minutes. Third came Lemond, riding with Fignon in the old Renault team which Hinault had quit after a violent row with Guimard, its inspirational *directeur sportif.*

Of the notorious fiery temper – leading riders' protest walk-ins, pitching into blockades of striking workers, fists flying – there is little sign now. He is charming, polite, friendly. He gave me a lift to Compiègne in his official car, helpfulness itself. An aristocrat of sport, one might say, exactly in the mould of what were called *les grands,* in whom courtesy was a badge of rank. But it is a mark of the man that he quite clearly assesses situations with scrupulous care – to his self-interest, for sure, but as Marcel Bidot, (French team manager '50s and '60s) said: 'There is no room for sentiment in this sport, else you will get flattened.' Hinault hasn't got an ounce of emotional flab in his lean professional nature.

'Do you still ride a bike?' I said. He hit the question full force on the volley: 'Non!' and smiled. A hundred km per year, maximum, and charity rides. When he climbed off for the last time (a cyclo-cross in

November '86) the bike became a thing of the past. A page turned. As a rider he had devoted himself 100 per cent to being a *real* rider and did nothing else. But he believes it important to make his image as an athlete *after* competition as complete as it was before. 'Image'? Well, there is no question he is acutely aware of his own place in the pantheon with a record probably second to none bar Merckx's, but also of the very personal responsibility it imposes. It was, he said, important to show youngsters that you can do sport but that you can do other things, too. If renouncing the machine that brought him such glory is a mite sad given the happy pedalling of many retired greats, it is another sign of his capacity for total commitment to the moment. Anquetil was the same: he became, like Hinault, a much-respected older statesman in the sport. As Hinault – now advisor to the Tour de France, in charge of Exterior Relations for Paris–Roubaix – said: 'If I didn't have a passion for sport, of many sorts, I wouldn't be here.'

Passion is central to him, however mildly expressed in the polite exchange of even an informal interview. In 1985 he came back to the Tour, Lemond now his lieutenant, and took huge satisfaction from riding Fignon into the ground over the Pyrenees. ('My turn to make you suffer, mate.') With that victory he elevated himself into a very exclusive club of quintuple winners. Aggression can harden into vindictiveness and true on–offs like Fignon and Hinault have a highly solipsistic vision of things, a powerful logic attuned to that one irrefutable certainty: *their* victory.

There was, undoubtedly, a powerful sense of destiny at work in Hinault, a near mystic ability to decide on a win. Fifteen km from Roubaix, in the leading group, a small black dog trailing its red lead (he remembers that vividly) darted out across him and he went down. He'd already fallen seven times (in that race everybody comes off) but lose to a *dog*? Fired up beyond even his own supernormal levels of rage to win, he chased yet again, rejoined and, after 260 km of misery, added the *cochonnerie* to his *palmarès*.

Hinault was four times Super Prestige Pernod winner in succession (the old world ranking), and when he retired he effectively left French cycling bereft. No worthy successor has appeared and it is my impression that, aside from his faint deprecation of the modern bunch (grumpy old pro, what's new?), in talking of change as an inevitable part of history's turning pages, he is consciously isolating himself in the context of that change: the last true boss of the old-style *peloton*; the last super-champion with a rich list of victories; the last Frenchman to win the Tour when it was still uniquely French. He is a man wholly content with the past, untroubled by the present, drawn to the future. Impressive, whichever way you look at it.

11. SEAN KELLY

JULY 2000. TOUR DE FRANCE. CARPENTRAS.

I'm prowling the barriers round the *Départ* enclosure. Once more I find myself at the bike race with interviews to do and *no accreditation*. The place is crawling with gendarmes, traffic police and Tour organisation officials. There are no gaps in the circuit; only one entrance, heavily guarded. Team motor-homes and cars pass through. I need to speak to Pascal Lino (Festina) and Jacky Durand (Lotto). I'm in a fix. The team vehicles trundle past down the side street leading to the paddock. I lean over by the window and ask each driver to deliver a message but, though they nod at my request, I fancy the chances of either rider bothering to join me for a homely chat over the barriers are no better than mine of racing them up Mont Ventoux today or any day (1,583 m of climbing in 21 km). I did it two days ago, got to the top before it was closed down – swirling fog and a danger of icing on the eastern slopes. It's 33 years almost to the day since Tommy Simpson died up there in furnace heat. This morning the thermometer read zero at 8 a.m. Mistral tearing the sky to bits in readiness for some bludgeoning of the Tour riders.

I'm on my way back to the paddock, hopes dwindling, when I see the Cofidis van pulling to a halt alongside the barriers: a blind spot. Now or never. I join the crowd, flip the bike over the rails and follow it. In.

Once in, I can mingle with a crowd of journalists, Tour motorbike pilots, cameramen, visitors from the town (furnished with the necessary laminated passes) and I pass unnoticed. I lean the bike against the Lotto team motor-home and watch as two elderly fans ogle the polished aluminium (goblin silver) frame then tap it gingerly to test its mettle.

I talk to Durand – he and the rest of the Lotto men are swathed in the most pungent orange-toned massage-cum-tan oil of a pretty odoriferous selection. Durand has won two yellow jerseys in the Tour, three *mallas amarillas* in the Vuelta, an early season classic Tour of Flanders in '91, tenth stage Tour de France in '94, and a late season classic Paris-Tours '98. Nowadays he goes out on his own delighting in *le punch*. And, he says, better the *lanterne rouge* than the anonymity of the middle order. Bad for pride, bad for sponsors. He told me he likes mountains in training but not in races. Why the attack onto the col de Marie Blanque, then? 'Ah, that's a bitch' he said. (It is: the sort of climb that looks nothing bad but does terrible things to you.) He shrugged. 'Well, you feel something, you do it.' And the consequences? He shrugged again. Never think of so banal an item on the agenda as *consequences*.

'The best moments are the moments you can't foresee, the fugitive moments. To win on l'Alpe d'Huez would be *the* win but . . . you never know where else.' This had been a good Tour for him, an attacking Tour, and he appreciates the spirit abroad. 'There are few riders of my style around, and it gives me pleasure to attack. *Bravo à tous les échappés*. I don't mind being beaten; what I hate is being beaten when I haven't tried.'

I went over to speak to Lino. He looked a great hope early on: ten days in yellow on the '92 Tour and a stage win in '93 but he had a worn expression when I found him by the team bus. He's had to give up personal ambitions this Tour to work for Pascal Moreau, currently third overall and bearing the full weight of French expectations. Sure, the bad weather has caused problems. Heat and sunshine would make a big difference to them all, but team morale was high. He didn't smile. Why should anyone facing Mont Ventoux in a gale smile? Still, there was also the sense that Lino is facing the end of his career; the (regrettably few) glory-days are receding. Once a leader, he is a team man now, under orders, obliged to be content with the dreaded anonymity. Yet he didn't complain about my intrusion on this prelude to the suffering and answered questions politely if with no great show of enthusiasm.

He shared that public openness with most of the other riders I saw around the place, whether sitting on the car steps, on plastic chairs or slouched against the top tube of the bike, all of them fielding questions from journalists, greetings from passers-by – like the affable duo of veterans from Avignon, trainers of the local football team, who know many of the riders. They sent David Millar some champagne after the Prologue win. Old fans – just loving the atmosphere and the chance to rub shoulders with the new breed of heroes who look far too young to be doing anything so utterly mad, bad and dangerous as riding the Grande Boucle. And there were the other fans, getting the autographs, though from what I could see they all look the same: the illegible scrawl on the offered page.

George Hincapie lolls against a US Postal team car, pensive in mint-blue sunglasses. He's no climber and today is going to be murder for him and the rest of the autobus. In these conditions it's going to be horrible for everyone; but the Ventoux always is a terror, whatever nastiness the weather adds to the terrible gradients on that bare mountain. Hincapie fields the question amicably – he'll be working for Lance (Armstrong) as will the whole team – but his mouth is dry, his mind brooding on the imminent suffering in prospect. Yet he *does* answer the questions. Like most of them, he's polite and generous with his time and temper, even if this time of waiting, waiting, hangs about them all like an undelivered job contract. They are accessible as no other sportsmen are to the fans and the media.

A sudden rush of bodies – microphones and cameras bristling, a mob of press men flocks to the emergence of Marco Pantani, double winner of Tour and Giro d'Italia in '98, disgraced and eliminated from the Giro in '99 and back now after a miserable year full of lost confidence, ambiguous enthusiasm, inadequate preparation. He is here to test himself once more against the best but with no thoughts much beyond getting to Paris. He's a star, though, and everyone wants a bit of him. No point in my trying to join that scrum.

As I stroll on down the open corridor between the parked cavalcade of following cars, the start only a few minutes away now, Jan Ullrich rides past, and, in the green jersey, his team-mate Erik Zabel, who is leading in the points competition and is going for a record fifth win, but has no stage victories as yet in this Tour. As he passes the very Cofidis van which saw me in, the driver's door swings open and nearly takes him out like a sideswipe of the Tashkent Express, mad Djamolidin Abdujaparov, weaving about like a wind-up mouse, his head down, bugger everyone else in the final sprint. But Zabel hardly blinks; merely rolls his shoulders, leans the bike clear and rides by, impassively. He's seen it all before in the stampede to the line, day after day. He did get his stage win finally, and he beat the record, a record held by the great Irish rider Sean Kelly, who wore the emerald with such distinction.

I met Kelly on the 1998 tour of the Blazing Saddles, an eccentric cycling club which every year embarks on a three-week ride to raise money for the blind of Ireland. Kelly is the ride leader and heads a *peloton* of around 150 cyclists and club hot-shots down to Sunday morning leisure pedallers. What unites them all is love of the bike, a taste for good company (and the fine beverages which lubricate it) – and the 'craìc', all gathered up in a cheery willingness to convert the push of their pedals into cash funds dedicated to those for whom the riding of a bike solo is not possible. There are blind cyclists who join the annual tours – Europe, America, Indonesia – on tandems piloted by sighted riders and it's no small part of the Blazing Saddles spirit, that cooperation on the bike. Kelly does the rides because he loves the bike and one would be maligning the man if one only mentioned that he's not principally celebrated for the craìc (he is, after all, one of the few people to be credited with answering a question in a radio interview by nodding). On a bicycle he becomes almost voluble with speed, and like many of the best in the *peloton*, he prefers his bike to do his talking for him. The air rushing past in his slipstream was often more interesting than whatever hot air issued from between his lips.

I joined the Blazing Saddles for the ride from Lourdes to Lisbon. My friends Nick and Jan had been employed to plan the route (no easy task given the state of many roads in Portugal) and they had asked me to be back marker: it would be my job to ride at the rear of the long snake of the bunch and come in last, to make sure everyone was in safely. Sometimes, given the broad interpretation of the epithet 'leisurely' amongst certain sections of the ride, I found myself riding so slowly I thought gyroscopic motion must surely fail and I'd be toppling off sideways onto the tarmac. There were some seriously steady, even stately, cyclists toiling up those roads, I can tell you. However, one afternoon, taking my responsibilities by the letter, I found myself waiting for Kelly himself to catch up. Now the man may not have been at the peak of racing fitness – he'd not even shaved his legs, for heaven's sake – but my humming and hahing by the verge waiting for one of the finest riders in the history of cycling, the papers of his last contract hardly yet yellowing with age, needs explanation.

Kelly seems to be ready at the drop of a bidon to divest himself of superfluous items of racing gear while in the saddle. This is a necessity in the *peloton*, of course, where even urination often has to be done on the move. This particular post-prandial interlude having turned out fairly hot, he had decided he did not need an undervest and, his usual quick-change artistry deserting him, had, in divesting himself of the article, inadvertently discarded it by the wayside and he stopped to retrieve it. He rode back up to me and I tagged on behind him. We started to chase after the bunch ahead tipping over the far horizon like a final mouthful of Guinness and, after a few hundred yards or so, I reflected: 'Good gracious, now, I'm riding in the slipstream of Sean Kelly, no less.' And then:

'So we should share the work, shouldn't we?': a reasonable assumption I think you'll agree. This found me a few seconds later with the man in *my* slipstream. I can't think of a better example of his love of the bike than for an illustrious champion such as Kelly to be sharing tows uncomplainingly with the hoi polloi. As to his uncompromising mastery of the bike, here follows one version of the story.

Kelly's career – the mere recital of which is to unscroll most of the racing honours on offer – makes for a good example of the way a professional rider learns self-confidence in the lengthening of his experience. Gaining self-confidence may seem an odd subject for education in the professional *peloton*. Surely men such as Kelly are clearly riders of top flight from the outset? For sure, they may take time to get into their stride but the victories begin to accumulate steadily and you can, perhaps, hardly imagine they ever want for so apparently earthbound a commodity as *self-confidence*. But there is a world of difference between finding you can keep up with the rest – and on glorious occasion, leap ahead of them – and the discovery of that secret assurance which imposes your will on them, which makes the rest of them keep up with you, to look to what *you* are doing, and to seek out *your* wheel because they know it's the soundest one to follow.

As a youth Kelly was a tall, gangling, awkwardly-muscled individual, but however unprettily he rode, he could ride fast and if his ambitions were slow to mature, he certainly knew about the world of continental racing, far off as it seemed from the glens and downs of Waterford. The great Seamus Elliot (stage winner in 1963 which put him in yellow) had led the way from Ireland to France and, as for many boys born into farm life, the lure of a high-earning career doing what they were exceptionally good at, even for a limited time, was powerful. It was, though, a far call from the future he had grown to expect (an apprenticed bricklayer) and he doubted the possibility. But there is always that leap of belief – of imagination, even. So when the man who was to be his first *directeur sportif* in the Flemish Flandria team, Jean de Gribaldy, contacted him and proposed flying over in his private plane for talks about a contract, Kelly was suspicious. De Gribaldy, '*Le Vicomte*', haggled with a taxi driver to take him all the way from Dublin airport to the remote family house 160 km away, asking the way up the muddy tracks from passing tractor drivers. There must have been some comic exchanges there, Belgian to Irish and vice versa . . .

They talked and the *Vicomte* offered Kelly four thousand pounds. Kelly argued with himself that if the man were *that* keen to come so far and no easy journey he was probably worth more and asked for six thousand. Three weeks later, the tough farmboy found himself installed as a lodger with a couple whom he came to regard as his continental family in Belgium. He says he had never planned to be a pro; certainly he was extremely cautious about entering the ranks. He'd ridden a race under a pseudonym in South Africa, at that time ostracised from the international sporting community because of Apartheid. A *Daily Mail* photographer covering the latest marriage of Richard Burton and Elizabeth Taylor there thought it'd be fun to add some cyclists to the picture and Kelly was found out. Banned from competition by the International Olympic Committee he missed the Montreal Olympics and was heartbroken. That extreme reaction to the disappointment must have helped harden him to any show of feelings aroused by anything to do with the bike. He became impenetrable and that mask of impassivity served him well; no one could get to Kelly. His face might have stared on the Gorgon, so little did it reveal of his inner reactions: there was only ever the distorted grimace of total absorption in the work and the sunburst of delight at the finish as the arms went up for another win.

The early days in Belgium must have been lonely, but he did not let that get to him. He was there to learn a trade. He trained and rode hard; went to bed early; spoke on the phone to his girlfriend (later to be his wife) back home. He was in Belgium to do one thing: to become a professional bike rider, and nothing else must be allowed to intrude. It's an attitude, a monkish approach, which doesn't sit well with many young riders contemplating the demands of the sport nowadays. Poulidor made the point from the outside and David Millar from the inside: it's hard work, unrelenting, taxing on time, patience and youthful exuberance. The partying still goes on – in and out of season – but all-round, all-season winners have to set their own agenda and it's an ascetic one. In recompense for the isolation in a foreign culture, Kelly put what is the routine argument: doing what he loved *and* being paid for it was the best reward anyone could dream of. Besides, riding a bicycle beat bricklaying any day. Sean Yates said the same: earning a pittance doing something you didn't care for held no charms, a no-hope job destroys all lust for life, and Poulidor always asserted that no day on the bike ever lasts as long as a day on the farm during harvest.

The trade was not an easy ticket nor had it ever been. Kelly found working as a *domestique* punishingly hard – the riding itself and the particular responsibility, the unquestioning subservience, even to a leader as richly-talented and rewarding to ride for as Freddie Maertens, the Flandria star of the time.

Of Maertens, Kelly said: 'He had so much class. For getting into position and sprinting clear he was the classiest rider I ever saw.' His *palmarès* bear some resemblance to Kelly's: classic one-day races, the Tour of Spain (Vuelta), Paris–Nice and the green jersey on two Tours. But Maertens was a prolific stage winner – which Kelly surprisingly was not. He won eight stages in 1976 and five in 1981. He also won the World's Road Race championship twice, in '76 and '81. He was a perfect rôle model: dedicated and hard-training. He would ride to post-Tour criteriums, for the extra miles.

As with every relationship between leader and the rest, the humbler lights of the team had to grind themselves senseless in an effort to protect and launch the leader, only to find themselves dropped off the back as the bunch sped away and then toil home, minutes adrift. That yo-yo-ing back and forth like worker ants ate into their reserves, their determination to persist, their pride. In some ways they might justifiably have concluded that they were, effectively, riding a completely different race, a race in which they had no personal interest at all; their position on the board almost an irrelevance – except that, their labour for team interests accomplished, they also had to produce enough continuing evidence that they were still worth the contract and that their abilities might, when unleashed, come up with more substantial results than 'worked hard, also ran'. That is the start of ambition and a pro rider is nothing without ambition. Self-belief is another matter. And it is easily bruised.

On the 15th stage of his first Tour in 1978, 10 km from the broad avenue finish in St Etienne (a favourite with sprinters), Maertens told Kelly he was not feeling too good, so that Kelly could have a go himself. Nearing the *arrivée*, Maertens rode up. He'd changed his mind. He had a sniff of a win so Kelly must lead him out. With 500 metres to go, Kelly jumped as he sensed a rider on his wheel and assumed it to be his boss. It was actually Bernard Hinault, in *his* début Tour and, when Kelly pulled over to give him the gap, watched in misery as the Frenchman stormed past and took the win, robbing Maertens. These were painful lessons: they put iron into your soul at the time, and iron into your will later – if you have the character to absorb it.

Kelly greatly admired Maertens – the epitome of the professional rider, leaving nothing to chance, preparing wholeheartedly for every race. There could be no more compelling example for a young rider

Charlie Holland in 1938, breaking the Liverpool–Edinburgh record (set by Frank Southall), by 12 minutes in a time (rounded up) of 10 hours. Immaculately groomed, he is clad in the black tights and alpaca jacket worn by time-trialists of the day to render them inconspicuous. Note the racing bike with bell.
(*Cycle Sport*)

RIGHT: Tour de France, 1958. Nicolas Barone, riding for Paris-Nord-Est, chats in French with his trade team-mate – and still his friend – Brian Robinson, riding for the Internations team: learning the language, doing the job. (Author's collection)

BELOW: An illustrious breakaway quartet climbing the col du Tourmalet, the first Pyrenean stage of the 1963 Tour de France: (left to right) Raymond Poulidor (8th overall), José Perez-Frances (obscured; 3rd), Frederico Bahamontes (2nd) and Jacques Anquetil, who won the stage and the race. (*Cycle Sport*)

ABOVE: Barry Hoban bursting through ahead of a clutch of ace sprinters, 8th stage into Bordeaux, Tour de France, 1975. (*Cycle Sport*)

BELOW: Tour de France, 1972, 17th stage. Eddy Merckx in the foreground, in the yellow jersey, alongside Frans Verbeck (no. 131), Cyrille Guimard (green jersey, soon to abandon), and Lucien Aimar (winner, 1966). Bernard Thévenet took the stage. (*Cycle Sport*)

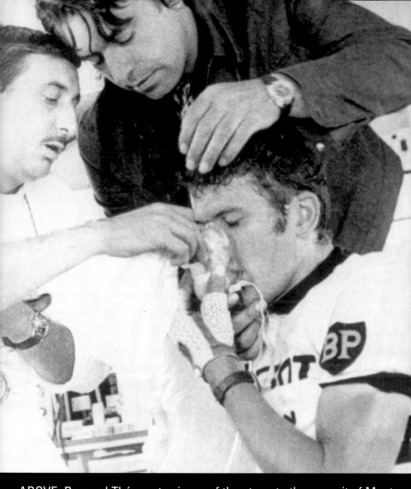

ABOVE: Bernard Thévenet, winner of the stage to the summit of Mont Ventoux, Tour de France 1972, succumbs briefly to lack of oxygen, and to heat and exhaustion. (*Cycle Sport*)

OPPOSITE PAGE TOP: Newcomer to the Tour de France, Paul Sherwen, gets his first taste of the high mountains, the enthusiasm of the fans, the heat and the need for unwavering concentration, 1978. (John Pierce)

OPPOSITE PAGE BOTTOM: Giro d'Italia, 1982. In the mountains. Bernard Hinault (the eventual winner, already wearing the leader's pink jersey) bracketed by Lucien Van Impe (in the leading climber's jersey) and Silvano Contini (3rd overall). (*Cycle Sport*)

ABOVE: Sean Kelly leading the way on the *pavé* of the Hell of the North, Paris–Roubaix in 1984. He took the race from Rudy Rogiers, a Splendor rider, perhaps on his wheel here. Riding straight along the crown of the cobbles road is rougher but offers the most direct route. (Graham Watson)

BELOW: Sean Yates out on his own in bitterly cold conditions (one entire team abandoned that day) to win the second stage of the 1988 Paris–Nice race into St Etienne by 2 minutes, 15 seconds from Sean Kelly, the eventual winner. Stars like Laurent Fignon and Charly Mottet came in 15 minutes adrift. (*Cycle Sport*)

ABOVE: At the *Départ*, Chris Boardman, distinctly unimpressed, makes a brave face of having his picture taken alongside 'the Devil' for somebody's private photo album – souvenirs of the Tour de France. (*Cycle Sport*)

BELOW: The author (right) with Raymond Poulidor at his home.

Phil Liggett (left) and the author relaxing on the
Cudlee Creek run, Adelaide, January 2001.

embarking on his career and it is no surprise that Kelly saw himself, like his first team leader, as primarily a sprinter. Maertens, however, was careful to go down to the Alps to prepare himself and, if he didn't turn himself into a climber there he did at least reduce his fear of the mountains. He spent ten days in yellow on the '76 before surrendering overall lead to Lucien Van Impe, the eventual winner, on the stage up to l'Alpe d'Huez.

Kelly's early concentration on sprinting probably marks a certain caution. The larger demands of what he called 'the 100 per cent race', the Tour de France, were, at least to begin with, beyond him. Better therefore to limit his objectives, make an intelligent assessment of his own abilities and the kind of experience he'd need to expand his aims. This is no more than an indication of the slow flowering of his confidence, though he took to the rough-house of the sprint finishes with obvious relish. It drew out the larger depths of his spirit and temperament. There, in the scramble for the gaps, the pushing and shoving, the elbowing and testing of nerve, the quiet-spoken young Irishman with little to say off the bike found a glorious touch of his native eloquence; a natural expression of his ebullient strength. He was a great and confident handler of the bike and showed skills no doubt schooled on the rutted tracks of his home territory and what he called 'Paddy weather' – the rain and wind lashing the bogs of Ireland. When he found himself riding along with his chain-ring submerged in water, through torrential rain, he could feel almost nostalgic. I myself watched in amazement as he punted cardboard boxes into the verges with a sideways flick of his back wheel, a big grin on his face. I've no idea how he does it but it's a favourite trick. As we rode down a long section of cobbles in Portugal one day, he was chatting to Nick in the following car. Suddenly, Nick cried: 'Watch out, Sean, pothole.' Kelly didn't bat an eyelid, flicked his bike, jumped over the cavity and carried on talking. He did, after all, win the Paris–Roubaix twice and there's no more bruising trial of a bike-rider's handling skills.

He is on record as saying that 'there is no such thing as a straight sprinter' but that may be no more than his way of describing the ruthless business of contesting the finishes down the long strait between the barriers in a large pack, wheel to wheel, densely squeezed into what seems to be a diminishing space, going for the narrowest of gaps, holding a line against immense pressure from other riders, constantly on the alert against the madmen who ride with their heads down, weaving about dangerously – and illegally. To embroil oneself in that level of close-order combat at the same time as avoiding being toppled in the crush takes huge nerve and physical strength. As Barry Hoban said, there is no place for real skulduggery, no criminality: that would serve against all riders and all riders are earning their living. Terrible accidents have happened in the final metres but generally through the idiotic carelessness of a spectator. In 1995, at Armentières, Laurent Jalabert was brought down when he collided with a policeman taking a photograph outside the barriers, but miscreancy amongst the riders is rare. In 1999, Tom Steels flagrantly shouldered Jan Svorada into the barrier before jumping past Mario Cipollini. He was relegated to last position and protested that this was unjust. Svorada had been strong enough to ride the shove and stay on his bike. Had he gone down there would have been carnage. (Steels has a very short fuse. He was disqualified in 1997 for hurling a bidon at another rider metres from the line.)

On the other hand there is an inflexible attitude to racing which the locked-in duelling of the final sprints does engender, depending as it so often does, on tiny photo-finish margins on the very line. Phil Liggett told me that even racing in the Carrick-on-Suir Christmas Hamper, the annual charity race round Kelly's home town, Kelly won't willingly accept defeat, even if his intransigent disbelief at even the possibility of losing to anyone may the man's idea of a joke. Every year Liggett joins him at the Carrick-on-Suir Christmas Hamper. First prize is something in the region of an Irish punt. One year Liggett got into a break near the finish, hung on and beat Kelly by a lap. Kelly refused to believe that he'd come only third. He argued and swore blind that he'd clipped the upstart on the line, whacked him, he'd come second not third and how could the cheating, conniving, interloping spalpeen dare to be thinking he could beat the fellow, and in front of his cheering home public, too? He was still protesting when the tannoy announced that Liggett had indeed done the business after all. At which point Kelly smiled and gave up. But the race was that important to him: whether for the price of a small glass of Guinness or for the rainbow jersey. That's the attitude. Kelly is a hard man, for sure, and he's totally direct. He's like a kid on the bike: he simply loves it. And his smile is not about giving in graciously, rather he's thinking of the next time when he'd take his revenge. There is never time to mourn defeats. Chewing over what is eating at you – the narrowest of losses, the ill-luck of the race, the snatching away of what you had in your hands – eats up your mind and spirit. Should you lose, you work out how you might have won and set your targets again; there is always another day.

He took time to flower. At the World's Road Race in Goodwood, 1981, he took the bronze behind Giuseppe Saronni and Greg Lemond.

His team manager, de Gribaldy told him that he'd ridden like an amateur. Chasing every attack, he wore his strength out. He was still clear of the other two when Saronni jumped some distance from the finish, and Kelly had nothing to answer either him or Lemond. It was the closest he ever came to a World title and he said, in praise of the support the young Stephen Roche gave him that day, that if he could split the medal in two Roche would have had half. Six years later, Kelly repaid the debt and helped Roche to the rainbow jersey in Austria.

Kelly's fearless sprinting matched his fearless descending. Like many others he relied on recouping time on the downhill that was lost in the uphill. I've seen him at it. On the last day of the Blazing Saddles tour, six of us went out for a three-hour ride from the old town of Tomar. Kelly had ridden himself in by then. He'd shaved his legs and taken a bit of a tan. We rode side by side and chatted amiably. He really does get quite garrulous on the bike, clicking away at the gear changes as his energy trickles out of the tips of his fingers, used to the limbering up for the big charge at the end. Towards the end of the ride, the pace hots up and cyclists with any competitive instinct are like horses when they sniff the approach of home, and it was a pleasure to be drumming up such a speed, all of a gallop, pretending that there was a red kite ahead of us announcing the last kilometre into the barriers, a cheering crowd and a nice prize – instead of a shower and a glass of *vinho verde* out of the tap at the bar round the corner from the hotel. We hit a descent and (quite against the run of the ride) I dropped off the back. I was riding on half a brake, I tell you, the front one – the back one had seized like a frozen shoulder and I was hopelessly disadvantaged. Heart thumping at the likelihood of missing the line of a bend, I watched Kelly hurtling round the corners on the wrong side of the road, one foot out of the cleat dragging on the road surface to check the speed and sway of the machine under him. Still in for the cut of risk, still, like Albert Ramsbottom, 'not showing a morsel of fear'. Speaking of what went through his mind at such times he would say that you think of winning, not of hospital. Indeed, once the reverse is true, it's time to stop.

Some incidents yelled caution at him, nevertheless. He speaks of the crash which cost the New Zealand rider Paul Jesson his leg. Descending too fast in the Dauphiné Libéré in 1980, Jesson collided with a car and smashed his knee. The wound turned gangrenous and the leg was amputated. Things like that frightened him; sharp reminders of how vulnerable riders are on their bikes, especially when dicing with extreme speed on fast, tricky, switchback descents.

Kelly had doubts from the beginning: doubts about his own ability and about his capacity to survive. But such uncertainty is common and it's the major hurdle. People who do not know the pro game will write off such difficulties as if they were fiction or excuses, a needless trouble. ('You joined the profession: what did you expect?') But even the best simply do not know what to expect. The transition is always very hard: the physical demands are so much greater than anything they've ever experienced and there's the psychological pressure, the mental strain. Kelly faced what every new rider faces: the simple fact is that you shape up or ship out. Some fail their own promise and it is almost always the extreme rigour of life in the professional *peloton* which defeats them: the racing, the training and the discipline. It is not a simple choice to make, however stark the demands. Timid spirits will haver and let some fatal weakness seep in. *Sometimes in life you have to take risks* and the risk-taking has to be wholehearted. That is the single characteristic of all these men I have talked to, their strength in that decision: to hold nothing back, to risk all and to go for broke.

The pattern of Kelly's career shows how he progressed to the top ranks from the slightly diffident *domestique*, the young Irishman abroad, living like a hermit. One season he spent down in the south of France in almost complete seclusion. He cannot have been happy. Phone calls back home sustained his spirits but homesick or not, if this rather bizarre existence was what being a pro rider demanded he must get on with it.

Kelly's consummate ability and racing intelligence made him *the* complete bike rider, even if he did not win the Tour de France. He did wear the yellow jersey, however, and came fourth in 1985 (his compatriot Roche came third) and in the top ten four times. Concentrating on the green points jersey he probably sacrificed a greater tally of stage wins, winning only five in all. Perhaps he compromised his chances by the excessive generosity of his effort. He did, too, ride for teams who did not make the French Tour a first priority – and team cohesion is essential to victory in any stage race. In 1983, for example, the young Australian Phil Anderson, in excellent form, looked like the best bet for his (French) Peugeot team, but he was under orders to work for Pascal Simon who was in yellow as the Alps approached. Even when Simon fell and fractured his shoulder blade and was clearly not going to make Paris (he eventually abandoned on l'Alpe d'Huez) the team, Anderson included, had to slave away in his lost cause. Had Anderson been French he would undoubtedly have become acknowledged leader and had the full support of his co-riders. Internal muddle has wrecked many a fine rider's chances and

Anderson, a class rider (he wore yellow jersey and the white jersey of best young rider in his first Tour), was particularly unlucky in 1983. Kelly won the points jersey that year without taking a stage. He missed a win on the Champs-Elysées by a whisker to Gilbert Glauss, that year's *lanterne rouge*.

Kelly raced and won all season round. He trained harder than most in the off-season and invariably came to the start of the racing year in unbeatable form. He won seven Paris–Nice on the trot. He ducked nothing and it was perhaps the case that this reduced his potential for Tour victories. He was caught between the drive to win everything else and the exaggerated, exclusive demands of a victory in the Tour. He thought of himself as no more than a sprinter, content to ride along in the anonymity of the pack, even to limit his efforts in time-trials to save the green. As he himself put it, much of the time he was content to do just enough against the clock, rather to coast than drive himself to the limit for a race he couldn't win.

It wasn't until he rejoined de Gribaldy in the small Sem team for 1982, that Kelly, with guidance, began to think of himself as more than just a sprinter. De Gribaldy built the team around him and suddenly he had to take on a larger sense of his own abilities. On the final day of the Paris–Nice, Kelly led the race ahead of the Frenchman Gilbert Duclos-Lasalle, a noted time-trialler and winner in 1980 by a mere second. They faced a time-trial here up the col d'Eze, which climbs to some 500 metres in 11 kilometres. For a man not known for doing well against the clock, this long uphill drag posed quite a test. Kelly batted away predictions about how he'd perform. Sure, he was in cracking form but the time-trial didn't favour him and besides his ambitions didn't include winning the race. It was routine bluff for the dead-pan Irishman. Duclos-Lasalle, on the other hand, showed every sign of confidence; Kelly had never shone in time-trials; he'd have that second and a heap more on top.

In fact Kelly trounced him by 44 seconds and the runner-up, Alberto Fernandez, by 14 seconds. For such a short course that was a whopping margin.

Tour winners are a breed apart, and Kelly did shy away from the absolute responsibility of leadership in the early days. Perhaps he left the ruthless task of Tour responsibility too late. He did, after all, take the tough Tour de Suisse and the Vuelta a España, neither of which are short of mountains to climb. The Tour, though, is different. Even so, he was the world number one three years in succession and won the Super Prestige trophy between 1984 and '86.

He was always too much his own man, disinclined to look to others, a rider with a voracious appetite for winning and a psychological toughness which no one could breach. Until his last season, when it appeared that he was tiring and was no longer impervious, there was no getting to Kelly. He was the man to beat, the man they all trusted, the man they respected; utterly dependable and utterly inscrutable. He trained without consideration of anything so pathetic as bad weather, for instance, and it was the disciplining of the inner strength which made his stupendous *palmarès* possible.

The day before the *Départ* from Carpentras (a rest day) I'd gone down to see Phil Liggett and Paul Sherwen and, sitting at a table outside the Channel 4 caravan, I felt a tap on my shoulder. It was Kelly, he'd come to share the Eurosport commentary with David Duffield. Kelly would be there to fashion the intermittent pauses in the virtually non-stop Duffield stream of consciousness, as well as to supply a shrewd reading of the race – an arcane literacy not learned by many, and certainly not with his fluency. He smiled and we chatted a bit; Duffield pitched up and the conversation widened till duty called and off they went.

One morning on the Blazing Saddles ride, we set out from Bilbao, home of those luckless Spanish children who, the year before, had been on holiday in Northern Ireland and were tragically killed in the IRA bombing at Omagh. It fell to Kelly to speak for us all. We stood in silence by our bicycles in the street outside the hotel, the whole phalanx – cyclists and support team; a small civic deputation grouped alongside Kelly at our head, a few hotel staff and pedestrians stopping to wonder what was going on. The air was warm and still, the normal chatter and bustle of the day's start paused and in the quiet of that morning, our last in Basque country, with thoughts of other terrorist bombings crowding at us, Kelly delivered a moving tribute to the innocent dead and a blunt reminder of how senseless the continuing violence is. He spoke in English and then in the Castilian he learnt when he was riding for Spanish teams. He did it with perfect grace: a man of his word, a man of the bike.

Kelly retired from the *peloton* in 1994, after 18 years as a professional and 194 career wins – 32 of them in 1984. His last race was an open invitation to honour him in Carrick-on-Suir. 1,200 riders signed up. The whole field was allowed to race at 24 kph for 80 km but for the final 16 km only the first 50 raced and it was to go to the fastest. Kelly caught the leaders as the race hit town, past Sean Kelly Square – and won. Several ex-pros came, buddies from his racing days, including Laurent Fignon,

Stephen Roche, Roger de Vlaeminck and Eddy Merckx – who summed up the way Kelly was regarded: 'I am very busy' he said 'but I had to come. Sean is such a great champion.'

Kelly, still full of the sheer fun to be had on a bike after those years of hard trade on it, said that day in his home town: 'The people have done me a great honour turning up in such numbers and that riders such as Merckx have spared the time makes me even prouder.' That is the man: tough as nails, unbeatable in his day, and despite all his victories, modest. May the wind be always at his back – as the bunch so often was.

12. PAUL SHERWEN

When I phoned Paul Sherwen at his goldmine near the Kenya–Uganda border in late December, he asked me if I could call back in ten minutes. Father Christmas had just arrived from Nairobi.

We first met in Compiègne, on the eve of the Paris–Roubaix one-day classic. Sitting over a coffee in a café next to the square in front of Napoleon's Imperial Palace, the departure point of the race, he told me how one time – in the days of toe clips and straps, he'd ridden the race on track pedals, with no quills at the side to enclose the straps, so his feet were double-strapped in. He came off nine times. This isn't untoward. The Paris–Roubaix is nothing without the cobbles, the rain, the crashes, the pile-ups, the grime, mud, dirt, dust and what seems like the entire population of Picardy out to cheer the riders through the 'Hell of the North', encouraging them in the local patois, the *ch'timi*. This is their home territory, so often the battlefield of Europe and their patrimony – the Paris–Roubaix *peloton* celebrates the land and the folklore as nothing else. After the race I was given a lift to the station by a man, Daniel Carlier, who turned out to be a local poet. He sings the praises of the Hell:

> Même un coureur su sin vélo
> Malgré qui treuf' cha redoutappe
> Dins 'Paris–Roubaix' ch'est ch'gros lot.
> Un pavé de ch'Nord ! Comme ch'est biau.

> Even a rider on his bike,
> Though he may find it daunting, gets an inestimable reward
> In Paris–Roubaix; it's *the* first prize.
> A *pavé* of the North. What a beautiful thing.

(The French use 'beautiful' to mean a variety of things, but of the suffering of a bike race? Well, observe David Millar's comments on this *beautiful* sport in chapter 16.)

Well, when Sherwen came off for the ninth time that day, and lay there face-down, tangled up in the bike, feet still locked onto the pedals; wet, cold and daubed in mud, it's as well the argot poet wasn't there to sing that rhapsody in his shell-like ear. Instead, Sherwen thought: 'Bugger this, that's that; I'm not getting up again' only to find himself and the bike being lifted bodily by a bunch of bystanders. Having got him upright once more, they pushed him forward and, with whatever reluctance, he was back in the race. They were doing him a good turn they thought. How could he let them down? He got going and, that day, came 15th.

He was riding for the La Redoute team and, he said, the Paris–Roubaix was the race they all went potty for. The *pavé* sections cut through bleak, open farmland and long stretches of ancient woodland, including the Arenberg – a gloomy, dense Druidic wilderness of forest, where the black trees overhang the dilapidated old cart track which is the *pavé*. Traversing it, the bikes get shaken to botheration, the riders get bruised, battered and filthy, like sewer rats chasing freedom on two wheels.

The La Redoute headquarters were in Roubaix and the week before 'the Hell', the whole team was hyper; so excited about what they thought of as their 'home ride'. In the days leading up to it, they'd do the Gand–Wevelgem and ride back afterwards, another 60 km on top – then the Grand Prix de Denain (the Denain *pavé* section lies just beyond the Arenberg) and 40 km home. Sherwen won the Denain once and quite obviously loved the absurd challenge of the cobblestones for the cavalier exhilaration it drew out of them all; the particular pride in saying 'we did that one, all right', as if racing on flat, smooth, endlessly long roads over hideous high mountains at a pace to break your heart wasn't already hard enough.

Sherwen was born in Africa and came to England to be educated. He lived as a pro cyclist in France and Belgium and, after the *peloton*, went back to the African bush to live and work. When he tells people that he used to be a cyclist they laugh and say 'Oh, right. Ever ride the Tour de France? Ha, ha, ha.'

And he says 'Yes,' pauses and adds: 'Seven times.'

It's curious this idea that the Tour de France is something any of us who ride a bike can just turn up for. I've been asked countless times if I ever rode it. Such ignorance (nearly inexplicable to even a mild fan) does prove one thing, however: the Tour de France is *the* bike race that is almost universally known. The regular Channel Four coverage (now, criminally, axed), for which Sherwen joined Phil Liggett as commentator, has opened the event up to an even wider audience who actually *see* the race (and can therefore, surely, have no illusions about who gets to ride it!) but there are still those who make no connection between the Tour and the everything it represents to the pro cyclist.

That is how Sherwen put it to me, when I asked just what it *is* about the Tour that's so exceptional. First there is the unique *history* of the race. This really is one of the legendary events in the sporting calendar – and that's not just the French making extravagant claims, either. (Not all modern riders accord that history due respect. The flourishing of Stars and Stripes is a regrettable annoyance of misplaced jingoism, I believe. Winners of the Tour de France wear yellow not national bunting.) And as for the race itself: 'It's everything,' Sherwen says. 'It's the race with the greatest prestige. The climbs aren't harder than in the Giro, the stages aren't longer, the whole race is probably no more punishing overall *but* it's the one every rider wants to do. A stage win in the Tour puts you into the record books; wins at the Vuelta and the Giro don't mean nearly so much. Even to get to the start, to find yourself riding in the Tour goes beyond everything else in the sport.'

To illustrate the point, take that day on his last Tour, in 1985 – stage 10, 204.5 km, Epinal–Pontarlier, heading for the Alps. Bernard Hinault had attacked from the start, the speed was crazy. Only 5 km out, one of Sherwen's team-mates, Jerôme Simon, touched a wheel just ahead of him and started to go over. Sherwen grabbed his shirt and hauled him up before he fell but in doing so, lost his own kilter and swerved into the roadside barriers. He fell heavily across them onto his back. Two members of the team stopped to help, Régis Simon and Alain Bondue, World pursuit champions in 1981 and '82. They got Sherwen back on his bike and tried to relay him. After another 5 km, Sherwen realised that he simply could not hold their wheel, he was in such pain. Ahead of them, Hinault had sat up, having made his point ('I'm in charge and don't forget it') but the bunch had, collectively, decided that the point was worth turning round on him and were keeping the speed high. Sherwen's difficulties might eliminate him, but the team could simply not afford the loss of two others in what looked like a vain attempt to save him. He told them to clear off and leave him to it. This was a classic professional dilemma with one horn decidely shorter than the other: whatever friendship dictated (Bondue was Sherwen's best man) it must not be allowed to impede team duty. They left – and Sherwen, in a crippled state, faced a 190 km solo ride.

Had this been a Giro or a Vuelta, Sherwen told me, he would almost certainly have climbed off. But it was the Tour de France. You don't abandon the Tour de France, that's how compelling it is, how important. His ride was probably doomed, but he kept to it, the broom wagon churning along behind him. It was the presence of that vehicle, the motorised Grim Reaper of the Tour caravan, hovering like a vulture, which helped to keep him going – the car of his humiliation just waiting to open the doors. Even if there is some spurious romance attached to the last man in the race, the *lanterne rouge*, that tail-end red lamp actually more frequently shines in a stricken rider's face like the feverish STOP light of the torture train receding inexorably into the distance.

The rest of the *peloton* were already across the line 40 minutes before Sherwen reached the foot of the last climb up into Pontarlier. Down the hill past him on the other side as he heaved his pain-racked frame up to the finish streamed the cars, Coca Cola vans and motorbike outriders of the Tour caravan. He came in way outside the time limit for the day of course but, with a stroke of generosity and in commendation of the honour his courage had done the race that day, he was reinstated and made it to Paris. Sherwen's bravery here encapsulates what the riders feel about the Tour: it's the one race where every rider forced to abandon will probably break down in tears. This event shows the nobility of the Tour's often capricious deployment of rules and is testimony to the strength of mind, spirit and sheer will of a fine rider, a man who rode most of his career as a *domestique*.

There was precious little riding in Africa when he was a boy. He had a bike to ride a mile or so to the shop, but the rutted tracks were not suited. ('I really should get a mountain bike,' he said when I asked him if he still rides a bike. An ideal machine, I'd have thought, for an ex-Paris–Roubaix hard-labour man negotiating the rugged African turf.) His sport was swimming. He came to school in Cheshire when he was 14 and here began to take bike riding seriously for the first time. As with so many others, it was the attraction of the surrounding countryside – the green hills and quiet roads – which stimulated more interest in 'the liberty machine'. And, as with countless other riders, the man at the bike shop got the more serious things started. He suggested a bike club and Sherwen joined the Weaver Valley Cycle Club.

And then it was time-trials, those inevitable time-trials. Not Sherwen's thing. He did a few 10s and 25s but got sick of the monotony of the mindless out-and-back and got stuck into road racing. By the time he went to the University of Manchester Institute of Science and

Technology (to read paper technology), he was a promising rider and came under the direct tutelage of the legendary Harold 'H' Nelson, the university cycling coach.

He had first met 'H' Nelson at a Weaver Valley training session when he was 15 and asked if he could start work with him when he was 17. Two years later, Nelson had a phone call; it was Sherwen on the eve of his 17th birthday asking if he could come round. 'Eleven o'clock sharp – if you're a minute late forget it.' Sherwen rode 26 miles to get there, mooched around so he could arrive on the dot and when Nelson asked him what he wanted, he said: 'I want to be a pro and I want to ride the Tour de France.'

Nelson replied: 'That's easy' and when one of his boys asked him later how he could be so blasé about it he said: 'His face is hard, he'll do it. Besides – we mustn't disappoint him.'

Nelson was far ahead of his time in training methods. A doctor at Manchester University had been carrying out ECG tests on swimmers; Nelson was curious and suggested some tests on cyclists (it was much drier work). The doctor said he'd need around 20 riders to make the tests viable. No problem, Nelson said, and his experimental training methods were launched. Long before the days of heart-rate monitors and wattage read-outs, he was applying an empirical approach: checking the pulse after hard exercise by holding his hand over the rider's heart, deploying an ancient Euler ergometer from the Max Plank Institute, (which could measure from 30 watts of work up to 500 in incremental stages) and matching the effect of various intensities of effort to the heart's performance. In a thoroughly scientific way, he taught the young athlete how to judge extremes of power and energy use – you might say almost by listening to what the heart and body were instructing you to do, or to delay doing.

Sherwen joined Nelson's stable of riders; they did chain-gangs, riding bit and bit. The youngsters were never treated harshly but were always tested. They did work on the rollers, overload work on big gears to build deep muscle power. It was an ideal set-up for a young rider brimful of energy and ambition. He rode alongside professionals, amateurs, Milk Race winners – all men who were inspired to ride the bike and were devoted to the discipline which Nelson instilled into them. Nelson has a fiery spirit, too – and that shows in the buccaneering style of Sherwen's riding. 'You've got to attack these devils from the gun' he'd say, give them no time to think, hit them hard and hit them early. Sherwen soon got a reputation for attacking from the gun in races. There was also the discipline. One morning at the hotel during the Isle of Man races, Nelson asked Sherwen where he'd been the night before when he was supposed to be tucked up in bed. Sherwen looked askance. 'I know you went out – clubbing, was it? I stuck a hair across your door and it disappeared' Nelson said.

Some years afterwards, when Sherwen was managing the Raleigh Banana team, he and the riders gathered for dinner, immaculately turned out in team uniform. Nelson and a friend turned up in scruff order. Sherwen said: 'Mr Nelson, would you mind going up to change for team dinner?'

Nelson complied but later that evening Sherwen took him aside and said: 'H, what was all *that* about? They all know our relationship.'

Nelson told him that he had wanted to make the point that there was *no* preferential treatment; that they all had to learn that everyone was subject to team discipline.

It is clear from the way that Sherwen speaks of 'H' Nelson – a man who became a father figure, a deep influence on many aspects of his life beyond the bike – that this kind of training, a development of mental and physical capacities in equal measure, suited him. It was a combination of scientific method and common sense. Nelson would always make sure his riders got proper rest and would refuse to allow them to race if they weren't in tip-top shape. Like that other great inspirational trainer, Eddie Soens of Liverpool, Nelson could lift a rider to extraordinary heights of achievement. Another of his men, Graham Jones, like Sherwen had a distinguished career in the continental *peloton* – five Tours de France. Barry Hoban, meeting Nelson for the first time at a dinner, introduced himself and then congratulated him on turning out Jones and Sherwen. 'Finding one is hard' he said 'but finding two is a miracle.'

Like all the other riders I talked to for the writing of this book, Sherwen is a man of sharp intelligence. I make no comparisons; the brainpower of some exceeds others as do their *palmarès*. Yet, they all *think* and if some showed less evidence of mental vivacity early in their careers, life in the *peloton* certainly honed the mind in an impressive way. Henri Desgrange said that to be any sort of a rider it took 'head and legs'. A large part of the joy of writing this book has been the company of what must be some of the brightest men in sport – men who know themselves, men of extraordinary poise.

Another of the crucial lessons Sherwen took from 'H' was self-discipline. This might seem to be a *sine qua non* on the job-description of any pro; yet, there are many who don't have it. Laziness, temperament, excuses, being gifted but spoiled . . . there is a long list of flaws which can corrode self-discipline. 'H' brought what is often sniffily dismissed as 'old-school' virtues to his young riders. This amounts to self-respect – above all, a sense of responsibility to one's own talents and the determination not to let them slip or go to waste. From that flows a tutoring of one's foibles away from missed effort; the ability to overcome periods of penetrating doubt; the moral strength to see through hollow effort, anything less than total application. It is, even for a professional, all too easy to be playing at it; pretending you're really trying your hardest – honest, sir. What 'H' taught Sherwen was to regard your own standard as the last recall of excellence. Fail yourself and you fail all.

Gradually, the riding bug bit. He trained harder: Wednesdays, Saturdays and Sundays that were free of lectures. Even in wintertime, he'd set out from Manchester at 6 p.m., ride out into the Peaks of Derbyshire, over the long climbs up the Goyt valley to the Cat and Fiddle pub at Wildboarclough (the second highest pub in Britain, a favourite venue) and back through the Macclesfield Forest, past Pott Shrigley to Manchester – a round trip of around three and a half hours (one time into ice on the top of the hills so thick that he had to get off the bike and walk).

In the autumn of 1976, during his last year at university, he won the Pernod Star Trophy for amateurs, a season-long competition, and was invited to collect the prize in Paris at the ceremony for all the trophy prize winners of the race. Among them was Freddie Maertens, who won Super-Prestige for best pro all-rounder. At the ceremony, he met some people from the ACBB club, that cradle of so much foreign talent (although the club was not exclusively for cyclists: they had rugby and football teams, and rowers). They had heard about Sherwen and invited him to join them there and then. He explained that he had Final exams to sit the following summer. They proposed that he come for three weeks during the Easter vacation.

He rode and won the Pernod Grand Prix, a 160-plus km road race near Beaconsfield in Berkshire, climbed off the bike and got into the car with the ACBB to drive to France. In his first race in their colours he fell off, but won the next three races, concluding with the Tour de l'Essonne in the undulating country south-west of Paris. It was a remarkable initiation. He then went back to Manchester for his last term. Immediately after his final exam, one Friday in early summer, he travelled to Paris for a race in Vichy. He got battered. The next day he rode the amateur Paris–Roubaix and came third. He had launched his sojourn in France.

At the end of that first full year as an ACBB amateur, he came second in the Merlin–Plage prize for best accumulated results and was approached by Raphaël Géminiani, former team-mate and *directeur sportif* of Jacques Anquetil. Gém offered him papers for the Fiat pro cycling team and the following summer, in his débutant year (1978) he rode his first Tour de France for the team which had signed Eddy Merckx for his last Tour in 1977. Three days out from the start in Leiden, Holland, Sherwen got into a break which made it to the *arrivée* and shot up to ninth on general classification. He recalled this with immense pleasure: a spunky 21 year old, mixing it with the best in the world and coming ninth in a huge field of 110 of them. Bernard Hinault won that year in his début Tour, and riding in the same *peloton* with the 'Blaireau', ('the Badger'), he counts as a singular privilege.

'Hinault was really tough,' he said. Sherwen was near him the one bad day he ever knew him to experience. Hinault himself has said that if he had a bad day that was when he would attack hardest – so as never to let the opposition know he was suffering; but this was different. He had crippling tendinitis and his knee was buckling. He was going through real agony. One of his team, Pierre-Raymond Villemiane was wearing the French champion's jersey. (The French Federation insisted that the jersey be left completely clear of any advertising which didn't please the sponsors. Hinault had won the title in 1978 so the Renault management had lost an entire year of publicity from their star rider. They told him he wasn't to win it again and, that June in 1980, he had set up victory for Villemiane.) This day, then, Hinault was in real trouble; he'd won two Tours and wouldn't give up, but Zoetemelk (never a particularly audacious or adventurous rider) was at last turning the screw on him, knowing probably it was a real chance for time gains. It was the only time Sherwen ever saw Hinault lose his rag: screaming at his team to get up the road and tow him back.

'Villemiane! I gave you the French title – get out there and chase them.' He climbed off a few days later. Zoetemelk took his only victory. But the man had such a will.

The day after he crashed and broke his nose in St Etienne, the 14th stage, 1985, four Tour wins already, the Colombians of the Café Colombia team really turned on the pressure. (Plastic-framed Oakley glasses had just come in and most riders had contracts to wear them but Hinault was still wearing steel-framed Ray Banns: the frame broke the bridge of his nose). They went off from the start at knock-out speed, aiming to polish Hinault off. So he got the entire team with him, rode to the front of the bunch and put the hammer down as only he could for 40 km, the *peloton* hanging off the back for grim death. Then he sat up, turned to the rest of them who had *dared* challenge his supremacy and told them that, injury or not, he was still in the saddle.

The esteem of men like Sherwen is particularly significant: it marks their love and respect for the sport through their high regard for its greatest champions.

Another rider Sherwen regards highly is Sean Kelly simply because he was racing at the top of his powers from February to October. Such a hard man, a tough competitor, a real all-round champion.

If Kelly has a successor in the *peloton*, it is Laurent Jalabert, now coming to the end of an illustrious career with a host of classic victories: the yellow jersey, points competition, Vuelta, World Time-Trial Champion and World number one for the past few seasons. He took the yellow jersey in the 2000 Tour but hit a dreadful reality on the cold, wet day up to Lourdes Hautacam. He spoke of the misery of being dropped early on during the long mountainous stage across the Pyrenees in terms which may sum up the affront of suffering to a rider of his class:

> You just have to get on with it, you can't afford to lose the pedals. It was hard to accept that I couldn't follow the wheels ahead of me when we were so far away from the finish. It was not something I expected and it was difficult to accept it but there was no choice. I put everything else out of my mind – avoid thinking of what you are losing, what had happened. Stay concentrated. Stay at the limit. Push on. Go as fast as you can even knowing that it's never going to be fast enough. I slaved like a madman. I want to see my kids and look where I am, I couldn't hear the time gaps, I couldn't hear the people shouting at me to go faster. I was a blinkered horse with ear plugs in. I just had to swallow the kilometres.

I have spoken elsewhere of the impossibility of giving advice on many aspects of riding the Tour – and Jalabert's words, if they capture vividly the *misery* can still hardly prepare anyone for the endurance. There are, though, areas where advice is salutary and one rider whom Sherwen speaks affectionately of is the man who was a veteran of the *peloton* when he was a new boy: Barry Hoban. Hoban was much respected by many riders of all nationalities, but he was particularly helpful to the English speakers – Sherwen, Kelly and the American Jonathan Boyer – when they pitched up on the continent, learning the trade. 'Get yourselves to Belgium', he told them 'ride the *kermesses*. Find the local man in the race, he's going to be looking for a win and he'll know the circuit like the back of his hand.' He tutored them in the masonry of the *kermesse*: the cliques who rode for each other, the best wheels to follow. One idiosyncrasy of the time-keeping – almost certainly designed to keep the intruders on the hop – was something Sherwen experienced in his first race. The starter's gun for a race billed to start at 2 p.m. would go off a second or two before time and the entire bunch, who knew the drill, was off down the road flat-out before Sherwen was even on the bike. It took him an hour to catch them. Good lessons in staying on the *qui vive*.

Sherwen got to know Hoban's wife (Tommy Simpson's widow), Helen, very well, and also her daughters by Simpson. Sadly he was too young to have met the man himself but Simpson occupies a fond niche in his memory: the example he set, the brilliance of his riding, the strength of his character and personality. It is of profound sadness to him that Simpson is remembered by a wider audience mainly for his tragic death that was probably related to taking stimulant drugs. (He had been dosing himself with extra glucose during the Tour and had so soured his stomach he could hardly eat any solid food. A more experienced manager would never have allowed him to ride on and he almost certainly did take some amphetamines.) But this was a sportsman of enormous talent and charisma; a great ambassador for Britain in a country not always amiably disposed to Britons. The French loved Simpson for his humour, his joy in their national sport and, above all, for the exuberance and strength of his racing. The first Briton to wear the yellow jersey (and there have been only four to date), World champion, Olympic champion, winner of a pile of classic one-day races – Simpson deserves a better memorial than the grubby slur attached to his name by the ignorant masses.

Cycling today, says Sherwen (repeating a discussion I have had with him and with several others), is taking a bad rap on the drugs issue. Other sports are quite blatantly keeping the lid on the problem. It is *no* proof or excuse to say 'we haven't had anyone testing positive'. The fact is that cycle sport is (in Sherwen's words: hyperbole, perhaps, but only just) 'doing 1,000 per cent more than any other sport to tackle the issue'. He even cites his own rather short-sighted approach during his days as advisor to the Motorola team. When they were getting hammered by the Italians, complaining that the speeds they were riding at were just impossible to match, Sherwen would scoff: 'Stuff and nonsense – you eat rubbish, you drink Coca Cola. Train harder.' But, the fact is, that they were riding at a disadvantage and there are other riders in this book who suffered from that inequality. It was, says Sherwen, simply too easy to turn a blind eye to the drugs issue – to call for more work, more training, better preparation, fiercer competition on the road. However even before the Festina affair, there was a large groundswell of opinion which revolted against the taking of drugs – and that opposition to the cheats is now in strident (if not always articulate) voice. There will always be cheats and Sherwen is not the only one to make this bald statement – sadly, it was, is and will always be so. But it is incumbent on all sporting organisations to reduce the number of cheats by every means in their power. Cycling is doing this with a will and, so far, some success. What drugs tests do rugby players undergo? Formula One racers?

I asked Sherwen what he regarded as his finest moments in a distinguished racing career. Fifth on the Champs-Elysées in 1979 . . . chasing a break of four riders on a Tour stage which finished in the Roubaix *vélodrome* (he nearly got back on but won the sprint for fifth place in that sacred temple of the northern racing scene) . . . stage wins in the Four Days of Dunkerque and the Tour de la Méditerranée . . . but the best was the least expected one: winning the British National title in his final season as a pro in 1987. He did everything wrong in that race.

He rode as team captain and was already signed to be manager the following year. The team tactics, which he outlined before the race, were that they should ride for a young Raleigh rider, Dave Mann. He was in tremendous form – flying, fantastic, a real bet. Sherwen actually told them all: 'We're going to ride for Dave.'

During the race, a break went clear with four ANC Halfords riders; ANC had three teams in the race and Sherwen joined the break to monitor it. He sat at the back, did no work, keeping the seat warm for Mann for about 48 km. It became apparent that the rest of them were weakening so Sherwen attacked. No one followed. They were all spent for the time being, and there was the usual uncertainty with the combinations – riders jockeying, unwilling to help others back to the escapee.

Sherwen had about 40 km to go, clocked his speed at around 48 kph over one period of 12 minutes and, no one close to him, took the win. Sometimes the team tactics simply don't pan out: as the race develops tactics must change or adapt. It was, though, a fitting end.

This 'riding for others' is an element which many people outside cycling find hard to fathom. Sean Yates, for instance, fashioned his entire career on riding for others. Sherwen reminded me of something he'd said that rest day in Carpentras. (He knows Yates well from their days in Motorola.)

'All the medical tests carried out on Yates proved him equal to Merckx physiologically. But you can't put the Cannibal (Merckx) into anyone.'

But Yates didn't enjoy riding for himself. Leadership wasn't his bag and if he was told to take it on he went to pieces. Yet if his leader *told* him to take the lead, he'd ride like three men. During the 1987 World's Road Race, Stephen Roche, already winner of the Giro and the Tour did everything he could to get the win for Sean Kelly; riding hard at the front, chasing every break, attacking like a fool. But he found himself in the winning break and popped out of the pack, still strong enough to go for the line and took a famous triple victory equalled only by Eddy Merckx in 1974.

This generosity of riding for others is unique in sport, especially in pro cycling. All pros, by their very definition, look to themselves; such is the extraordinary nature of life in the *peloton* that their job requires them, *obliges* them to look after their fellow riders too, to a greater or lesser degree. Even Hinault gave victories to team-mates who had ridden selflessly for him.

It's all one facet of the great fraternity of cycling. At a cocktail party up country in Kenya, the British High Commissioner introduced himself to Sherwen, they exchanged pleasantries and the conversation somehow turned to bikes and, at once, they were chatting nineteen to the dozen.

13. SEAN YATES

Sean Yates's preferred method of steering a following team car is with his left knee: this leaves the right knee free for balancing the address book and both hands available for pouring the coffee from the flask preparatory to rifling through the address book and making a call. This I discovered when I was travelling in the team car with him of the now defunct Linda McCartney pro cycling (Yates was their *directeur sportif*) during the Giro d'Italia. Laid-back isn't in it. And, when the phone rang as we hit the one-in-ten hairpins at 80 kph on the run down into Genoa, Yates fielded the call and drove on one-handed. I wasn't scared (the feelings transcended mere fear), but I did get some inkling into what drove the man, and that was very far from being one-handed.

I asked him if he'd always been a good descender on the bike. 'I don't know' he said, and this response was typical. Sure, he got a reputation as one of the maddest, fastest, focused downhill men in the *peloton* but the skill came out of necessity. He had never been much of a climber (his manager at Fagor said: 'That bloody Yates can't get over a hump-backed bridge') and, besides, the mountains on the continent were so vast in comparison to what he was used to in England. He encountered them in a race for the first time in the Midi-Libre and knew he had a problem. But, typically, he went to the heart of the problem and took the only solution that presented itself: since he could never get up them fast, he had no choice but to learn how to get down them fast, to limit his losses. Later, riding the Tour de France, he would analyse the profile of a mountain stage – say three major climbs – and calculate that so long as he got to the bottom of the final climb with the main bunch he'd be okay. They were all paranoid about getting eliminated in the mountains but, as he said, 'you'd never lose 20 minutes in 20 kilometres. You just had to give it everything on the first climb, do the descent as hard as you could and hook up with the bunch for the valley run. Even if you were 300 metres adrift you'd have to work like hell just to stay in touch, or try to get back on. But if you were in the pack you were safe; you take a wheel and you need only be working at 80 per cent. The important thing was to conserve as much energy as possible for the next day. I could never do the mountains but that wasn't my job; I had to stay in the race to be ready to do my job later.'

That job was as one of the most highly-regarded *domestiques* in the *peloton*. The word means 'manservant', equivalent to the quaint English 'retainer', and the stock epithet 'faithful' applies. The *domestique* – also known as 'gregario' and 'water-carrier' (because that's what they do, fetch and carry bidons) – is there to protect his leader, to ride for him without complaint or reserve, his own ambitions completely subservient to those of the leader, in whose success the whole team shares. Individual as it may seem, pro cycling is the ultimate *team* sport and Sean Yates was the ultimate *team* man. When I put it to him that he might have been a leader, he demurred. When he sized up what it took to be a leader – the physical attributes, the talent, the capacity to absorb the extreme mental pressure of the responsibility to win and keep winning – he knew that it was not for him. On the other hand, he did know that he could be a good *domestique* and was determined to be the best. 'You knew your work finished at the point where the leader took over and besides, if you were a good *domestique* you'd always be in demand. A leader can go a while without winning, but if it goes on too long, he's out. I didn't want that added pressure.' On good days he could compete with the best in the *peloton*, but he could never predict when those days would be: a leader must be able to rely on form or else exact it from himself by an unassailable level of self-confidence tinged with mystique.

His talent wasn't immediately obvious; in his early teens he sailed, at national competition level, and was just as keen on football. Only when his father had a yen to get into cycling, when Yates was about 17, did he try the bike. Educated at a Rudolf Steiner school, he had no interest in academic subjects. Did he like school? No, he hated it. But his wife Pippa pointed out that the one asset that he and the rest of the Yates family share as a direct influence of the Steiner educational principles, is the idea of doing only what makes you happy. Money ain't the thing. Nor is the idea of a career structure where, in the pursuit of a life's work, you follow a set path, from A to B to C, all mapped out to the journey's end. Phew, you made it . . . Now what? That might seem like a programme for pure ambition – maybe the truer emergence of self is to be found in the plumbing of deeper resources than those that can be charted in long-term plans. Yates has no long-term plans and never did. He works for the moment and on the move. He is a very easy man to be around: genial, charming, relaxed. You get the sense that he could field anything; a man of immense resilience and adaptability. Some might find this unruffled, sunny disposition entirely at odds with the fearsome reputation he had as a pro cyclist (they nicknamed him 'Animal'). I don't: it's what I have found about most of the cyclists I've met, talked to and grown to like. The hostile energy goes into the pedals; elsewhere, it has no place.

His original aim was to be an outward-bound instructor, but as a very small boy in the '60s he saw Tom Simpson ride, and the bike rides in the Ashdown Forest (his local turf) were by then surely stoking his latent interest. In 1976 he and his father went to Crystal Palace to watch Bernard Thévenet racing and that sparked the change. He cashed some premium bonds, bought a bike, joined a local club and started riding – and winning – the club ten-mile time-trials. This was promise and his father encouraged it completely. And, as it did so often, added stimulus came from a friendly bike-shop owner. Tony Mills of Sutton sorted out the equipment and, on New Year's Day 1978, Yates pitched up for the first ten of the year in all the kit plus specialised time-trial machine, and was unbeatable. He was working part-time as a gardener, 9.00–12.00, then one and a half hour's training followed by the serious business of the day: hanging out. This is classic Yates country – following your own path, taking it as it comes – hard or easy, in equal measure.

He went to the Archer Road Club, once a real force in London though at the time in decline, but there was sponsorship on offer there and a first taste of road-racing – round the local Frant circuit. He won a time-trial stage in the junior Tour of Ireland, turned senior, came 6th in the 4 km Pursuit at the National Track Championships, moved to the 34th Nomads and then got dropped at the start in the Folkestone–London race (a prestigious event at the time). An attack took place, which shredded the field and Yates found himself dangling off the back – out of it, nowhere. This came as a bad shock, his first bitter taste of serious racing pace and here he made one of many practical decisions: you get dropped? You train harder: five and six hours per day, in fact. His body tolerated the new work-load readily and his form improved dramatically. Virtually unannounced he took third in the 1979 National 25-mile time-trial (behind two established riders, Addie Atkins and Phil Griffiths), and decided to go for selection in the team time-trial squad for that year's World Championships. At his first session with the squad, up in the Midlands, there was no partner for him and he had to ride the circuit on his own. The next time, paired with Ian Cammish, he was 5 mph faster than the rest, clearly a hot certainty for selection, but the BCF officials told him he couldn't be in the team: 'You're the strongest but you haven't got the technique.' (This was double talk for: we don't want you ripping our guys' legs off and they've been around a lot longer than you so why should you spoil their party and have them give up their trips abroad?)

Typically, Yates, undeterred by this hypocrisy, decided he'd go for the track squad. The fabled Eddie Soens – always his own man, never a BCF stooge, a gadfly to officialdom, nor one to mince words – told Yates bluntly that he had the posture of a postman, sorted his position out, loaned him a bike and set him loose on the track. The technique of track-racing is much more technical than team time-trialling on the road but Yates learnt it. Talent you can't put in; technique is easy to acquire with a good teacher and a willing pupil – and Yates came second to Tony Doyle (later World Champion and one of the great British track men in the National individual pursuit). Doyle pulled out of the World's and Yates rode the team and individual pursuit after breaking the national ten-mile record.

He was by now winning most of the races he entered, but over relatively short distances. He was still suffering in the longer road races, though he had what must be called near-professional support from his father as combined driver, mechanic and *soigneur*. They drove all over the place for races. The time he went to Sunderland was typical. His mother woke him at 1.30 a.m., shoved him in front of a bowl of cereal and packed him into the reclining front seat of the car. His father drove and Yates slept and arrived quite fresh. But this was still part-time work, he had no plans. He came sixth in the Grand Prix de France time-trial (he went on his own bat), entered the team and individual pursuit at the Moscow Olympics in 1980 and the end of season Grand Prix des Nations Classic time-trial in France (open to pros and amateurs) – where he met Stephen Roche, then racing for the legendary ACBB amateur club in Boulogne Billancourt, a suburb in south-west Paris. Roche told him that the club were looking for talent and that he should send in some results. A short while later, at the Grand Prix de France, Yates came second, eleven seconds behind Roche and over a minute up on the rest of the field. Roche told him: 'Forget the results – you're in.'

The British pro scene of the time was a closed shop, very insular. It had little tradition and existed rather in limbo, a rump of the British League of Racing Cyclists which had always been at loggerheads with the BCF. One gets the impression that the political squabble exerted more leverage than the desire to make headway on the road. Certainly for a young rider crossing the Channel, there was no experience on offer at home which could prepare him for what would happen on the continent.

Travelling by coach to Paris with a rider from Manchester, John Parker, laden with bike and luggage, Yates had been told that a representative of the ACBB would meet him at the Gare du Nord. There was no one at the station. Parker, who'd been over before, said: 'They're testing you, to see if you can sort yourself out.' They had an address and no more.

That 'sort yourself out' was the pattern. Yates and another conscript, John Herety, were provided with an apartment, equipment, carriage to and from races and occasionally a sub on prize money. That was incentive enough to ride for primes – to make money to buy food. They trained on the nearby track round the circumference of the Longchamps race-course. No cars, just a huge *peloton* of anything up to 500 other riders screaming round at racing speed.

They were required to ride their bikes, simply that. It was a novel and not altogether easy routine to accept. Yates was not used to sitting around doing nothing in an empty apartment. He wasn't homesick, but he did put on some weight, overdoing a régime of press-ups and weight-lifting, eating Mars bars and indulging an erratic diet. He'd been a vegetarian all his life but he suddenly found himself being carted off to restaurants at 4 a.m., for an early race start, to chomp through a plate of rice and manky steak – blue with age and frilled with yellow fat and gristle. Dietary methods were crude. The accepted wisdom was that worn muscle had to be built up with heavy meat protein and so Yates ate what he was given without complaint. As ever, he thought, if that's what he had to do then he had better get on with it.

He went more or less directly from Paris to join the three-week ACBB training camp on the Côte d'Azur. Resident in the same hotel was a young French racer called Laurent Fignon. They went training together and Yates consistently gave him what for on the flat stretches, but every time they hit a climb, Fignon was off like a madman, Yates thinking 'who is this idiot?' Three years later, that idiot won the first of two consecutive Tours de France. In those days there were a large number of early-season races in the warmer climes of the south of France and in his very first taste of amateur continental competition, the Grand Prix of St Tropez, Yates won. It was a torrid baptism into riding in a bunch of between 250 and 300 riders. (In the UK the maximum for a road race was 40.) I asked him how he got to grips with what has always seemed a singularly arcane and perilous skill: being able to ride elbow to elbow and wheel to wheel in such large packs of other cyclists, with no room for wobbles or hesitations. He said that was another thing you just had to get to grips with there and then, when it presented itself, in the first race. You learned fast or you foundered. 'You get on with it or you're stuffed' as he put it. No time for bleating; no room for errors. That is part of what Antoine Blondin called *le coureur fonctionnel*: the capacity to adapt, to shave losses to the minimum, to conserve energy and to read a race and adjudge effort accurately. Jacques Anquetil was a supreme 'functional rider', moulding his racing style on the one hand to his strength – variable, even with such a fine rider – and the circumstances which confronted him which were always in flux. There are faults in such a policy: his *palmarès* show gaps, perhaps unmerited. But, in Anquetil's case, that was a fault in temperament; he reacted badly to suspicion and unpopularity. A failure of generosity in the public made him meaner, on the bike at least, than his huge talent might have otherwise persuaded him to.

Yates spent one year with the ACBB and was offered a pro contract with the Peugeot team. Transition from one to the other was well established and it was inevitable that Yates *would* move up, but his obvious strength and racing aggression gave him the lift early. The transition to the pro bunch was a big jump: the speed, the strength and quality of the riders, the distances they raced. In England, Yates hadn't ever raced much more than 80 miles and his grounding was in much shorter distances, excelling at what is often called 'the English disease' – time-trialling. French cyclists are weaned on road-racing; the only time-trials they do are in stage races.

With the pros, Yates was racing up to 270 km regularly. Another aspect of the pro life then was the requisite of self-sufficiency. Riders were given money for a first-class fare and told to make their own way to races. (Nowadays, everything is arranged.) The Peugeot team vehicle was a van with a 504 engine. Riders used to the massive motor-homes and de luxe travel all provided by the organisation simply don't believe Yates when he tells them about the 'fend-for-yourself' system of the past – 'Yeah, yeah, yeah, things were tough in the old days, grumpy old ex-pro, blah-blah-blah' supposing that he's making it up.

Yates identifies another essential difference between those old days and the current scene: the racing is more aggressive now, more open; the chances of winning are fewer and further between; the races are more of a free for all and the possibility of controlling the action is gone. The points system introduced by the UCI in 1989 put a premium on teams maintaining form throughout the season; riders cannot be scattered across the country riding races in their own interests, they have to answer central directives from sponsors who are more and more obsessed with results, therefore, and they are less and less in the sport because they love it. The entire show is driven by commercial imperatives dependent on team success. Their ranking also depends on this, and so also whether they are invited to the prestigious first category events on the calendar or not. Second-division teams stand little if any chance of racing in the Tour de France. This has also extended the season at both ends, though many pro road men in the past competed through the winter in cyclo-cross and six-day track events. Yates would go back to France in fairly poor shape after a winter in cold, wet Sussex, where he'd scarcely ever see more than three riders out training, (his mates in the *peloton* returning from southern France or Italy, bronzed and lean) and he'd suffer like a pig in the early racing, whereas present-day riders have to be in hot form in January or they're useless. 'You can't afford to be fat or slow. [There are dishonourable exceptions: Jan Ullrich, for example, whose singular and underperforming promise must, surely, be nearing its cash-in date.] When the rest of the *peloton* are flying you don't want to get your legs ripped off and there is nothing worse than suffering on a bike.' *Nothing worse than suffering on a bike.* That is, I should say, as close as Yates got to a personal definition of motivation. With such a man talk of motivation is irrelevant: motivation is bred in the bone.

Until the size of the field proved too unwieldy even for the grandeur of the Tour de France, up to 22 teams of 10 used to ride the Tour and there would probably be something for them all to scrap for, with the race's mountain-top finishes distinct from sprints and time-trials. Lone escapes were more frequent then; the bunch showed less interest in chasing down the fugitive. Nowadays, they chase much more readily. The glory on offer is too big to let slip. There are no gifts. Whereas there used to be more willingness to share out the honours, the current mood is, by contrast, miserly.

For most riders, the end of the Tour de France used to mark the beginning of the holidays, bar a few autumn races. (There were always great exceptions here – Merckx, Hinault, Kelly . . .) This no longer happens. The World Cup competition continues into October with the Paris Tours one-day classic and, latterly, the World's track and road championships. One thing *has* eased pressure on riders, and that is the dwindling of the post-Tour criterium season. These one-off circuit races, often starting at 9 p.m. (to promote large crowds of spectators in the small towns across France, Belgium and Holland), were contested by contracted Tour riders, stars and their chosen *domestiques*, riding for appearance money in a field composed largely of fresh-legged local riders

who hadn't ridden the Tour and were hell-bent on giving the prima-
donnas a good kicking. In 1984, when Robert Millar, a Peugeot team-
mate, had won the mountain stage to Guzet Neige and the King of the
Mountains prize, he asked Yates and the Australian rider Allan Peiper to
ride a round of criteriums in Holland with him. Yates doubled his
earnings for the season and practically finished himself off. The day after
the Tour finished in Paris they drove to their base in Belgium and the
torture started: 19 days non-stop of racing; to bed at around 1.00 a.m.,
sleep till midday and then set off again; one day off, then another 11 days
more or less without a break. 'The rest of them were mega-motivated'
Yates said. 'We were just turning up. I was totally knackered at the end
of it. That winter I was sleeping hours and hours, waking up not
knowing where I was.'

Peiper and Yates were based in Belgium so had not so far to drive each
day; riders in France might be flogging up and down the hexagon, from
Normandy to Nice, Briançon to Bordeaux. Yates described one such
journey to me: from Holland to Paris, fly to Manchester for a race;
straight on to Dublin for a track event; back to Paris for a flat-out drive
to Nantes for a race; from there flat out to Bordeaux and on to a
criterium in Toulouse, whence to Tours for a race and back to Holland
for yet another race. Incidentally, why he bothered to mention driving
'flat out' is a puzzle: Yates rarely drives at anything less than flat out.

He did about 15 criteriums in 1985 but very few thereafter; the
punishing effort simply became unendurable. One major benefit of
paying current riders a full wage is that it removes the necessity for this
circus. Of course, sadly for the public profile of the sport, another
consequence is to reduce the spectacle for smaller communities who
could turn out to see the Tour stars racing round and round their town.
That closeness between riders and the public was always a marked
characteristic of cycle racing, but the advent of high commercialism and
a ravenous media scrum has strained that frankness. There are still the
Départ paddocks behind open barriers, where riders wait for the start of
the day's pasting, but sadly more and more of the big stars hide up, like
movie actors or Formula One drivers in the big motor-homes parked
alongside the team cars, roofs bristling with spare bikes and phalanxes of
spare wheels.

A professional cyclist for 15 years, Yates rode three Giri d'Italia, two
Vueltas and twelve Tours de France between 1984 and 1995. (He turned
it down in 1996 – he'd had enough.) In 1988, he won the sixth stage, a
52 km time-trial, beating two aces, Roberto Visentini by 14 seconds and

Tony Rominger, later holder of the world hour record, by 23 seconds. In 1994, when the race crossed the Channel for a stage into Brighton, through Yates's home village Forest Row, he put on yellow. I remember seeing the picture of him at the end of the fifth stage, hearing that he had taken the overall lead by a second. (He'd been in a break; one of the riders jumped at the end and took a 20-second time bonus and, by that one second, had missed the yellow.) Yates is calling over to a friend off-screen in the crowd: 'Yell-ow'. There was no sound but the word was plain and the delight palpable. It was a seemly reward for so selfless a worker. He took some 35 victories all told, including stages in all the big stage races – Tour de France, Vuelta, Paris–Nice, Midi–Libre, Dauphiné, as well as the British national championship, Tour of Belgium, Grand Prix Eddy Merckx.

At the end of his first year he was completely exhausted. He was sleeping for 15 hours, and then was scarcely able to turn a pedal. He struggled for any kind of form throughout 1983 and, but for the advocacy of other riders in the team, might have finished without a renewed contract. But his form came at last and in 1984 he was in great fettle. His career showed the sort of vicissitudes which dog any freelance professional – uncertainty, above all. Was there a contract or not? Changes of management, promises suspended. In 1986, he rode the final race before the Tour de France. His team-mate Pascal Simon fell and hurt his wrist and, at the end of the race Yates was told that he would not be riding in the Tour. He was nonetheless told to report for team time-trial training in Le Mans, close to the manager Roger Legeay's home. Yates, bringing up the rear like excess baggage, swung off after the first lap, rolled up to the *soigneur*'s car and said: 'Take me to Paris.' He flew home. A day or so later, while he was at the swimming pool, Legeay phoned leaving a message to tell him to pack his bags: Simon's wrist had actually been broken. Yates was riding the Tour.

However, not wanting to risk being without a contract, and lured by a couple of ex-Peugeots who had signed for Fagor, he 'signed a bit of paper in their team hotel' one night during the race and next season joined what turned out to be an appallingly ill-managed Spanish team.

'Bunch of nutters,' he said. 'We had ten spare wheels for the entire team in the Tour. Had to borrow stuff from other teams, the mechanic who'd never been on a bike telling us what gears we needed for Mont Ventoux and there was this guy from the sponsors who didn't know a bike race from a bullfight turning up, leaning out of the team car shouting "Do this, do that, do the other." Bazat the manager was such a donkey, everything was screwed up. Robert Millar was throwing wobblers, took a wrong turn and missed a win on the Guzet Neige climb where he'd won a few years before – it's amazing we came away with two stage wins.' (His own and Johhny Weltz's on the Puy de Dôme.)

Bad management or good, they were, in the old days, under orders. It was, he said, like the army. One Milan–San Remo, it started raining and Phil Anderson went back to the car and asked for a raincoat. 'Get back and do your job' they said. A rider sent a message back to the team car, which was driving way back at the rear of the following caravan, for a helmet. The message came back: 'If you want it you can come back and get it.' Such peremptory treatment is unimaginable nowadays, as Yates, in his role as *directeur sportif* knows well. Riders have to be alert the whole time; the racing is nervous and jumpy. They need, and get, instant back-up. In the past, on the Giro for instance, the racing usually didn't get earnest until around 50 km from the finish, always signalled by the arrival of the television helicopter. That was the moment for the tempo to change from 'piano-piano' to 'belto ever-so'. Pros in the past were also more inclined to strike deals on the road. A man who had had a win might take money to ride for a rival who hadn't. The code served mutual benefit through cooperation: they were all there earning a living. Today's sponsors look askance at such curiously masonic loyalties inside the *peloton*.

Not the least winning facet of Yates's personality is the obvious pride he takes in his achievements as a pro. Merely to have *made* it as a pro is occasion for satisfaction, but the pride is set against an almost boyish cheerful dismissiveness about the whole caper, as if there was never any place for complacency. You are only ever as good as your next ride. Reputation doesn't win races, though it can spur even more daring exploits and punishing effort. I reminded him of something he said – to the effect that it was pretty astonishing, really, that he got paid all that money 'just because I can ride a stupid bike'. Well, maybe, and there is no room for wooliness in that trade. However, he does rejoice in his luck. A nine-to-five job never posed any problems for him but the offer to direct the McCartney team was too good an opportunity to miss. Besides it was, of course, nicer to be able to continue in the world he knows and loves; travelling, and being involved with racing; sorting out the myriad things it's his responsibility to attend to – things about which, as a rider required simply to cane himself on the machine, he knew nothing. That he has taken it on with such apparent lack of doubt, worry or puzzlement is no more than the measure of the man: the consummate professional who nonetheless bubbles with enthusiasm, loving the laugh of it all.

My favourite story about him, and one that sums up the no-nonsense toughness laced with good humour, is how after a final training ride before the Paris–Roubaix (the race he enjoyed best, one that suited his hard-riding style) he got back to find that all the hot water had gone. He took a cold shower, because that's all there was. No big deal.

14. FRÉDERIC MONCASSIN

At dawn on 1 August 1997, I cycled up over the col du Sérailler in the Basses Pyrenees. It's an easy enough climb, I was full of riding after a week in the high mountains and I topped the crest, just under 1,000 metres, as the sun began to lift into the clear air above the mists spilling up from the valleys. I rode on, down to the ridge overlooking the tiny commune of Cominac, the copper-sheathed coping of its church spire glowed in the warm sun and beyond it opened a magnificent view of a majestic chain of mountains which announces the high Pyrenees. Tour country. The air was still. Birdsong, a lone dog barking.

Cominac is where Fréderic Moncassin's grandfather lives, where Moncassin himself lived until recently. Through the adjacent woods twists and winds a vast network of mountain bike tracks and it was at a day of mountain bike racing in the small town of Oust, a few kilometres below Cominac that I first met Moncassin later that same year. He was changing a tube in his front wheel before the start; getting ready to race round with the amateurs of his fan club, which had organised the event, and a few of his pals from the pro *peloton*. They'd be celebrating the joy of the bike, riding for fun, having a laugh – the sheer pleasure of it. My friend Nick was with me that day and some three years later he drove me up into the Tarn region to interview Moncassin at home.

When I asked Moncassin what he felt about cycling tody (he retired in 1999), he replied with one word: 'Tristesse.' This seemed cruelly at odds with the impression I'd formed of him that autumn day, and it deserves elucidation.

Moncassin grew up in a family of cyclists – almost a dynasty. His grandfather was planning to ride the Tour de France in the days of the independent *touristes-routiers*, but could not afford to give up work. His father was a fine track rider and sprinter at élite level (on one occasion beat the great Tour de France fast man Jacques Esclassan) and Moncassin started riding the bike when he was eight years old and identified the passion which was to dominate his life. Between the ages of eight and 12 he went to cycling school in Villeneuve near Toulouse: no races here, just games for the youngsters to teach them bike-handling skills and the thrill of romping around on two wheels – slaloms, short sprints, a bit of cyclo-cross. When he was 14 he started racing but with no idea about serious competition – BMX, track, road, cyclo-cross, all for fun – 'just like that day in Oust' he said and laughed. Moncassin punctuates much of what he says with laughter: it's an entirely biddable trait in him.

He discovered mountain biking and added that to the other disciplines before army discipline (the mandatory military service) interrupted the increasingly hectic racing programme. Racing for GSC Blagnac, his earliest great rival was Laurent Jalabert. They formed, he says, a regional ensemble even in the national amateur team, road-racing through the summer, cyclo-crossing during the winter months, track riding every Saturday.

Shortly after he left the army, he entered the first mountain bike championship of the Pyrenees at St Isabel, outside Toulouse and, in that French way of pointing out the surprise and heightening the delight, he said: 'And it was I who won!' That same year came one of the most significant victories of his life: the amateur Paris–Roubaix. He was 20 years old, riding now for the Persan club; his team had ridden for him knowing that he was their best hope of a win. He was already possessed of startling speed and, an essential for the rough-house of the Hell of the North *pavé*, his bike-handling was second to none. This is a guy who can dance jigs and execute gymnastic leaps on a bike. There were, inevitably, pro outfits interested in him and the first to make an approach was Roger Legeay. However when Cyrille Guimard (then with Système U) expressed interest, Moncassin's *directeur sportif*, Bruno Le Bras, advised him that there was none better to turn pro with and repeated the high praise you will find elsewhere in this book. Guimard, who has a merited reputation for spotting talent early, was mightily impressed by Moncassin's abilities *and* his temperament.

It was a dream come true: to get paid to do what you love doing. Moncassin turned pro with the Castorama team, now managed by Guimard, and became a team-mate of Laurent Fignon, twice winner of the Tour de France in 1982 and '83. He made a dazzling début: five major wins in his first season including two stages of one of the most prestigious races in the calendar, the Dauphiné Libéré. He capped the season by riding well in the World's cyclo-cross and then Guimard said: 'Since you like the track so much too, you can go and do the Six Days of Grenoble.' After such a heavy season he suffered considerable strain in his lower back and had to have an operation to ease it.

The relationship with Guimard was good so long as the results came in. He had three victories in his second year and another three in his third – but it began to deteriorate as Moncassin's form slipped and he lost favour. I know from other riders that this is a common complaint: when they are riding high, no time or effort is spared to serve their every need; they're first onto the massage table after a race and so on. When they struggle though, it's free-fall down the snake to the bottom of the board. This seems to be traditional in bike racing, part of the ongoing psychological toughening. And, as Moncassin stresses, *directeurs sportifs* tend always to be hard on young riders, bent on teaching the spoilt brats discipline, moulding character as well as directing physical and mental focus. In the 2001 Tour Down Under (of which more later) Neil Stephens, joint *directeur sportif* of the Linda McCartney team, ordered their two new Spanish signings to attack one day; they didn't. At the finish he ordered them to ride the 50 km back to the hotel. When David McKenzie, a veteran of the team chipped in that he thought Stephens had been joking, he found himself out of the team car and on his bike, too.

After three years, Guimard grew impatient with what had, initially, seemed a considerable plus in Moncassin's make-up: his exuberant energy. Now it seemed more and more like lack of professionalism. 'Ah,' he said, 'you're not serious, you do more moto than bike, you're not professional.' The moto, or moto-cross, is another of Moncassin's passions and it accorded badly with Guimard's ascetic view of how strictly professional bike riders should conduct themselves. But, Moncassin said, he needed to do something other than just with the bike. After the full racing season, cross-country events on the motorbike helped him relax and refreshed his spirit. When the disagreement with Guimard became an entrenched conflict, he even contemplated quitting altogether.

The switch to Wordperfect, managed by Jan Raas, gave him a much-needed boost; he rediscovered the bike, or rather the pleasure of riding it, in a sympathetic more easy-going team. For instance, where other teams provided bread, honey and sugar at the table, Raas allowed them all the trimmings – mustard, mayonnaise, ketchup and Nutella (that gooey chocolate spread beloved of French kids and, it seems, bike riders off the leash). He, the 'little Frenchman' (he used this expression a couple of times) found himself teamed with some of the classiest sprinters of the current *peloton*: Franz Massens, Erik Vanderaerden, Jelle Nijdaam, Erik von Houydonck. To be associated with such guys –

especially Vanderaerden who had been his childhood hero – inspired and lifted him. In the Dauphiné Libéré that first year he beat Vanderaerden to win the criterium stage. It is a sweet continuum of respect and emulation to lionise a rider and then ride with him – even beat him.

There were less happy moments. On the Champs-Elysées that year, the sprinter from Uzbekistan, Djamolidin Abdoubjaparov, known, with scant affection, as 'the Tashkent Express', pushed him twice in the sprint for the final stage of the Tour de France, very nearly decked him and stole the win by a hand's breadth. For all their aggression the French and Belgian sprinters have, generally, adhered to the old code of mutual safety. There are notable exceptions, but Moncassin's natural instinct had been confirmed by the example of the men he rode with as well as Raas, himself a noted fast man.

'Abdou is a dangerous sprinter. He and Rolf Nelissen. They ride with their heads down, they can't see where they're going and have no sense of where the rest of us are. That time in Armentières [in 1995, when Laurent Jalabert collided with a policeman who had stepped out in the finishing strait to take a photo] it was Nelissen who caused the accident: he didn't see the gendarme and obscured Jaja's view.'

Such close brushes are unnerving and must have added to the general malaise. No, he never felt fear in the early days – competitive fire ruled out fear. They were all immortal, weren't they?

On the Friday evening before the 1994 Tour, coming off the stage from the team presentation, Moncassin slipped, fell and broke his wrist. The rest of his season tailed off lamely, but in February 1995, impatient to recoup, he savoured what he regards as his finest memory: victory in the 49th edition of the Kuurnes–Bruxelles–Kuurnes.

The day before, he'd come 13th in the Het Volk, drawing on a careful winter of preparation – Raas had asked them all to come to the start of the season at their peak. Their methods he left to them. Moncassin asked Raas at the beginning of his contract how he should train. Raas said: 'You're a professional. You know what to do. Carry on doing what you did to get here.' (Part of Moncassin's speed training had always been to train behind a motorbike or scooter, his wife often driving.)

It was a foul day. Jacky Durand, one of Moncassin's best pals from the *peloton*, a man of imperturbable good humour, rode up alongside Andre Tchmil early in the race and said: 'Time for you to attack; it's not raining any more. It's snowing.' There was snow, hail, ice on the road, and a blustery wind. Moncassin looked round the bunch and saw all the heads go down against the snow stinging their eyes and whipping their faces; even the hard men, the *flahutes*, ('flat-outs') as the French call the beefy-shouldered Belgians who love the ill-surfaced roads, the shocking weather, the draining marathons across the wind-swept roller-coasters of Flanders – even they flinched from the hail beating at their legs. Moncassin thought: 'Time for me to go' and he went. He'd put a slick of oil on his legs, sufficient to keep them warm. Most of the others wore leg-warmers.

He was in terrific form. The sole Frenchman – *le petit Français* – up against the bruisers, but the winter's hardening had given him a solid base of endurance. 'It was the first time that I'd taken the initiative to attack *de la sorte*. The win gave me a confidence I never had before then.' Here is the risk of advancing into unexplored territories of will, strength and self-knowledge.

During the following winter, he fell and broke a scaphoid but he trained harder than ever. He had signed for Legeay's GAN team (GAN are a French insurance firm) and was super-motivated. 1996 turned out to be his most successful season ever: stage wins in the Paris–Nice, first and third in the Midi Libre, first and fourth in the Route du Sud and, best of all, results in the Tour de France. He won the first stage, wore the yellow jersey for a day, spent six days in the green and took the 19th stage into Bordeaux. Watching him in the crowd was a man to whom he had been compared when he first showed his paces in the *peloton*, a rider of enormous class. Moncassin, cooed the French, was 'his worthy successor'. It was André 'Dédé' Darrigade – World Road Race champion 1959, winner of 22 Tour stage victories, three green jerseys and one of the finest sprinters of his generation. Darrigade met him as he came down from the podium. For the French, Bordeaux is one of the Tour's traditional homes; it has staged an *arrivée* more than any other city. Moncassin's astonishing burst of speed brought the race in for the 75th time – and a sprint victory here ranks especially highly with every Tour rider. It is, as they say, 'a consecration'. This is French Tour vocabulary; anyone who does not understand the exalted level of feeling behind it misses completely the hold that Tour mythology has on riders and public with its core of mystique. Darrigade greeted Moncassin warmly. He is a noted tactician himself. Like many of the greatest sprinters, he is not heavily built. He congratulated Moncassin's perfect reading of the sprint. Moncassin said that such praise from a rider they all revered and admired was a 'sacred compliment'. Darrigade had been their model; in his day, riders had to be especially gifted tactically. They did not use the huge gears which allow modern riders such devastating speed.

In the sitting room of Moncassin's house stands a memento of that glorious summer: a small winged armchair coated in a *maillot jaune* cover.

At the 1996 Olympics he fell in with the Sunn VTT team (*vélo tout terrain*: a mountain bike) and they told him they had a place in the team entered for the Tour de France VTT to be held that August/September. This race evokes the pioneering spirit of the first Tours de France: the riders sleep in tents, do their own repairs, move from race start to race start under their own steam. Moncassin discussed the proposition with Legeay, the President of the French Federation and Jean-Marie Leblanc, director of both Tours de France. There were contractual obligations to consider but Moncassin was given permission (what he called 'a gift from Legeay') to ride the off-road Tour in Sunn colours. Normally, he would be required to wear the GAN strip. He won a stage and was overjoyed. Then, such is the nature of this enthusiast – this generous-hearted man driven by boyish glee, enthusiasm and sporting good humour – he entered the Tri-cross de Dole, near Besançon in the Jura mountains: a 10 km run, 30 km VTT with 3 hours of motocross. He won.

He laughed. It was his best year. It gave him such pleasure.

In 1997, he stood on the winner's podium more frequently than any other rider in the *peloton* yet took not a single victory. Chris Boardman, his then team-mate, felt for him: the disappointment of no wins began to sap his morale; it was very hard on his spirit.

Twice eighth ('95 and '97) in the Paris–Roubaix, the race he calls '*le top du top*', he came fifth in 1998, and, though it can never be proved, the strong possibility is that Moncassin was pitted against rather more potent stimulants than energy drinks. As Brian Robinson put it to me: 'You don't win the Belgian Classic one-days on Eau Vittel.' In his day and Simpson's too, dope was freely on offer in Belgium.

Moncassin, like Boardman, has always been outspoken about the taking of drugs, adamantly opposing the whole shady culture. Perhaps riding clean cost him victories, it is impossible to say, but it is certain that the drugs scandal ('the famous year of '98') destroyed his appetite for racing in the *peloton*. The pharmaceutical companies have abetted the scandal, too. At virtually no cost they could add inert chemical markers to medicinal drugs used illicitly by atheletes which would show up instantly in tests; this they refuse to do and, Mancassin claims, (an unconfirmed) 57 per cent of EPO is sold to sportsmen and women. He had more or less decided to quit at the end of the season. He fell heavily in the Four days of Dunkirk and began to suffer severe back problems; he didn't want to continue but rode the Tour, tumbled off on the descent of the Tourmalet and abandoned soon after.

He went home and tried to resume training but the pleasure had gone. He found it increasingly hard to leave the house, his wife and his children. It's a common syndrome: riders who marry young and have the full-hearted support of their wife often find it easier to cope with the protracted absences. Those who marry in mid-career find the jolt of new family ties versus the austere demands of racing and travelling hard to absorb. An obvious sign of his growing disenchantment was in the hesitation, (albeit fleeting), in his final sprints; the abrupt glance at the barriers hemming them in – the thought that if he crashed there he'd be a goner. Throughout his career, Moncassin never had anyone to lead him out in the sprints. Whereas Cipollini could rely day after day on the red train of the Saeco boys, Zabel on his Telekom myrmidons, Moncassin was on his own. That made an incalculable difference. So when fear, imagination's stepchild, began to whisper caution, he knew he could not last. Safest never to analyse.

Moncassin is no dewy-eyed dreamer. When I asked him if riding in the *gruppetto* (he was a hopeless climber – five minutes on the climb and he exploded) forged special bonds, he said: 'No, it's mutual help . . . *ça rend service.*'

He had reached a dead end. 'No one laughed any more,' he said. For him the jaundicing of what had always been a passion – the bike – was intolerable. Had he not had a contract for 1999, he would have quit then; but, he said, 'you don't dishonour a contract.' His last win came in the team time-trial of that year's Tour Méditerranée.

'I had no wish to ride again, not even VTT. I needed a complete change' he said. He even wanted to move from Toulouse, the same roads he'd ridden for so long. As he put it, he 'took back his Sundays'.

In 1998 a new team-mate, the Australian Stuart O'Grady from Adelaide won stage three of the Tour de France and held the yellow jersey for three days. He freely acknowledges that the genial Frenchman's help and influence has been of major importance to him and others. When O'Grady and fellow-Australian Henk Voigt signed for the GAN team, Moncassin cheerfully became their cicerone in France, helping them set up home in Toulouse, introducing them to the local social scene to palliate the harsh process of adapting to a foreign culture. As he said, the cycling is good out of Toulouse and the discos and cinema are good *in*

Toulouse. It became quite a scene: the GAN team *chez eux*: the training rides together, the partying . . . There is danger inherent in the dolce vita – more patrolling of the wine bars than serious gripping of the handlebars – but O'Grady thrived. In the 1999 Tour, he became the first Australian to wear the green jersey.

I went to Adelaide in January 2001 to follow the third Tour Down Under and write various articles about the race. O'Grady, the local boy, who had won gold with the Australian World's team pursuit team, took overall victory in the first edition: this and the fact that he'd been seen in the leader's yellow jersey on television coverage of the Tour de France gave a huge fillip to the popularity of what has become the highest ranking race in the southern hemisphere.

I had hoped to talk to him in France when I went down the previous autumn but he had already left for home. I did speak to him briefly a few times in Adelaide but he was buried under a media scrum most of the time and, in the frustrating way of trying to synchronise watches with riders who hardly know what day of the week it is, the interview never materialised. However I saw him ride to the final yellow on the closed city circuit, his slender lead of two seconds carefully patrolled by one of his team-mates, a rider whose recent career illustrates quite poignantly the depth of feeling behind, and aptness of, Moncassin's *tristesse*.

In the 1998 Tour de France, Bobby Julich, riding for the French Cofidis team, came third behind Marco Pantani and Jan Ullrich. It was an astonishing result for the American rider who, five years earlier, then 24 years old, had had no pro contract. Ninth in the 1996 Vuelta a España, 17th in the 1997 Tour de France, suddenly he became the compelling new prospect and got the highest placing in the Tour for an American since Greg Lemond's win in 1991. Much was expected of him. However there were sceptics who questioned the validity of his success in a Tour shaken to its roots by the Festina scandal. Not only had a batch of riders been evicted from the race, but the psychological damage done to many others could not be discounted. Julich had, some claimed, merely reaped an easy harvest. This was horribly unfair to a racer of undoubted talent but the last two years have been miserable, aggravated by the emergence of his fellow countryman Lance Armstrong: unquestionably dominating, although to some thoroughly obnoxious.

Armstrong was contracted to ride for the French team Cofidis (he'd been spotted by their man Guimard) when he fell victim to testicular cancer. Cofidis initially confided their support but, visiting him as he lay in hospital undergoing the chemotherapy (which, together with his indomitable will, miraculously saved him from the disease) they annulled the agreement. The luckless Paul Sherwen, who had known Armstrong from their days at Motorola, when Sherwen acted as advisor to the team, had to deliver the message from the French-speaking manager. Although the contract required him to be fit to ride, Armstrong has, ever since, vociferously denounced this *betrayal*. He even obliquely dedicated his first victory in the Tour, in part, to the traitors – 'they know who they are'.

Since then, it has become quite apparent that he rides in France on a mission of small-minded vengeance. He has lived in France for some years – a fact he used to rebut charges of illicit drug-taking during the 2000 Tour: (he was, he said, subject to the same stringent French Federation rules and tests as the home-born riders) yet he speaks no French worth the notice; this is a snub. More insulting, Armstrong *does* no French, either. He is brash all-American, stiff with the hometown narrowness bred of that particular jingoism. He it was who unfurled the first national flag ever to flutter over the victory ride in Paris. He was recently quoted in an American paper as regretting the fact that the greatest bike race in the world had to be in France and, although renouncing the Tour was not an option, he moved house to Spain and scratched all racing in France from his season's objectives. This calculating and appalling act of spite he later diplomatically softened by announcing that he would, after all, ride the Ciruit de la Sarthe, an early stage race.

After his extraordinary attack up the Hautacam climb in freezing rain in 2001 (out of the saddle for something like 8 km, pedalling at a cadence of nearly 110 rpm, eyes goggling, a monomanic show of willpower and raw physical force), loaded questions were asked. I've ridden the climb myself – it's an absolute pig – and David Sharp, a journalist friend, told me that they waited in the press tent at the top shivering, half frozen. As Marco Pantani remarked at the time, it planted them all in another reality. The French press continue to cast doubt on Armstrong's integrity and, after murmurs about boycotting even the Tour de France, he has spitefully renounced all racing in France in 2001. And, against the traditions of cycle racing, he blockades himself off behind a screen of intermediaries, refusing all contact unless it is filtered through the defence barrage.

Armstrong's cure from cancer was a miracle (apparently doctors gave him virtually no chance) but it did nothing for his personality. In reproof of the adverse criticism levelled at him after his unspeakable behaviour on and after the Mont Ventoux stage of the 2001 Tour, he snapped: 'This is a bike race, not a popularity contest' thus effectively rubbishing the way the French – media, cyclists and fans – feel about this great trial of physical strength, endurance, character, racing intelligence – *and* the weight of history, tradition and legend it carries with it. On Mont Ventoux he waved Pantani through to take the victory, then claimed that 'everyone knew who was strongest on the mountain' thus belittling his rival's courage in a very public forum.

The man is as insensitive as he is obsessive; the product of a very American force-feeding, from the cradle, of 'greatest, bestest, strongest, onliest' which produces remarkable performers and utter monsters. When Kevin Livingston, who had ridden for Julich in the Cofidis colours during the '98 Tour and then for Armstrong in the US Postal team, left his fellow-American to join Team Telekom in 2001, Armstrong compared this to a defection comparable to General Colin Powell siding with Communist China. This is absurd as well as pathetic.

Julich may be a lesser rider but he is a far more rounded man, has weathered a torrid time of disappointment and psychological pressure – the weight of expectation under which no rider can perform or, at times, even believe he will ever perform again. It remains to be seen how Julich has emerged. He has said that he is more chilled now. Like Boardman, he has recognised the intensely damaging effect of focusing to manic distraction on the Tour de France. Moncassin's implicit warning – that when you stop laughing you are in real trouble, might be more widely broadcast.

The Tour Down Under is, reckons Patrick Jonker, one of the best-organised races in the world. I spoke to him one morning at the *départ* and he's ridden most of them. He left US Postal, after a wretched time with injury (latterly, tendinitis, the curse of all bike riders) to ride with the French Big Mat team. As a *domestique* for a Tour winner, he would be earning up to $80,000 on top of his retainer. Now his horizons are reduced, but not his energy. He rode strongly in the TDU, showed up in many of the breaks and delivered what turned out to be a decisive attack on the last major climb of the Tour, in a chasing bunch with O'Grady, various other contenders for the overall win *and* the current yellow jersey, Nikolaj Bo Larsen. On a hideously oppressive day (air temperatures in the 40s, wind, dust and scorching bitumen to increase the misery) Jonker, responding to the roadside banners 'Go Pat Go' flew off up the climb, split the field and left Bo Larsen for dead. O'Grady finished in the chase on equal time with the stage winner and the next day, the final stage, seized his chance.

Some while ago, O'Grady went through the kind of despondency which most riders go through even if they don't admit to it. He was sitting with some friends in a restaurant in France, the walls decorated with champions' cycling jerseys. Look, they said, that's what you want to be part of – don't give up. In the Tour de France 2000, he was decked by another rider some 80 km from the finish on stage four. He fell heavily and was in dreadful pain but rode on in the bunch of back markers. He struggled on every climb but the *lanterne rouge* of the day, Jean-Patrick Nazon, helped him along, whilst the guy who had floored him bitched constantly that O'Grady was doing no work. (X-rays later showed that he had broken his shoulder in four places.) Fortunately O'Grady is a rider of immense courage and a man of proven willingness not to take things altogether too seriously (despite a horrendous mugging attack made on him in Toulouse a while ago).

Each morning during the Tour Down Under, a bunch of us – the local bikies with Phil Liggett, his wife Pat and a group led by the former pro cyclist Australian Phil Anderson – gathered in front of the hotel at 6 a.m. for a two or three hour ride. On the last day of the race, we rode up the Gorge along the route taken by the race on its first day – a long climb through groves of gum trees to our turning point at Cuddlee Creek. On the big climb, Anderson was off the front, hammering away as he always did in the *peloton*. Liggett was going well, too. I stopped off to look at some wallabies.

They called Anderson the 'Kangaroo', not only because he came from Australia but because, with 2 km to go to the *arrivée*, he'd be the one jumping off the front, the restless attacker, always up for the chance of a win, riding with exuberance. He rode and finished 13 Tours; (Joop Zoetemelk holds the record with 16 completed Tours). In his first Tour he came 10th and won the white jersey as best young rider under 23. He took his best placing, fifth, the next year and wore the yellow jersey for ten days. In 1983, he was probably the strongest rider in his Peugeot team, but team loyalty came first (see page 132) and he came ninth, *what might have been* is of no account.

He had a long career (retired in 1994 aged 36) and was the first Australian to win a Classic race in 52 years when he took the Amstel Gold in 1983; (Herbert Opperman had won the Paris–Brest–Paris, then a professional race, in 1931). But here he was, riding with a bunch of enthusiasts for the sheer fun of it.

The day before flying to Australia, I returned home from Combloux in the French Alps where I'd spent four days with a party of skiers, among them Raymond Poulidor, André Darrigade, Henri Anglade, Gianni Motta, Brian Robinson, Joseph Groussard, Jean Stablinski, Michel Jouhannet, Nicolas Barone, Jean-Claude Theillère, Francis Rigon – all of them ex-Tour riders of varying eminence. Every January they all get together for the Arc en Ciel week, many with their wives, at the lovely village resort of Combloux, ('the pearl of Mont Blanc in a jewel-box of glaciers' as Victor Hugo described it), to ski in the loom of the mountain, its skirting ridges, Aiguille du Midi and the fretted crests which tower over slopes in parts still thickly overspread with pine forests.

The gathering is a celebration of friendship, a camaraderie established in the *peloton*. On the Tuesday and Wednesday, they take part in the Trophée Robic – slalom and cross-country races commemorating the 1947 tour winner who was tragically killed in a car accident shortly after Sallanches, the town in the valley below Combloux, hosted its second World's Road Race in 1980 when Bernard Hinault took the rainbow jersey. The first time was in 1964. Janssen took the pro title, ahead of Adorni and Poulidor; Merckx his first – amateur – rainbow jersey, to which he added three pro titles. Merckx usually comes to the indaba in the snow, and I had hoped to meet him at last. Alas, he was in England. I had arranged to go to Belgium in October to his factory; then was told he'd be going to Manchester, for Boardman's record attempt on the track. I went to Manchester; Merckx stayed in Belgium. It seems entirely appropriate that having been uncatchable on the road, he should prove as elusive off it.

Brian Robinson encouraged me to go to Combloux and the whole event is open to anyone who fancies a race downhill between the sticks in company with the *anciens coureurs* and any of the other entertainments organised by one of the best Offices du Tourisme I've ever encountered.

Robinson couldn't ski five years ago but Jouhannet, the *professeur*, leader of the party up on the pistes, and Barone, both former team-mates, took him out on the slopes one morning, taught him how to go downhill and left him to practise. They came back and found him hurtling to the bottom with the unstoppable force of the TGV. Second lesson: they taught him how to stop, told him to practise and left him to it. Robinson's nearly 70 now but still possessed of the unshakeable nerve they all have, these pro bike riders. Necessity bade them ride fast downhill so they did. Robinson, from the start a wonderfully skilled and daring descender (and no bad climber, either) would let the lead group head him over the col by a minute or so, take some food and drink, wipe the sweat off and catch them with ease on the way down.

Early in his career, Tom Simpson was riding with Robinson, the man who had inspired him to try his luck on the continent. Robinson told him at the top of a descent to take his wheel and follow. Simpson did so but, in the agitation of trying too hard he came off. Robinson waited for him. Simpson got back on but, a bit further on, came off in the gutter again. Robinson nursed him back. Simpson admitted that he might well have given up – not just the race, the entire business – without Robinson's help. With what riches he rewarded that thoughtfulness.

In very different circumstances, I enjoyed the same encouragement. Robinson coached me down several descents and, one particularly difficult afternoon, waited for me to guide me back in to safety at the bottom. (Motta, who insisted on calling me Ken, gave me a lesson down a slope one afternoon. He took me the easy way round. I fell off anyway.)

One evening, Poulidor partnered Jacques Anquetil's widow at belote (a card game) before going off to win the big tourney (part of the week's competitive fun) with Jouhannet. Introduced at an event staged in the Office du Tourisme as the 'eternal second' next evening, he stood up and, to general applause and laughter, cried: 'Not at belote!' The next morning, over croissants at breakfast, he said he'd put on two kilos during the World's at Leicester in 1970 – 'all those English breakfasts'.

It is a mark of their *joie de vivre* that these ex-riders do gather for the fun of it and there is very little nostalgic harping on the past: there's too much still to do. As Barone said to me, echoing Sean Yates: 'I only do what I want to do, what gives me pleasure' and this is not a late discovery: it is an attitude which, quite clearly, has coloured the thinking of everyone in the *peloton*, including Poupou, with whom I stood in line at the ski lifts.

One time I rode up with Anglade and Robinson. Anglade was talking about an old mate from the *peloton*, Jean Forrestier, now a neighbour in Lyons: he had been reluctant to attend a special reunion of athletes for the millennium celebrations. Anglade had persuaded him, but intimated that Forrestier had been sickened by the recent drugs scandals. And, just as Guimard had said that cycling changed radically with EPO, Anglade shrugged and added: 'They take different sweeties nowadays', meaning something altogether more deadly than the occasional amphetamine which were on issue to United States Airforce pilots in those days, for heavens sake – just to help them stay awake.

And Moncassin's 'Tristesse'?

The problem, Moncassin said, is that cycle sport is all getting too serious now. His cousin is in the national French track and road team and another is French national track champion and both of them started training behind a motorbike at the age of 15 – something he did only as a pro. The youngsters don't go out dancing or to have a good time in case it interrupts their training programme; when their parents go off on skiing holidays or to the seaside, the kids stay behind to cosset their pulsometers. It is becoming a job as soon as they sit on the bike; there is little or no *pleasure* any more and pleasure is a much better base on which to found a career in bike racing, that lovely dream of being paid for what you love doing . . . so long as you can go on loving it.

15. CHRIS BOARDMAN

I always believed Chris Boardman had it in him to win the Tour de France. Greg Lemond, who rode his last season alongside the new professional in the GAN colours, thought the same. That he did not fulfil what seemed an extraordinary potential I imputed to lack of preparation. He didn't go to France to live and race in the heartland of pro competition. He didn't take himself off to the mountains to harden himself physically and mentally. He chose to ride under his own terms, to retreat to his home on the Wirral as often as he could. Moreover, he insisted on training as he had always trained rather than accepting the traditional methods of continental riders. He ignited much adverse – and derisory – comment when, instead of going to the mountains to train, he went into the laboratory, mounted a bike tilted on an inclined treadmill, visualised an alp ahead and pedalled for set periods. There were the computations, too: on an ascent of the Tourmalet a loss of 1.5 kg of body weight would save 46 seconds and, projected over the whole Tour de France, that was a total of seven minutes. 'That information was dynamite to an info-junkie like me' he writes in *The Complete Book of Cycling*.

He has been much-criticised (I declare my own fault here) for this kind of techno approach to things that simply cannot be charted on graphs (at least not by me) and it *has* given rise to some comic anomalies. In the same book, for instance, he offers advice on climbing mountains while admitting it's not a subject he's highly qualified to advise on. Instead, he quotes the recommendation of Robert Millar, winner of the King of the Mountains prize and fourth overall in 1984: 'Ride up hills.' Boardman comments revealingly: 'But that can be soul-destroying.' The fact is that Boardman's soul was *not* in continental pro cycling; nor do some of its demands make much sense to him. Yet that is *not* the reason why he never won the Tour. By Boardman's own admission, we were wrong about his abilities. I cannot think of his *not* winning the Tour de France as a 'failure': the lustre of his amazing career absolutely refutes such a notion.

Never set on becoming a professional cyclist, in the end he really had little option. He was, simply, too good, too fast, too dedicated to winning, *not* to accept the offer of Roger Legeay, the *directeur sportif* of the GAN team. Legeay, a highly-regarded rider in his day, rode every Tour between 1975 and '81 and has become one of the most respected team directors in the *peloton*.

Boardman was an astonishingly able time-triallist from the start. At 16 he became the youngest rider ever to be selected to represent Great Britain in the World's track championships at senior level. The list of his victories on track and against the clock between 1985 and 1992 is dazzling. At the Barcelona Olympics in 1992 he lapped his opponent, the German Jens Lehmann, to take gold in the 4,000 m pursuit – Britain's first Olympic cycling gold medallist since Ryan and Lance took the 2 km tandem race in 1920. In the World Championships the year before, Lehmann had suddenly produced a ride of 4 minutes 22 seconds, 9 seconds faster than any of his rivals and 10 seconds faster than Boardman. It tested what Boardman describes as a fragile morale; he could not imagine bettering the German's mark. But, typically, he analysed it. As he did throughout his entire career, he wanted to know why he had lost and in so doing makes the important distinction between wanting to be the best and wanting to be the best that *you can be.* The one you can control; the other is quite beyond your control – and control fills the very core of Boardman's psyche. If he is set a training schedule he wants to know specifically why it will improve his performance. If he sets a goal the goal has to be circumscribed in as much detail relating to its possibility as can be gleaned from physiological and technical tests. He has a restless, inquisitive mind and is driven as much by this constant questioning of himself and his advisors as by any fear of failure.

He focused on what he suggests is an essential difference between wanting to win and needing to win. The need to win is insatiable; victory only sharpens the hunger. Need is for the nutters, the obsessives. This is a terrible famine to live with and Boardman, who knows what damage it can do, has exorcised those ghosts. The strong possibility was that he might have succumbed.

In 1993, at the insistence of his long-term coach Peter Keen, he made his first attempt on the world hour record and chose as the venue the *vélodrome* in Bordeaux on the day the 18th stage of that year's Tour finished. If he had powerful doubts about becoming a pro, this was surely *not* the way to allay them. The choice of Bordeaux was (as usual) calculated for maximum publicity but, for that very reason, it added pressure to what was already a huge gamble. Pressure is another of those elements which Boardman sees either as a negative or a positive force: it can squeeze the best out of you or it can flatten you. Only a week before the Bordeaux ride, the pressure tightened: another amateur, Graeme Obree, broke Francesco Moser's existing *professional* mark of 51.151 km in Norway. Having failed at his first attempt he nonchalantly went out the day after and set a new record of 51.596 km. Boardman had aimed for a distance in excess of 53 km but, because of the heat, decided that was unrealistic and set what he called a pretty conservative 53 km. Amazing, in truth, to think that such extravagant physical and mental achievement can be so monitored. In the event, he raised it to 52.270 km. That same evening Boardman shared the Tour de France podium with the man in the yellow jersey, Miguel Indurain. A year later, after his first day in the Tour, he himself stood on the podium in yellow.

Legeay buttonholed Boardman that night in Bordeaux and agreed a rendezvous in Swansea in August when the GAN (Groupe Assurance Nationale) team would be riding the Kellogg's professional Tour of Britain. Legeay seemed to be wholly unconcerned about Boardman actually saying *no*. He arrived at the meeting with a planned schedule of races for the following season (no Tour de France yet) and that was that. I recall Boardman once speaking of his profound uncertainty about the idea of being a pro. Sitting in a hotel lobby somewhere, he'd seen a salesman launching into a pitch with a prospective customer. He saw the desperate need to impress, to clinch a sale, and then traipse off somewhere else and do the same again . . . and again, and again – and thought: 'No, I can't do anything like that' but it was, finally, the sense of having achieved virtually everything within grasp at amateur level and there being really no option but to turn pro. The world didn't attract him: he knew how painful and hard it would be; he also knew he was exceptionally gifted and, if things didn't work out, he could walk away. Besides, the 'what if?' question is not one a man like Boardman could ever walk away from without testing it.

In September 1993 he signed a contract with GAN, the French insurance firm, one of the longest-serving sponsors in the sport and, a short while after, he won his first three professional races, all time-trials, beating some of the most illustrious names in the established *peloton*: the Grand Prix Eddy Merckx, Chrono des Herbiers and, with Laurent Bezault, the Duo Normand. It was some début.

At his first training camp he told the management that riding six hours a day wasn't going to put any more speed into his legs. This was revolutionary. Long hours in the saddle had always been the way for a pro cyclist to train. No one questioned it; it was more than tradition. Endurance sport demands endurance training; the best way of preparing for something is to do it. The cricketer John Edrich made the point that modern athletes may be stronger and faster than ever but they are, in general, not so hardy or resilient; they break down more frequently than they did in his day. He walked long distances as a boy (to school and back) and that daily routine exercise toughened his frame in a way that no formal training in later years could ever have done. Cyclists, though, need to weather themselves with lengthy exposure to physical and mental stress; without that steeping in the hard labour of their trade, they don't acquire the essential ability to recover quickly. Recovery rates vary according to physiology but the power of recuperation can be increased. In his first Tour in 1993, Lance Armstrong, already winner of the World Champion Road Race, won the eighth stage into Verdun. A few days later, after a pitiless flogging in the Alps, he lay on his bed unable even to speak. He hauled himself onto the bike next morning, encouraged by his team-mates, but he was simply too battered to continue and, a short way into the stage, he climbed off. Seven years on, he has survived cancer, submitted what is admittedly an iron consitution to the routine conditioning of the best in the *peloton* and won two Tour victories.

Boardman argues against the validity of this conditioning for himself and, latterly, tests have shown that he suffers from a hormone deficiency which seriously impairs his ability to recover from extreme fatigue. Ordinarily this weakness would have been exposed quite early in his career. The irony, he points out, is that had he followed the conventional route into continental road racing he would never have made it into the professional *peloton*; his frame and constitution would not have been up to the punishment meted out. As it is, the kind of racing to which he was accustomed never stretched him far enough beyond a limited recovery rate to suggest any problem. He arrived in the pro ranks as a champion. This did not make for an easy ride. He had to win his spurs, but his record was hard to argue with and he was allowed to train *his* way, with scientific methods constantly and exhaustively applied: kilojoules, Newton metres, watt read-outs, detailed records of pulse, weight and fatigue. He even sought to prove the depth of his passion by a flow diagram: passion feeding self-belief flowing into evidence with an added supplement of coaching, analysis and planning. This is Boardman's way and I do find it difficult to square such cool appraisal of what happens to him on a bike with what he actually *does* on a bike. There are no statistics for passion; the proof lies only in action and Boardman – logical, intelligent, meticulous and scrupulous about *everything* necessary to his profession, his bike and his body – is as passionate a man as ever mounted a bike. Forget the diagrams. Here is an athlete of uncommon brilliance and dedication.

On reflection, he says, he could not have done more to extend or enhance his professional career. He tried every approach – though he would do nothing unless there was tangible cause for doing it. Just riding miles for the sake of riding miles made no sense to him and in summary, he says he squeezed out every drop of what he calls 'a narrow talent'. 'My particular ability was being able to apply myself' he says. That is certainly true but it is astonishing, given what he achieved, that his modesty is as large and full as the engine nature endowed him with.

He had very limited experience of road racing and was used to fairly short rides against the clock and now faced the enormous workload of a racing pro cyclist. It is a measure of what the GAN management thought of him – indeed *expected* of him – that Legeay gave him permission to live in Cheshire; an indulgence that was almost unthinkable, but was essential to his temperament. He has, of course, pondered what a difference it would have made had he turned pro earlier and served the rigorous apprenticeship holed up in an apartment somewhere in France, hardly ever getting home (he and his wife, Sally, have known each other since they were 16). He would, he is convinced, not have lasted six months.

Living in England made not a jot of difference to his commitment. From the very start he was committed to succeeding as a pro and that meant focusing on the Tour de France. Boardman's focus is as sharp as the set-up of his bikes. As he put it: he ate, slept and dreamed the Tour de France. Everything revolved round that goal. Nothing else in life counted but arriving at the start of the Tour de France in peak condition. He became obsessed. His moods swung violently; he was totally wrapped up in the mania and it very nearly cost him his marriage. Such can be the price of enslavement to an exceptional gift and the terrible frustration of not fulfilling it.

However, he joined the GAN team as a star and in his first season his eccentric training methods, entirely foreign to the rest of the *peloton*, reaped marvellous rewards. He took the Prologue of the Tour of Murcia in spring, showed well in the Midi Libre and was in cracking form in the Criterium du Dauphiné Libéré, a favoured warm-up stage race for the

Tour where he won the Prologue time-trial and two stages. Wearing the leader's jersey, but dropped on one mountain stage, he nonetheless shrugged off the bad spell and, showing huge courage and grit, rejoined the leaders on the col de Coq. This unexpected maturity in a rider of such individual class as yet largely untested in the *peloton* convinced Legeay that he should, after all, enter the Tour, if only for ten days, for experience.

Once more Boardman demonstrated what extraordinary powers of concentration, nerve and self-belief he harnesses with an equally egregious physical strength and cultivated economy of effort. At a record speed of 55 kph he won the 7.2 km Prologue, beating a galaxy of Tour-hardened time-trial specialists. He beat Miguel Indurain by 15 seconds and thus became only the second Briton to wear the yellow jersey. (Tommy Simpson held it for one day in 1962.) Suddenly he was besieged by the media. There was a mad scrum of journalists waving microphones for sound bites. Pressed by one (a Belgian he thinks) to say if he thought, after such a tremendous performance on the first day of his first Tour, he could win the race, he replied to the effect that he had two arms and legs and he'd certainly try, but that that was a long way off. This, in the way of things, became a statement of intent with which he was, to his weary irritation, saddled for a long time.

He climbed off a day later than planned, halfway through stage 11 on the first day in the Pyrenees up to Lourdes-Hautacam. He'd wanted a taste of the mountains but began to suffer early on and decided to stop before he blew up. It was, he recognises now, an error to have embarked on the stage and not to ride to the finish. A failure of respect for the Tour. A few months later he took one rainbow jersey in the World's time-trial and another in the 4,000 m pursuit.

His standing made him leader of the GAN team and his second season increased speculation about his long-term prospects. He dismisses this as unfounded. What people reckoned to be only the tip of the iceberg (a clutch of high prestige wins in his rookie season) he claims was all that was ever on offer.

He singles out his best memory of the *peloton* as the day in his second Dauphiné Libéré when, having won the Prologue again, he was lying second to Indurain. He rode with great nerve on stage four over Mont Ventoux in baking heat and lost only 1 minute 17 seconds on the leaders. Two days later across two alpine giants – up into snow on the Galibier, on over the Croix de Fer in freezing rain, 143 km from Briançon to the mountain-top finish in Vaujany – he stayed with four others, some of the best climbers in the bunch (Indurain and Richard Virenque among them) all the way up the final 7 km of steep hairpins to the *arrivée*. This was fine riding indeed on a very tough stage, a 'real Tour stage', Indurain called it. Boardman reckoned it was if not the best race of his life, very close, and certainly the most satisfying (not enjoyable, but *satisfying*).

Boardman provoked much criticism for saying that he didn't really *enjoy* riding a bike, but he did derive much satisfaction from it. Perhaps the admission was naïve; fans expect their heroes to mirror their own enthusiasm. It's not encouraging to hear a man of Boardman's gifts relegating the talent to a sort of gloomy 'Devil's bargain': his talent for fabulous and richly-rewarded results came via sheer purgatory. Champions are not expected to suffer like us sublunaries; or, if they do they shouldn't acknowledge it. They hand out the punishment and absorb it too with disdain and indifference. (Such a response is not confined to Boardman. The writer Robert Graves said that he did not actually like *writing*; what excited him was *rewriting*. I rather concur.)

In the 1995 Tour Prologue, on a road slick and treacherous with drizzling rain, Boardman crashed and broke his ankle in six places. It was a dreadful way to go out of the Tour that year but exemplified his total commitment to all-out effort. Knowing the risks, he took the gamble. Convalescence gave him the first real rest from bike-riding in years: a time to reflect, to enjoy his family and to plan for the following season. It started well. He had victory in the Critérium Nationale time-trial (third overall) and a stage win in the race to the sun, the Paris–Nice. He then came fourth in the Midi Libre before he took to the ramp for the Tour de France Prologue. The roads were wet, he reined in slightly, eased on the corners and came second. He was still in the race but the mountains nearly finished him off. On the 263 km stage to Pamplona, the second day in the Pyrenees, the race crossed seven major climbs: Soulor, Aubisque, Marie Blanque, Soudet, Port-Larrau, Jarietta, and l'Alto de Garralda. Fighting to stay with the *gruppetto* at the distant rear of the *peloton*, Boardman told himself incessantly that he couldn't go any further. Even as you tell yourself you have to stop you fill time and continue, somehow, even though you still go on telling yourself 'enough, enough, enough'. With five or maybe six hours left to the finish it is, he says, 'very difficult to be positive about the situation'. He was riding on the very edge. 'The worst day I've ever spent on a bike.' I remember the pictures of him in the Channel Four coverage: gaunt, wasted, battered, deep in that awful misery you know you have to endure for compelling reasons beyond logic. Way ahead of him, the great Spanish champion

Indurain was suffering his own torments. Already winner of five Tours, it seemed he was heading for certain defeat by the Dane Bjarne Riis. His arrival in his home town of Pamplona was greeted with commiseration not acclaim. As a mark of respect for the Spanish champion in his home town, the Tour organisers invited him to share the podium with Riis that day, and Riis handed him his leader's bouquet.

Boardman did survive and eventually made it to Paris, his first Tour de France completed. But, whereas he had set himself a target of finishing in the top ten, he came 39th. This was a disappointment and the first sign that he was performing close to his absolute stretched limit – on the roads at least. He simply could not recover fast enough to take such atrocious a beating day after day after day. In a race in Spain though, when they rode the mountains on the first day, he was in terrific fettle, driving the lead group up the climbs. But he never had the deep reserves necessary to stay at that level.

> The Tour becomes a very personal challenge to the individual rider. During my nightmare stage I became very emotional. I know that if I had succumbed it would have been psychologically difficult to have faced the Tour the following year. I would have felt a beaten man. The fact that I stuck it out is very pleasing to me. I think you can only say you've beaten the Tour if you win it, but if you finish then you can get on with your life with the satisfaction that the Tour – at least this year – failed to beat you.

Boardman would not see 'satisfaction' as at all derogatory or as evidence of confined ambition. It is a realistic description of what he does supremely well, balancing the huge personal sacrifice of effort against the fleeting joy of success. Such terseness is not widely understood. He is accused of arrogance, indifference, aloofness and a certain chilliness as if even his responses were hitched up to a pulse rate monitor and not allowed to exceed fever pitch. This, though, is to do the man a gross injustice. His opinions are articulate, considered and unforced, entirely without artifice. Exhilarated by winning he is modest to the expense of rhetoric and there is, in my view, no doubting his immense generosity of character and achievement with a noble, genuine reticence in his pride.

There can be no underestimating the desperate effort it took to reach Paris in 1996. In his specialist field, however, he was still near unbeatable. He took the bronze medal in the Olympic time-trial in Atlanta, victory in the Grand Prix Eddy Merckx and, six days later, came to the

Manchester velodrome, his home track for the World's titles, and won the 4,000 m pursuit in a new world record time of 4 minutes, 11.114 seconds. Seven days after that he was back again in Manchester. In one hour when everything conspired to perfection (a perfection that could never be reproduced – air pressure, temperature, his own position and physical condition, the purpose-built bike, even the luck that attended him that remarkable day), he shattered Tony Rominger's hour record of 55.291 km (itself an apparent miracle) by over a kilometre to set a new mark of 56.375 kms. He even enjoyed the ride. Braced for the suffering that comes from riding fractionally below the threshold of anaerobic effort (like walking a tight-rope, as he put it) requires complete concentration. He could not have gone any faster. Two stunning world records in a week – a magnificent triumph of pure athleticism, dedication, preparation and technical efficiency.

Scandalously, most of the British press ignored it.

He won his second Tour Prologue in 1997 but, though he had believed himself capable of finishing the race in the top ten, he was already suffering undue fatigue even before they got to the mountains. He crashed heavily on the descent of the col du Soulor in a dense Pyrenean mist and, though he carried on, the pain in his back became unendurable. He abandoned and, he says, driving with Legeay's car up the slopes of l'Alpe d'Huez later that same day, seeing the crowds of British fans gathered to cheer him on was a bitter disappointment; profoundly depressing. He felt he had let them all down and sold short the immense demands he had made on himself and the faith placed in him by the GAN management. These were the first signs of the debilitating physical decline which dogged the last three years of his professional career. He began to lack any kind of consistency: a strong ride one day; totally drained the next. He was no longer in control.

In the winter of 1998–9, a specialist doctor in Liverpool carried out bone scans. The density was below what it should have been; he diagnosed osteopenia – a wasting of the bones, which could easily worsen into osteoporosis, and prescribed hormone replacement. This was unpleasant news, but at least it was a relief from the anguish of not knowing why he felt in such poor condition and he had been told that something could be done to reverse the decline. The specialist prepared a full dossier of proposed treatment and medication, including HRT patches and infusions, and submitted it to the UCI doctor who vetted and agreed to the treatment. However before he had commenced the course of low-dosage medication, the UCI changed its mind and told him that if he continued to take the drugs he would have to stop racing. This was a touchy time: the Festina drugs scandal had made the UCI extremely nervous of anything possibly untoward and, whilst Boardman sympathised with their decision and the sensitive reasons for it, he never agreed with what must have been, for them, a very tough choice. He might indeed have taken the case to the Court of Human Rights on grounds of equality (most women pro cyclists are permitted the fairly run-of-the-mill HRT treatment of oestrogen) but the process would have been expensive and lengthy. Time was against him. He obeyed the UCI ruling.

I asked him what he would say to any rider who was thinking of turning pro in the continental *peloton*. He replied: 'Don't do it', acknowledging just how hard the life is. Not only did he suffer physically, the psychological stress nearly finished him off. This bike riding became so deadly serious there was no glimmer of enjoyment in it. Obsessive to the point of mania about the Tour de France, he very nearly broke himself and his family relationships. Nothing else mattered but Tour de France; there was no other perspective. This fanatical drive to succeed in the Tour, akin to the same fury which killed Tommy Simpson, was shaking his mind and body to pieces. It was a fearsome lesson in the difference between wanting to win and the intemperate *need* to win. Somewhere in the balance lies sanity.

He won a third Prologue in 1998, but crashed near the stage finish in Dublin two days later and was out. He finished only his second Tour in 1999, but the last two years were comparatively bare of other results. As leader of the GAN team he was expected to perform much better. He was paid far more than the other riders, but because of poor form seemed not to be justifying either his high contract salary or his status. It was bitterly upsetting for a man with such high ideals of professional obligation. He was letting everyone down and that hurt. Worse was the growing sense that he was reckoned not only to be failing his best but not *doing* his best either. Such recrimination, even unspoken, cut him to the quick.

The idea for his last flourish was mooted as early as 1993. The plan was to ride the hour on a bike as close in design and manufacture to that ridden by Eddy Merckx when he set a new record on the track in Mexico. Legeay raised it again over dinner in 1998 and, since things had been going badly for him for some time, it seemed a great way to sign off. The notion appealed to Boardman, not least because he felt that Legeay had not been getting his money's-worth for some time. Here was a way to recompense his faith and to go out in style. It was a gamble, but

Boardman took it on with all the passion that had informed his entire career.

The UCI had erased all records from the books – Boardman's 1996 mark included – and ruled that all future attempts would have to be made on UCI-approved machines, insisting in particular that the frame should conform to old-style conventional lines, equal-sized, non-disc wheels and so on. This posed acute problems for Boardman's team. Merely equipping the bike he was to use was difficult given that some of the materials used to build bikes 30 years ago no longer existed.

On Friday, 27 October 2000 at 3 p.m., Boardman, wearing Crédit Agricole colours (GAN had given up their sponsorship and Legeay had turned to the French bank) came out onto the track at the Manchester vélodrome, rode a single lap and stopped on the line ready for his last outing as a professional cyclist. The years in the *peloton* had reduced him. He actually dreaded this last bout of extreme suffering but it was a way of paying tribute to the fans who'd given him such support, cheering him when he took the record to an unimaginable distance on the same track four years earlier. He wanted to set a new record that would hold for other riders to aspire to. However 12 hours before the ride, the UCI told him that they regarded this attempt as replicating (and/or attempting to beat) Merckx's Mexico hour. This conflicted with Boardman's purist idea but he had no choice and the attempt was billed as 'versus Merckx'. The muddle and confusion this caused cannot have helped his mental state but he is, above all, possessed of a considerable cool.

Thirty minutes into the ride he knew that it would come down to a sprint. I asked him what he thought about. He said that you don't think about anything other than holding your effort at exactly the right level. Once you push just a little too hard and tip over into anaerobic effort you are done for. There is no escaping from that merciless expenditure of oxygen. It is like bailing a sinking boat: the same quantity goes out as comes in.

Information came to him from the electronic board and his coach Peter Keen at the side of the track as he paced out the gains and, nearer the end, the deficit. Lap by lap the gain – at one point some 300 metres – dwindled, until Keen actually steped back into territory that had been lost. At this point Boardman's wife Sally came to the edge of the track to cheer him on, something she had never done before and it very nearly unnerved him. He felt a rush of adrenaline: 'Attack it now Chris.' But it would have been a disaster. He checked the moment and prepared himself for the final surge into oxygen debt. I watched from the press stand in amazement at the heroism of this tussle with his patience, his physical distress, his nerves and his self-belief. There was now no room for error; the final burst had to be timed to the second and he made it – by just a handful of metres. It was, for him, finished and as a cycling exploit it will rest in my mind as a unique personal statement of his admirable dedication to a sport in which a narrow ability produced incredible dividends. It also puts into even starker relief the incredible ride that Merckx produced 28 years earlier (admittedly at altitude). Experts say that was worth an extra kilometre.

I have corresponded with Boardman for some years and he happily agreed to write for my last book something his secretary, in a letter, propitiously misspelled 'Forward'. After the crash outside Dublin I wrote to send him my sympathy and to wish him a speedy recovery. He replied, thanking me and saying that such sentiments from a fellow cyclist meant a great deal to him. ('Fellow cyclist'?)

Boardman's time as a pro may not have been very happy – the highs were astronomical and the lows ruthless with his life, mood, mind and body. It shows just how hard a race the Tour de France is, and how it can dominate the sport too. His candour about it is instructive and whilst he did lack the honing of the conventional early years, his record in the great race is a fine one. He refused to enter the drugs culture at a time when only a few cyclists resisted. He raced clean and was always at a disadvantage (not that he offers that as any excuse). He did all he could with what little he had, no effort spared, ever. He was a man and a rider of immense integrity. He wouldn't have done anything differently and, from now on, will do only what he *wants* to do. He feels it important to be able to walk away. He is not sad that it's finished, knowing he gave it his all.

* * *

Having retired, Boardman can now follow the prescribed HRT treatment freely and diagnostic tests show that the bones are already responding well. He gets out on the bike 'once a month or so' (chuckling) but is doing a lot of gym work; the vital thing is to stress and flex the bones to strengthen the skeleton. Running and hard walking achieve a similar effect whereas cycling is all weight-bearing and inhibits the improvement of bone density.

16. DAVID MILLAR

David Millar's fiery passion for the sport shows both in his riding and his reflections on it.

'I've always thought of cycling as having an epic, romantic scale,' he says. 'It's a beautiful sport, a great sport. I've always liked the epic nature of all that suffering. That appeals to me a lot. In one race in Italy we went up and down the same mountain six times. It was zero degrees at the top and snowing. I had convulsions for half an hour after the finish but I really enjoyed it. To me that's what it's all about.'

As statements about the powerful lure of professional bike racing go, David Millar's appreciation is impressive – but this was before he rode the Tour de France in 2000. At the end of the stage into Briançon (249 km, three huge mountains including the fearsome col d'Izoard) he said: 'Eight and a half hours on the bike is not sport. It's ridiculous. They are burning us out. It's sado-masochism on a grand scale . . . crazy . . . outrageous, and I hope someone hears what I'm saying.' The following day involved 173.5 km over the cols du Galibier and de la Madeleine, finishing with the long climb up to the ski station at Courchevel; the day after that, 196 km of alpine gradients to the towering peak of the col de la Joux Plane. That is the reality but how can anyone put that into words which come close to the experience of actually doing it?

There was no advice for Millar before the Tour – either from those members of his Cofidis team who had ridden the Tour, or the *directeur sportif* – only the fact that he had been picked to ride the race and had the confidence of men like Cyrille Guimard. A 'You can do it' from those who have done it and know what is entailed is the best that anyone can expect. *How* to do it is another matter, but Millar has talent, class and courage. He is outspoken and forthright. His berating of the Tour organisers at the finish in Briançon is evidence of a formidable nerve and self-possession. No wonder he caught the attention of the man who spotted and nurtured the talent of Bernard Hinault, Laurent Fignon, Greg Lemond – men who had ten Tour victories between them. This man had 'the instinct and the profile of a winner', as the French say.

Till he was 15, Millar lived in Hong Kong – not an obvious cradle for the budding cyclist. He got a mountain bike and kicked around for fun and like countless other youngsters was drawn to the local bike shop: the gleaming wheels, the glossy enamel of the frames, the smell of tyres, the bikie chat around the counter. He joined the crowd and met other kids his age who raced the off-road machine (roustabout, hair-raising, devil-may-care stuff) and thought he'd give it a go. He took to it at once and did well in races. It was good fun. He then got more serious and switched to a road bike. There are road-bike snobs who are sniffy about the off-road machine; this is short-sighted. Many pro riders take to the hills for off-season races and training: it provides great conditioning and a light-hearted change from the treadmill. And certainly the love of the mountain bike has nurtured the talents of David Millar and Fréderic Moncassin.

Millar's parents divorced and he went to live with his mother in England. He was 15 and uprooted from what he had always known (and still regards as home), had no friends and no contacts. His mother suggested he join the local club, High Wycombe Cycling Club. It would be something to do in the holidays and would provide a ready pool of kids his own age with his own interests. His talent emerged almost at once. He very soon joined the National junior squad and went to the World Championships in San Marino. Here he had his first run-in with the organisation. 'Organisation' is not a word that sits well with his view of how best to nurture individual talent and nor is he alone in that. The best riders are those with an independent spirit who know what advice to heed but, finally, won't be dictated to. The British Cycling Federation seems to have a natural genius for laying down inflexible organisation law, telling riders what to do and effectively crippling them, without any real appreciation of what the riders have already done or may well do if they are left to their own devices. Riders are selected (and dropped) on the basis of their willingness to conform. They are required to train according to the BCF manual and if the methods do not suit their style, they are out, amounting to a kind of 'sovietisation' of the training régime.

Millar's speciality was the time-trial; he'd been selected originally as a time-triallist but the BCF rota system chose to forbid him to ride that and entered him for the road race instead. His description of his performance in it was colourful. It went, in précis, *badly* and this was a failure he found impossible to accept. The incompetence of the so-called organisation had effectively hamstrung him. He had gone to the competition with only three weeks' riding in his legs; he was denied his preferred race and 20 minutes before they were due to go to the line there were not even any numbers for them. He knew he could do better but maybe a combination of inexperience, frustration with authority and a sense that he had not managed things well provoked his anger and that is the kind of anger that gives you the edge. He *knew* he was good; he wanted to *prove* he was good. Until that first appearance on the big stage, everything had come easily to him. The disappointment was hard to bear. Hitting failure for the first time he decided to try real cycle racing: road racing on the continent.

He had a place at art college but the desire to explore his true worth in something for which he had an outstanding talent was too strong. Like all truly gifted riders, he has an entirely objective opinion about his abilities. Bragging is, after all, ridiculous in such a context: you can't quarrel with results. So he did what only a few British riders have done before him: still only a junior category racer, he went to northern France to see what he could do.

Millar told me: 'If anyone's interested in road racing they should forget Britain. They haven't got a clue. It's a total waste of time. They know nothing about it, the riders and organisers, and they do everything to discourage you. Before I went to France people were saying "Don't go, you'll only get your head kicked in" but I wanted to go. I knew it was there or nowhere. The fact is that Britain has *nothing* to offer pro cycling. If you want to ride as a pro the best you can do is get out of the UK as soon as possible.'

That winter of 1995–6, he raced as an independent in and around Ypres in Flanders, the heartland of pro cycling in many ways and one of the toughest breeding grounds. It's the chosen patch of many riders from across the water. This is *kermesse* land: round-the-roads lap racing in every local town, cheered by enthusiastic crowds, a bounty of racing against hot competition, and the best nursery for an aspiring pro.

Millar lived like a monk and hardly went out, applied himself to the non-stop training, training, training with intense determination. He received some money, just enough to get by on, every month from the Dave Rayner Fund – set up, by public subscription, in memory of a rider of outstanding talent tragically killed in a motor accident. Millar was the first beneficiary of the money devoted to promoting young riders bent on a professional career in cycling.

To France came the man who was to be Millar's mentor and great advocate, Mike Taylor, formerly British junior team manager. (Millar reckons him to be the finest judge of new talent in the UK but the British Cycling Federation didn't recognise that – he didn't conform to the prescribed pattern and, as they say, his services were dispensed with.) Several French clubs had shown interest in him but nothing materialised. The year grew old. Millar was left dangling. This was a waste. So Taylor contacted his friend Paul Sherwen, ex-team-mate of Alain Bondue, now part of the management of the French Cofidis team. Millar was an extraordinary prospect, he said. More phone calls found him taken up by the VCC St Quentin, south-east of Ypres in France. He spoke no French but the opportunity could not be passed up. Neither had he ever ridden more than 160 km in his life. Suddenly he found himself *racing* such distances.

That second winter on the continent, he lived in a tiny village. It snowed a lot; it was bitterly cold, but he was, he said, on a mission. This was what he knew he wanted to do, could do, *had* to do. His focus was direct and acute. Scratching out what he euphemistically called a 'basic life-style', he was nourished by that sense of mission. He had *such* a goal, he told me. He was driven, no question about it; he sacrificed a lot – this is not something every lusty teenager would be prepared to do. His friends in Hong Kong, a pretty hedonistic crowd, were setting up for university and the commencement of career plans: study leading inexorably to a steady job. Millar did suffer pangs of anxiety: what kind of a *job* was he committing himself to? But, the results came, with praise from every angle. His talent was recognised and rewarded and the sacrifices were, deservedly, winning dividends.

He had, too, what he called a particular advantage in this bizarre existence he had adopted. Born in Malta, removed to Hong Kong and thence to the UK, he had very few deep ties to any one place. His sojourn in France, lonely as it was, did not weigh so heavily on him as it would have done on many of his contemporaries who might have found quitting the homeland far more difficult. They were, he said, 'wrapped in cotton wool'. He understands the process of mental hardening. Called up as a first-year pro, at only two days' notice, to ride the Tirreno–Adriatico in Italy, one of the hardest stage races of the year, he said: 'I've never suffered so much in my life. I came out on my hands and knees. It was horrific, utterly horrific.' He adds: 'It made me tough, though.'

The Rayner fund backed him for a whole year, a year which gave him essential grounding in continental racing. As Poulidor pointed out, the major difference between the amateur racing scene of his day and the one today is that the élite riders – the top category of amateurs – are racing at a level nearly comparable with that of the professionals. The leap from amateur to pro *peloton* is still enormous but that is more to do with the very nature of professionalism in whatever sphere, where the demands are all-consuming, constant and rigid. A professional is *always* expected to be at his or her best: reputation counts for little, only results matter. Mental toughness is what marks out the true pro and Millar, even so young, was clearly possessed of that as well as being a rider of exceptional class. The Director of the St Quentin club, Martial Gayant, winner of the yellow jersey in 1987, told Bernard Quilfen, *directeur sportif* of Cofidis that he had a 19-year-old kid 'with two Gayants in each leg'. He'd just won a big amateur race, the Tour de Courèze, on the back of an astonishing time-trial victory. Quilfen sent Cyrille Guimard to St Quentin. He watched Millar race and took him out to lunch.

Millar was, not unnaturally, in awe of the man. It was an enormous compliment to have such an acknowledged genius of bike racing interested in him. Guimard brought him to Cofidis and, at the age of 19, Millar was a professional rider. This marks another difference between the modern era and the past. All the teams are, by and large, better financed and a few have such backing that they can afford to take on a rider with promise and carefully nurture the talent gradually as an investment for future performance. That is an approach that Guimard always advocated, even with Hinault – to delay entry to the Tour de France until he was ready to win it. Today, the preparation period can be extended further. Charly Wegelius, another brilliant young prospect, has signed for the Mapei development squad in Italy to learn his trade before moving up to the senior ranks.

Millar was identified as a possible Tour winner, but his bosses at Cofidis were ready to wait. The first year as a pro was very hard, he said: *ride, ride, ride; race, race, race.* Much of the time he was a team reserve which meant phone calls the day before a race telling him to get himself to the line. It was taxing but even if it was erratic, it's the kind of schooling no pro rider can do without. It was sink or swim. There were unfortunate additional pressures too. The team management was not functioning well, there was a confused and confusing command structure. The commercial boss of Cofidis operates as boss of the cycling team which makes the job of the *directeur sportif* and his assistants extremely difficult at times. They are, on occasions when their direction is of paramount importance, effectively sidelined by the intervention of someone who does not know the sport as they do. This is a problem by no means unique to Cofidis but it is symptomatic of the changing nature of sponsorship in cycle racing: the advent of the money men, balance sheet decision-making and pro cyclists as a commodity.

'It's run completely like a business enterprise, now, not a sport,' says Millar. 'There's no leeway. The team is the Cofidis boss's pet project and he runs it just like the company. He doesn't understand cycling, he hasn't a clue and he's ripping it to bits. All we're doing is a job, that's what he expects from us – just do the job.'

It hasn't made life easy. As he said, when the results are good, the team's morale is high; when they're bad, everyone gets stressed – riders, *soigneurs*, managers, and if the big man 'who knows nothing' is on your back too, it can be a nightmare. Why, then, does the boss of Cofidis – a French telephone credit company – run a cycle team? Advertising, publicity, high-profile image. In France, cycling is *the* glamour sport.

Guimard, in particular, was experiencing considerable difficulty that first year of Millar's contract. He had always been head honcho. Now he had to accept a subordinate position in an irritatingly cumbersome headquarters operation. He is, though, in Millar's view, still the best; his reputation is well-deserved and he deserves still better from it.

'In the car Guimard is fantastic, there's no one to touch him for reading a race and telling you what's what. His tactical understanding is brilliant. Sure, he's opinionated and highly intelligent and that sometimes leads to clashes between us. I'm not a French peasant boy and he can't treat me like one.' Guimard responds ably to that brand of self-belief and assertiveness. It was his own, after all, and he has always looked for a rider who is prepared to argue. Independence of spirit is what distinguishes the very best. Millar's team-mate, David Moncoutié, another rider being groomed for the future, is exceptionally strong – a rider of sheer class and yet of very limited ambition.

'We're both capable of getting into the thick of races and doing well, but he's not interested in winning much. He just plods along, chooses a couple of races a year to win. He has no material obsessions. All his family are postmen.'

Millar has been a pure professional for four years: he has had virtually no amateur or junior career. He is, moreover, very alert to the privilege that he has enjoyed (and earned) from the beginning. 'I've always had a huge amount of faith put in me.' He is sufficiently strong and single-minded to translate this faith into stimulus rather than pressure. He is a natural leader, not averse to arguing with his bosses, though in general his own objectives match those of the team director; there would be little point in riding for the team if they didn't. The aim is to move up notch by notch – marking goals and attaining them and for the most part enjoying it, doing what he's got to do. Very few teams have the luxury of setting their neo-pros specific objectives; the common case is for the young riders to hang on, survive and, perhaps, if they're lucky, mature into riders of some standing.

In his first four years, Millar has taken seven time-trial victories, including the opening stage of the 2000 Tour de France. The enormity of that win reduced him to tears – he had beaten the 1999 winner, Lance Armstrong, into second place – and rendered him temporarily articulate in French: babbling answers to questions he had forgotten the instant they were asked. He had considered the win a possibility: the distance, 16.5 km, was ideal, but the night before the ride he would not think about victory. 'I didn't want to put the fear into myself.'

Fear? This is the fear instilled by expectation. *Expectation* has no place in the mind of the winner; it occupies too high a level of consciousness, suppressing the vital subconscious which supplies the deep inner desire. Only at that level can the complicity between moral power and mental focus be complete.

There's plenty of homespun wisdom on that subject, but Goethe puts it well:

> Whatever you can do, or dream you can do, begin it. Boldness
> has genius, power and magic in it. Begin it now.

Some ten days before the first stage Tour ride, he'd won the opening 14.9 km time-trial in the Route du Sud by a huge margin (46 seconds) for such a short distance. Such wins extend possibility to new ranges, unexplored territory. That is where the fear lies – but also the adventure of advancing to another level of the collusion between self-confidence and aspiration. Objectives go higher but, at the outset of a career, they must match a realistic scale. (Miguel Indurain's career was nursed along in this way: he abandoned his first two Tours, came 83rd in the 3rd and then won five in a row.) It was *not* realistic for Millar to think of wearing the yellow jersey for long. His initial aim had been to take the white jersey for best rider under 25 from the first stage. This he knew he would do; he had no rival. Making the start for the Tour de France was already a special moment. Winning the yellow jersey as well as the white and the green for that remarkable ride was almost beyond belief: 'taking it by beating Lance Armstrong [he might have added Jan Ullrich, Laurent

Jalabert and Abraham Olano too, all champion time-trial specialists] is an immense honour. It's very moving. I'm lost for words.' The unlooked-for triumph did not deflect him from the main target which had to be sensibly limited to getting to Paris. He nearly didn't make it.

Soon after the *départ* for the 13th stage to Ventoux a rider came off and the bunch ahead of Millar suddenly seized up. He jammed on the brakes and went head-first over the bars and landed on Udo Bölt's spinning front wheel. The tyre burnt his chest and neck and an X-ray the following evening revealed a dislocated collarbone. With such injuries, he might well have struggled to stay in the race. Those three cruel days in the Alps which came immediately after Ventoux brought him nearly to his knees – and, as if the stage into Briançon hadn't been bad enough, he and others in the team car were held up in dense traffic jams for two and a half hours at the end of the race. The roads to the team hotel, 25 km away, were completely blocked with cars from the Tour caravan and television vehicles. He spent 12 hours in racing kit and went on record denouncing the lackadaisical management of the Tour organisation. 'Their first priority should be to get the riders to their hotels instead of worrying where the VIPs are staying.' He refused to knuckle under. Everyone was tired, though some idiots out there in the bunch just kept attacking from the gun. The day after Ventoux, before Briançon and the Izoard, there were 19 unsuccessful attacks, all of which had to be chased down and snuffed out. But this was Bastille Day and only 12 Frenchmen had claimed victory on the national day in the past 50 years. The racing frazzled him but his mood was defiant. 'There was no way' he declared, 'I wasn't going to make it.'

Millar is very bright, good-humoured, relaxed and passionate about racing – a debonair individual who knows his own talents and knows how he wants to use them. 'That is the way I am and the way I want to be.' He held the yellow jersey for three days, despite a crash near the end of the third stage. He avoided colliding with some crashed riders and opted for the hay bales – that took the deft skill and bike-handling that he'd learnt on the mountain bike. His chain had come off though. All fingers and thumbs he fumbled it back on, remounted and, showing incredible nerve, managed to race back to the main field in time to preserve his lead. He lost it in the team time-trial, but he had worn the jersey with confidence. Trying it on for size, you might say. Since the Tour though, things have been difficult. He was candid about his disaffection, about the nagging pressure of people getting on his back, concerned that he might throw away his talents. They misread him he insists, but the unwieldy burden of that has bitten into his spirits. It is, he says, difficult not to be cynical about the sport when you find that you are seen only as an object, a fast racer; the wearer of the yellow jersey. This is the weight of other people's expectation and it comes close to suffocating his passion. Cracks appeared, and have reappeared since, in his composure.

He spent three months off the bike, chilling out and taking stock. He asked to be excused from the World's championships and couldn't focus properly at the Olympics. The yellow jersey had become a shirt of fire. He even came close to thinking about quitting altogether. Such is the penetrating mental distress to be endured. It is as punishing, in its way, as the physical duress on the bike. The trauma was worsened by the dread that cycling had consumed his life: everything – friends, entertainment, food and drink – caught up in the incessant turn of the two wheels.

In April that year, his *directeur sportif* Bernard Quilfen came to see him to talk about his attitude. He had not, in Quilfen's view, properly embraced the regimen necessary to the life of a professional; he had not concentrated hard enough on learning how to *faire le métier* (that phrase Brian Robinson used of his own self-instruction nearly 50 years ago).

'He told me that with my class I could make a living and have a decent career without much work. He also said that it was a little *unjust* to botch the gift I had been given. I took that to heart.'

They even discussed a move to Tuscany to live near his team-mate Massimilliano Lelli. There are a lot of pros in the vicinity and, he says, 'they could keep an eye on me'. Now he is determined to get stuck into the trade, 100 per cent, despite the good-time calls on his temperament. Millar was frank about his sybaritism: he needs to party, to visit his pals in Toulouse from time to time (O'Grady and the rest of them), to blow off steam and have a few beers.

'I am,' he told the French press, 'a bit of a dandy. There's no way I could live like Sean Kelly. We come from such completely different backgrounds. I miss my hedonistic days in Hong Kong sometimes; I get fed up with eating pasta every day for breakfast.' The racing season is long and arduous and he, like the rest of the bunch, is constantly on the move. The evening I talked to him he told me that it was the first time in many months that he had spent longer than three days at home. He *did* respond to Quilfen's counsel and, as is apparent from his first forays into the continental racing scene, he *is* a man of focus and dedication. He is also a fun-loving young guy who, as the French say, 'eats life in big mouthfuls'. The monkish asceticism of the Irish farmboy Kelly would so damage Millar's psyche that he'd go down very quickly.

In the spring of 2000, he had his first taste of the Belgian classic races. Two days after finishing the five-stage Circuit de la Sarthe (he came fourth) he rode the Paris–Roubaix (273 km) as a *domestique* for the team, protecting their main men before the *pavé* sections. He stopped to help when a team-mate's chain had jammed, but by the time they got back on, the *peloton* had disappeared out of sight. He climbed off, job done. Revealing another side of his passion for the sport, he expressed wonderment at the strength of Johan Museeuw, admiring of the sheer *beauty* of such a victory: 'I can't comprehend how he was capable of doing the ride he did.' Next was the Flèche–Wallonne (200 km), followed, four days later, by the Liège–Bastogne–Liège, (264 km). At the start, he was petrified. Reconnaissance of the final 100 km (an unrelenting roller-coaster of brutal ups and downs with a killer climb of the St Nicolas hill near the finish) had left him in a state of shock. Then in the race itself, they rode the first hour at an average of around 45 kph. He knew he wasn't going to last long, nor did he. Such is the wicked trend of the learning curve, and its season is unremitting. Until the Tour de France itself there's just racing and training – three months completely *bloc* as the French say.

We had met, fleetingly, in the *Départ* paddock at Carpentras, but I contacted him quite frequently in Hong Kong, Australia and Biarritz before we finally talked at length. I had hoped to see him en route in London but he went straight to France, bung full of a cold. I went to France, caught what may well have been the same cold, but couldn't get in touch. I came home and soon found a message on my machine. He'd been on a training camp when I was in France. I'm not surprised he hardly knows which day of the week it is sometimes . . .

Training camps tend to be soulless, mind-numbingly boring, harshly disciplined affairs. It's just ride, gym, pool, eat and sleep for eight days in a remote Spanish village – everything shut, nowhere to go even if they had been allowed out, which they weren't. The decree pronounced at the start of the long week: 'No Fun'. Any infractions and it's a fine, or worse off to Lille for a dressing down by the Headmaster. He got to the camp in the aftermath of the cold feeling dreadful. He hadn't been on the bike for ten weeks and the riding came as a bit of a shock to the system, but you get used to that.

The first time he hit the mountains in a race, he had no problem, but this was as an amateur, in the Tour de Corrèze in south central France; the climbs were only 5 km long. The switch to the professional way with climbing was brutal: a bunch sprint to the foot of the col, where the field sorts itself out. The reflex is to get into lower gears but no – the pros ride most of the way up on the big ring. The madmen at the front go at high speed; the middle ground is filled with riders testing their legs and their strength, forcing themselves into new areas of pace and suffering (just as Millar did in the Tour de France, first on the Hautacam climb and later in the Alps, even riding alongside his friend Armstrong to help on the col de Saisies). At the back of the *peloton* come the riders hanging on by that ever-stretched elastic, the survival merchants and the autobus. Wanting to see how well he *could* go in the mountains during the Tour, he knew, too, that he could not afford to 'go into the red'. If he overstretched himself he risked being forced to abandon, exhausted. Prudence vies with stubborness. It is a fine balance, but maintaing it testifies to a profound depth of character when the courage to continue sits with the dismay at the horrors of doing so.

Millar certainly showed a growing confidence in the mountains. During the Dauphiné-Libéré he went well on the ground he must conquer if he is ever to be in contention to win a Tour. During his début Tour of 2000 his weight dropped by three kilos and he was climbing better than he had ever climbed. His objectives for the next season are fixed: Paris–Nice, Critérium Nationale, Tour de France – with a hundred or so other races in between: routine riding.

A cyclist's racing weight is of crucial concern. Millar has been advised by the team doctor that he should drop to that only twice a year. Shedding body fat to nil puts the physique at its peak for performance, but also in constant danger of ruinous depletion of reserves. The diet has to be carefully monitored and balanced; he has to grow accustomed to being hungry. Even after a training ride, there is no greedy packing in the food to fill the hole gnawed in the stomach. It could drive a lesser person entirely neurotic, one imagines.

He made it to Paris, got into a break on the Champs-Elysées (he was there to race, wasn't he?) and the sheer relief and joy of making this, his first Tour finish, overflowed in spontaneous exuberance. He was doing what he does best: loving the speed, the exhilaration, the triumph over everything that had happened in the past three weeks, the wondrous high of the yellow jersey, the dreadful slog of the Alps and even the unbelievable fatigue as the days ground on and on and on. That is the spirit of the Tour de France, the great epic race, the climactic adventure into the depths of the soul and the sheer magic of its vast variety. Mountains. Courage. Endurance. Spectacle. And a peculiar generosity of spirit which Millar, in all aspects of his life, reciprocates. When he won the yellow jersey he said: 'Cofidis have invested a lot in me and I am proud and happy that I've been able to repay their confidence in me.'

If there is a central thread in the narrative of this book, I should like it to be that one quality which marks out all the best riders, all the riders I have spoken of at length herein, which is generosity. Generosity of spirit, of mind, of effort – in everything.

17. THE MECHANICS

May 2000. The Giro d'Italia. I'm sitting in a Linda McCartney team car heading for the Alps with Colle dell'Agnello on the Italian side, col d'Izoard on the French side and assorted nastiness in-between. The finish in Milan is only two days away. Next to me in the driver's seat is one of the McCartney team mechanics, Topper. Topper is wearing a pair of plastic turquoise frog-eye goggles which gives him the look of a diseased welder, very blue about the gills. Possibly this is to frighten the spectators as we pass. Another of the McCartney drivers is prone to leaning out of the windows as the cavalcade sweeps along the crowd-lined barriers to shout: 'Why aren't you at work?'

Ahead of us, round a long curve of the road, we see the *peloton* snaking through an avenue of Lombardy poplars; a glittering serpent of colour in the umber Italian sun. Steady speed, mountains ahead. Suddenly, another car screeches up and shimmies in, parallel to my elbow, wing mirror almost brushing ours. It's Sean Yates, slipping over for a chat. This happens a lot; it relieves the boredom and much of the day pulls through an uneventful longueur of inaction. We exchange a few ribaldries, our pocket version of team solidarity, in the jostling of the other team cars, some racing up the line in answer to a call for assistance from a rider, some pulling over for a roadside leak, others just looking for a bit of gay banter like us. And, whenever we pass 'the Devil' (the German nutter in diabolic drag who tows a giant penny farthing round every stage race in Europe and chases the *peloton* up the road waggling an oversized toasting fork) we yell: 'You're mad' which shows no more than a healthy respect for fact.

Suddenly the race radio crackles: '*Linda McCartney avance au peloton. Linda McCartney avanti*' – always in French, the international language of cycle sport and the home lingo. Yates swings out, hand on the horn and drives hard along the line of the following cars, ambulance, police motorbikes, cameramen, *commissaires*. They don't always give way immediately, but Yates can work his way through a tight bunch on four wheels or two, bobbing and weaving with a slippery swing that would have impressed the Artful Dodger himself.

On such a day, with big climbs to cross, we see more action in the second car. Following our riders at the back of the race as it strings out over the long drags into thin air, we do what we can to keep them going. Ciaran Power, riding his first major stage race, is up against it. We drive alongside him.

'Give me some Extran,' he gasps.

I reach for the carton of energy drink and start to open it.

'No,' he snaps, 'leave it.' I hand it out and he stuffs it in a pocket.

He later, quite needlessly, apologised for his rudeness – in extremis, still polite.

Colle dell'Agnello goes on and on and on. I feel for him. The Italian spectators give him wonderful encouragement. I shout out of the window: '*Spingere! Spingere!*' ('Push him.') It's what the partisan *tifosi* have always done for their riders; now the charity is spread wider and several fans here give the lad a good, long push. It all helps. Anything to relieve the agony in the legs and lungs. We check for red *commissaire* cars. There are none in sight. Topper drives up: 'Come on Ciaran, cop hold.' He doesn't want to, but needs must and the important thing is making it home inside the time limit. It's a small indulgence, to finish the Giro. He grabs the door post, Topper hits the gas and we propel him a hundred metres or so. Spotted later, he was fined the routine 50 Swiss francs.

Over the top, Ciaran lets rip. He's a manic descender and all at once it's quite another rider we see in front of us: his weight shifted onto his right leg, he crouches like a sprinter in mid-stride over the frame and flies down the hairpins. They call one of the Italians, Paolo Savoldelli, 'The Falcon' for the speed of his descents, swift as a stooping hawk. In the car behind Power I feel the lurch of the drop, Topper swinging the wheel left and right, bend by bend, like a skier's hips, tyres squealing. I go beyond fear; say to myself only that 'this is *happening* . . . nothing can be done . . . try to stay inside the moment without analysing it . . . hey-ho' and homely soothings of that preposterous nature. (Don't even think about it.)

Along the valley we're back to the supply of Coca Cola, water, energy bars and energy drinks, stoking him up for the last assault of the mountains. On the horrible climb to the Casse Déserte and the Izoard Power is faltering, right on the limit of his reserves, fighting hard but he's in a bad way and it looks as if it'll be touch-and-go. It's a 25 km downhill slope from the col into Briançon, for sure, but he's having to ride mostly on his own. A *gruppetto* formed on the flat but he's shelled out on the climb.

The crowds cheer and clap and cry '*Forza! Forza!*' ('Courage!').

I holler '*Spingere!*'

Topper leans out calling 'Keep going!' – we're all staying with him, encouraging him to stick at it, as he just has to.

I say to Topper: 'Tell him, if he gets to the top he's done the Giro. No – say *when* he gets to the top . . .' Think positive.

Later that evening, Power and the rest lie on the massage table, talking, as long as they still had the energy, to Serge. He's the *soigneur* from northern France who warms their muscles before the start of every stage, hands them their food *musettes* at the feeding stations, greets them at the finish to give them dry towels, clothes, drink and a bite of food even if they can hardly swallow it – a banana to remind the flayed system that eating has to be done, an immediate token replacement when they climb off the bike. Back at the hotel he gently kneads and stretches muscles hardened by the day's racing. Serge personifies the total support every rider gets: a listening post, encouragement, practical help, care, attention and good humour. The very word *soigneur* sums it up: the man who dispenses *soin* or care, watching over them, as parents would their children.

While he's busying himself with the rider's physical and moral well-being, Topper and the others attend to the bikes. The riders depend absolutely on the mechanics – for their safety above all.

1972. Amateur Tour de l'Avenir. The Alps. Phil Edwards, later a pro with Francesco Moser in the Filotex team, is on a ride. Leading over the col, he switches his brain off and lets it roll: a breakneck, switch-back plummet down the hairpins – crazy speeds, hectic cornering, knife-edge risks. Behind him the team car, driven by the manager Alex Taylor, is trying desperately to keep up, hurling the car round the bends, swinging perilously close to the edge and grazing the mountain wall. In the passenger seat sits Mike Mullett, the team mechanic, terrified. But for Mullett, the experience of the mad chase would be doubly horrific. Catching sudden glimpses of Edwards, slaloming down the hairpins, he was scared to death. 'Phil was my responsibility. I'd set up his bike, cemented the tubs . . . what if one rolled off? He'd be a goner.'

That scenario encapsulates the job of the cycling mechanic, the pressure on him and the scope of his duties. The machine is in his sole charge; if anything goes wrong with it, the blame falls squarely on him and him alone. In the rough trade of the professional *peloton*, the rider is protected little enough at the best of times, but if the machine he is riding proves faulty, he is in real peril. The mechanic, therefore, carries a heavy burden quite beyond the immediate task of the specific job he's paid for. To him, rider and bike require equal attention.

To find out how the job of the mechanic has changed since the early '50s, I spoke to four men who know the business inside out. (I also drew on Steve Snowling's excellent memoir about the life and work of a bicycle mechanic – *Bicycle Mechanics*, published by Springfield Books Ltd.)

Technological advances apart, the basic job hasn't really changed much at all, but the circumstances in which the job has to be carried out have altered enormously. Consider the complex team back-up which is routine these days: a huge travelling workshop better supplied with spares than many specialist bike shops; every facility for repair, rebuild or re-jig on constant tap. There's a full team of mechanics devoted to the care of the vast array of team bikes, with each rider's own machine tailored to his individual whim and physical peculiarity: a different mount for time-trial, flat and mountain stages. The Mapei support squad nowadays, for instance, far outnumbers the cadre of riders. Yet not so long ago even the first rank continental teams employed no more than one mechanic, one *soigneur* and one manager per team on a permanent basis – until the racing season when temporary extras would be hired as and when required. And in the UK? It's DIY.

Professional mechanics were operating on the continent from before the War, though the rules as to what they could and couldn't do during the race were quite restrictive. Till the late '50s, pro riders carried compressed air pumps and spare tubulars (tubs) looped in figures of eight round their shoulders. They were expected to swap a punctured tub by the roadside. Until 1964, no bike changes or swapping of components was allowed unless the machine was unrideable. This tradition of self-reliance was rooted in the idiosyncratic principles of the father of the Tour de France, Henri Desgrange. Up till a few years before his death in 1940, Tour riders were required to do all their own roadside repairs, without assistance, on pain of fines or time penalties. Desgrange did not admit the use of the *dérailleur* gear until 1937, partly because it would need specialist repair if it broke down during the race. (Campagnolo produced the ingenious Paris–Roubaix gear to reduce this risk. The rear drop-outs and the hub spindles were serrated, allowing the wheel itself to move to and fro by action of a lever and by back-pedalling, adjusting the chain tension for the ratioed freewheels. Bartali used one such in his 1938 Tour victory.)

Desgrange had already bent to appeals against the absurd purism of insisting that riders rode the whole race on the same bike – and, if it broke: hard luck. This infuriated one particular French journalist who denounced the injustice of subordinating a rider's talent to the chance of a broken machine. The *gendarmerie* began to accompany the Tour in 1933 and the advent of support cars in the 1930s for all the major continental tours offered riders rudimentary but dependable support. Around six lorries packed with spare equipment and workshop tools preceded the race to the finish and a single service *camion* trailed the riders to offer repairs they couldn't manage. But, as Benoit Faure (winner Tour de Suisse 1935) recorded, 'the rules of the race said that any rider with mechanical trouble had to wait until the last rider went through before he could get service'. This needn't be too damaging on the flat stages but for a leader in the mountains it could be a disaster. Who could forget the photo of René Vietto on the descent of the Portet d'Aspet, Tour 1934, in tears, waiting for the long-delayed service lorry, his own bike surrendered to his leader 'Tonin' Magne, Magne's broken machine at his side. He'd had to stop to help his chief less than 24 hours earlier on the Puymourens (a wheel swap proved impossible: Magne's axles were 8 cm, Vietto's 9 cm). His very real chance of victory squandered, the 20-year-old newcomer took the Mountains prize but those mechanical failures that were not his own seemed to bruise his will permanently. Bursting with talent, he never won the Tour; a precious resolve seems to have died with that wretched roadside wait. The philosophy of 'rider support' then took root.

Meanwhile, back in Blighty, the makeshift 'on yer bike' approach persisted. In 1953, Monty Young, aged 21, was hired by Triumph cycles to provide the mechanical support for their team in the *Daily Express* Tour of Britain (a precursor of the Milk Race). The chief *commissaire* was one Jimmy Saville, OBE: ex-miner, pro bike rider, wrestler and later celebrity DJ ('now then guys and gals, how's about a stage race?'). Monty started as most of them start: he fell in love with bikes, and wanted to know everything about what made them run fast and smooth. He taught himself the lot, wheel-building included, on a jig he bought in 1948 from the main stockists of the day, Brown Bros in the East End of London. It cost him two pounds and ten shillings, (about half a basic weekly wage at the time; the price of a decent racing bike was roughly twenty pounds) and he's still building wheels with it in the back room at Condor's.

He built the team bikes, with Reynolds 531 tubing (the first version of which appeared in 1935; the '5,3,1' referring to proportions of the main elements in the alloy steel); San Giorgio rims and tubes; GB bars, stems and brakes; Brummy Cyclo gears and hubs supplied by the team sponsors, Gnutti. The riders brought their own saddles, invariably a Brookes one which came in a flat shape. This Monty reshaped or 'butchered' by rounding it to form on a special template.

As mechanic, he rode a Triumph motorbike with two spare wheels mounted in front, replacement tubes tied to the petrol tank, *musettes* in the rear panniers. As the riders approached a feed station, he rode past to set up the hand-out of the bags, leaving his team to the care of the neutral service vehicle. Their own team car, an ex-army jeep, carried a quantity of spare parts and the main tool box. On one occasion Monty found a rider stranded with a broken bottom bracket. With the spare bike, he went on his way, while Monty chiselled out the cracked cup and replaced it, at the side of the road.

He was working entirely on his own and learnt that he had to sink or swim and fast. Often the job proved even harder than necessary. Some hotels refused to allow the mechanics to bring the bikes into the building. They had to stooge around until midnight, smuggle them into the bedrooms and get to work on them there.

(Steve Snowling was similarly debarred from one fancy establishment but without blinking simply set up a temporary workshop on the pavement outside the main foyer, in front of a fascinated crowd of spectators.) This added problem wasn't confined to the UK. Even on the Tour de l'Avenir, the mechanics were sometimes searching for digs at one in the morning; the bikes, as ever, the priority.

The pressure to clean and check the machines every night was the same in those pioneering days as at any time since, of course. Only, this was a ground-breaking operation for Monty. He had no experience of stage races but then hardly anyone in England did. One mechanic with some background in professional cycling was riding a motorbike as mechanic for the by now veteran Hercules team in that same '53 Tour of Britain: Bob Thom, later to become Team Manager.

In 1955, Bob crossed the Channel as mechanic with the first ever British team to ride the Tour de France: the Hercules men, led by Brian Robinson. It was quite an eye-opener. Used to the casual arrangements in Britain, Bob suddenly found himself part of a huge, well-heeled organisation. The Hercules outfit was comparatively very well set up, but on the Tour de France the pay was far better, the attitude more workmanlike, the conditions more conducive. On the continent the mechanic had long been a greatly respected member of a highly professional scene. To every team of ten riders there were assigned three mechanics: Bob, who spoke no French, was joined by two Frenchmen who spoke no English. They got by; Bob picked up some French and a great deal of additional expertise too. One of the Frenchmen, Louis Debruycker, knew all the tricks of the trade. It was an oddity of the rules at the time that if a rider punctured, unless the spokes, hubs or freewheels were damaged, his mechanic had to fix a new tube onto an empty rim before fitting the fresh wheel. So an alert mechanic had to be as quick at warping a rim as he was at truing it. If one of his riders punctured, they would always make sure a spoke or two were snapped, or else that the rim was dented. In this way, even with the *commissaires* hovering, the mechanic could produce one of the tyred wheels he had ready and the change was as quick as it is usually nowadays. Debruycker records how in one Giro, when Anquetil was riding in pink, the team car broke down on a mountain stage and rather than wait for a replacement car and risk Anquetil puncturing and losing minutes of time, Debruycker just mounted the spare bike and rode off down the mountain in chase, so as to be on hand if necessary.

One aspect of the ruthlessly professional forum which Bob found not so different from the domestic scene was the chaos at the end of each stage. It was the one side of the race that was least efficient. It was, if you like, a second contest outside the day's main action – a sprint against rival teams for the best space and facilities. Matters were generally complicated by the fact that they would lodge in a separate hotel from the team riders. At the end of the racing, Bob and his partners waited to collect the bikes from the mêlée at the finish, bundle them into the waggon, dash to their hotel (school, monastery or barracks) and scramble to claim any well-lit, large room, garage or corridor with water not too far away – even a courtyard near the kitchen or laundry – anywhere to spread out the bikes and equipment. Once, for Monty, this place was in a rainstorm near Dresden, standing at a wooden table in a tent with a stream of water pouring through.

The first job was always a thorough wash-down of the bike with hot soapy water to reveal any cracks in the frame or obvious faults that needed addressing. When the last bike was washed, the first machine would be near-enough dry and proper work could commence: the daily overhaul, from checking working parts to cuts in the tyres.

Habitually, they would go to the team hotel during dinner (about the only time they made contact with their men) and would compile the list of jobs to be done. Riders reported any squeaks, wobbles, or things that needed attending to like head nuts that needed loosening, brakes that needed binding, gears that were slipping, or requests for change of gear ratios. Changing gear ratios, crucially in the mountains of course, necessitated one of the most fiddly, lengthy jobs on the worksheet. There were no cassettes in those days – every block had to be dismantled completely with a couple of chain wrenches and the replacement freewheels were laid out in a row and the new combination built up. It took ages. The routine rarely varied: work till about 9.30 p.m., slope off for a slap-up meal and then back to work, sometimes till around 1 a.m., and then totter into bed. *Reveille* was soon after 6 a.m., two or three hours before the stage start. That was the time for the last checks, the greasing, oiling and inflating of tyres.

All riders rode tubs. For that '55 Tour, Dunlop had sponsored the Hercules team and delivered a large supply of new tubs – a generous donation in principle but riders would customarily keep their tubs for anything up to two years to harden or 'mature' them. The rubber on the new tubs ridden by the class of '55 was too soft for the rigours of the Course. The riders punctured wholesale and used themselves up with constant chasing to get back on. This was the main reason for the gradual collapse of the team – only two men finished. Robinson had no truck with that: losing time with punctures made no real difference when you were a long way down already. It was more a case of punctured morale.

Tubs were the descendants of the balloon tubulars developed by Dunlop and Michelin which had revolutionised cycle racing at the turn of the century. They made long tours possible by enabling the riders to effect their own roadside tyre changes. The tyres were fixed with sticky tape. The later tubs, much thinner in gauge, were cemented to the shallow rim beds with a mixture of shellac crystals and methylated spirits, a compound also used in French polishing. The glue had to be painted smoothly onto the rim making very sure to leave no gaps or air pockets which would inhibit the holding power. When it was dry, the tyre was rolled onto the cement and fixed into position. One application would serve several fittings. A well-stuck tub gave a smooth ride, with virtually no roll. The cement didn't react well to the wet though and doing this in the rain was difficult and dangerous. The chances were that the bond between tyre and rim would not be as strong as it ought to be, which made for not a very happy turn in the storm-ridden Pyrenees or the snowbound Alps. Incidentally, even up to the late '70s and early '80s, they used wooden rims on the front wheels in the mountains. Brake blocks around then were prone to catching fire with the friction of binding on metal rims in precipitous descents.

I asked Bob about his rapport with the riders and his reply echoed that of all the men I spoke to: the relationship was close and often quite intense. There was a mutual respect, with infinite care and consideration on the one side and gratitude and trust on the other. Steve Snowling records how much he appreciates the late night gift of a cup of tea and cake from a thoughtful rider. Both sides were, and always are, under massive pressure to do a good job. The riders are in the furnace of race competition while the mechanics are in the breech of the action during the racing and also in the lonely darkness after it, making sure of everything, setting up the bikes perfectly to instil confidence in the men who depend on them. No detail is too small. One old-school mechanic insisted on polishing the riders' shoes – the soles particularly. The temperament of a mechanic comes to the fore: a nervous rider has to be given every morale boost possible and this was a point emphasised by a man whom Bob Thom introduced to the world of cycle race mechanics: Harry Hall.

Harry rode as an amateur and did Brighton–Glasgow and Brighton–Newcastle. He dubbed himself a 'middle quality' rider, and became more and more interested in the actual machine than in racing it. Scraping together a few hundred quid, he gave up work in the haulage business and set up Harry Hall Cycles in Bellevue. Taught to build frames by a university-trained engineer (Rob Mitchell of Stockport), he insisted always on precise drawings, extreme accuracy and exact tailoring of frame to rider. Bob came to the shop frequently, as a sales rep with the Viking team, and invited Harry to go to the first Isle of Man pro race to look after the riders. He packed his tools and flew across. They piled into a Land Rover hired locally and so began a strong partnership between the two men. They worked as one, with the same drill – never flustered, cool, calm and collected, no matter what frustration was going through their heads. And just as the case still is these days, whatever reputation they had established, it had always to be earned over and over again. One collapsed wheel, one frame cracking at the wrong moment and a reputation is shot.

There were tricks, too, but just tricks of common sense and simple psychology, really: always polish the front wheel and the cranks especially well, so that when a rider's screaming with effort and his head goes down, he sees the shiny clean metal and, almost subconsciously, registers that the mechanic is making a special effort on his behalf, an effort to be repaid. And, if a rider has a bad day, put fresh tape on the bars. The next morning he collects the bike and it looks like new so he perks up. Steve

Snowling always cleans under the saddle for a similar reason. It is, says Harry, not only thinking about the bike itself but what the rider has to do on it that makes the job so demanding – but satisfying too. Even when people get het up in the stress of the moment and you're taking strafe, the one thing you don't do is react. Remain unfussed, unflappable: that, like sound work on the machine, is crucial.

The problem of equipment does not really affect the current mechanics so much: every team uses integrated bikes and components and every rider is uniquely catered for. In the early days, especially among the British riders, this was far from the case. In 1955, for example, the Hercules men rode their own machines, (Dave Bedwell was tiny: with only three spare bikes, what sizes should they choose?) and had their own preferred gears (Benelux, GB, Cyclo, variable length wheel skewers, different sized blocks). Most of the equipment was incompatible: a considerable headache for the mechanic who had to do his best to change as much as possible for some attempt, at least, at uniformity. The continentals knew nothing about the British stuff, nor did they want to know. The Tour service *camion* was amply stocked with replacement Simplex and Campag components and these were handed out generously. It was all good advertising for the prestige of the company, but was a devil to accommodate on bikes not set up for them.

And then there was the ignorance of the course. What gears to fit in the big climbing stages? Local knowledge would help – the other team mechanics were not all sworn to masonic silence; but even if they didn't tender advice, a bit of intelligent snooping to see what block sizes the foreign teams had installed would serve.

The top pros of that era usually rode frames specially built for them, irrespective of what team they were riding for – just as the many Sablière frames conceal alien trade markings beneath them today. And to show they were the aces, they kept the frames plain, without transfers – a mark of kudos; the man who carries no badges of rank because he is above them. Harry Hall built a frame for Robinson when he was with Gitane, for example; and there was Tommy Simpson too.

Harry had ridden with Simpson in their amateur days and he joined the GB team mechanic on the fateful '67 Tour. It was to Harry that Simpson said his last words: 'Get me on my bike.' It was the only Tour Harry worked on, though he did a whole string of other continental races like Classics and Tours. Riding for Peugeot, Simpson had a handbuilt Italian frame from Masi and, noted for his quirky sense of humour, enjoyed a neat trick on his rivals in the *peloton*. Most of the continental riders used Campag chainsets which went no lower than a 44 inner ring (not even a 42 in those days). Simpson had a Stronglight 93 with a 38 inner ring which enabled him to fit a straight-through block to only 20, or even 19. When the rest were slogging up the inclines pushing 24 on 44, they stared in disbelief at the Major surging up, twirling a 20, and thought: 'How's he pushing that? He must be strong. Get his wheel.' All part of the kidology.

Harry said nothing of that tragic day on Ventoux, but he did say that whatever anyone thinks about it, Simpson's record shows that he was one of those exceptional athletes who could drive himself beyond the normal boundaries of endurance; he had passed out several times during his career. He knew no limits to his ambition or his physical effort.

In those early days, the mechanics would often find themselves rattling about in the back seat of the following car changing tubs, truing wheels, all sorts – even rebuilding the whole bike. When the daily five-ring circus of work and running repairs on little or no sleep had been coped with, there was always the BCF to contend with. Theoretical selection, for instance: loading a team for the relatively flat Peace Race with climbers. For one Giro delle Regione, in north Italy, they presented Bob Thom, manager of the GB team, with a mechanic whom he knew to be a no-hoper. He asked for Steve Snowling, who had done the race, knew it inside out and was a first-class man. The BCF retorted that if Thom wasn't happy with the man's performance after the race (by which time it would be ludicrously late) he could file a report of complaint and simply dumped the idiot on him. It was a nightmare. Every stage finish the guy was wandering around aimlessly, asking questions, doing nothing to help, showing neither initiative nor energy when the rest of the team was swinging into action.

'Where's this?' he was saying, 'Where's that?', 'Where's the other?' to which the only (exasperated) reply could be: 'We don't know. *Find out.*'

Jobs were put off, left undone, botched: the effect on team spirit was disastrous.

Mutual reliance is vital to the material success of the team and to its morale. Every minute is precious. If there's going to be a delay between loading the bikes and making a transfer for instance, the space can be usefully employed: wash them, scrub the goo of banana and squashed sandwich off the tape, clean the wheels and frames ready for the maintenance work at the other end. Sadly not all team men match up to that overall devotion to the common welfare.

Mike Mullett, another man given a start by Bob Thom, recalled the phone ringing past midnight one time: it was the great Eddie Soens. Dave Lloyd needed some tyres for the Isle of Man, could Mike sort some out? Lloyd was a hell of a racer but had a rather brittle temperament. Mike didn't think twice about it. He got up and drove over. There are countless such stories which confirm the dedication, the mutual respect and professional responsibility of the best people in the sport; the loyalty and unthinking cooperation. Demands are made in exact proportion to the calibre of the people you make the demands of. Mistakes do get made. Dismantling Venix's bike after he'd taken gold in the *demi-fond* at Leicester in 1982, Mike failed to tape the seat pillar marking the position of the saddle. Venix had been adjusting and fiddling with it all week to get exactly the right height. A harsh lesson learnt. He once put Merckx's bike together before a meeting in Eastway in the late '70s. Like all the pros, notoriously exacting, Merckx watched him start the job to make sure he was on song and then left him to finish.

In the Peace Race, which all four men did, there was an unwritten code of mutual help between the teams; even a daily prize for the mechanic who did the most to help out all round. Steve Snowling won it four times and he brings the story up to date, the first and the only full-time bike mechanic in the UK as long as seven years ago. In the past, they were bike-shop men who took a break to go on the road and give up sleep for a week or two, satisfying that thrill which exploded in them early: the kid with his nose pressed up against the bike shop window, the smell of the gear inside, the glossy feel of cool enamel, and the obsession with the beautiful machines. As Mike Mullett put it to me: 'This isn't a sport, it's a disease.'

18. PHIL LIGGETT

During my mother's final illness, I regularly caught the train to Ipswich and cycled the 25 miles to the hospital in Aldeburgh, smart clothes in the saddle bag for a change out of the comic strip. (Returning from a ride a while ago, I stopped at the fruit stall in Sevenoaks market and asked if they had a ripe banana.

'We've got everything' the bloke said.

'I'll have a ripe banana, then' I told him. He came back and said:

'Tell you what, I'll give you that.' I asked him why.

'For having the courage to come out looking like that,' he said.)

On one occasion, David and Peggy, old friends of the family were at the hospital when I clumped in, all cleats and lycra. Taking stock of this low-tech apparition, David said: 'We've got a cyclist living next to us.'

'Oh,' I said.

'Yes' he said. 'Phil Liggett.'

Some months later I visited them and called on Phil, two doors along in the row of houses tucked away in wooded tranquillity in Hertfordshire. Since then we've exchanged e-mails, met in France on various occasions, and in October 2000 I went to the World Track Championships in Manchester to see the racing. For many people, Liggett is *the* voice of cycling and in terms of enthusiasm for and understanding of the sport, he is a very singular man. Each day we walked to and from the velodrome along the towpath of the Ashton canal and talked – about cycling of course, but also of sailing England's vast canal system, (which he does in the narrowboat which is his second love) and of wildlife, another passion. He had once wanted to be a zoologist and worked for a time as a keeper at Chester Zoo. When he and his wife Pat went on safari with Paul Sherwen, Paul's wife and the noted cycling photographer Graham Watson, Pat laid a secret bet that sooner or later there'd be a humdinger of a session of bikie talk. It seemed like a safe bet. But Sherwen was kept busy changing wheels and barking at marauding game; Watson was disinclined to take photographs – this was a holiday

– (though, naturally, he did and they were all gems), and Liggett didn't mention the two wheels once. Pat lost her wager.

Although cycling is Liggett's essential trade it is not the overruling obsession most people would imagine it to be. I know how he feels. There are times when I crave a break from velocipedomania – a writing assignment in Mongolia, writing and directing a theatre show, anything to broaden the horizon.

Of course Phil Liggett is *the* voice of cycling in Britain, often recognised in the pre- or post-race mêlée ahead of the renowned cyclists milling about the place. It's a constant embarrassment to be asked for his signature when there's a star of the *peloton* standing next to him. However he is a man without side, as happy to go for a weekend's spin with the Droitwich CTC (he's the Cycle Touring Club President) as to be reporting on the Tour de France. It was with the CTC that he started.

Brought up in the Wirral peninsula, that fertile breeding-ground of racers, he was induced to get on a bike by a school pal, for fishing expeditions. The family had no car and a bike offered the best – indeed the only – chance of independent mobility. His pal was a member of the local CTC and gradually came the lure of longer excursions. Going out on a Sunday had no charm to begin with; it was not worth missing Sunday lunch, a roast joint, the only meat meal of the week. The club regularly rode out from Merseyside into north Wales and the lure of exotic destinations was strong: Rainbow Pass, the Old Horseshoe, Moel Fammau mountain . . . a bike took them briskly away from the anonymous back-streets of Bebington into the green wilderness.

The club rides made no concession to youth: the bigger men rode hard and expected everyone to try to keep up. No one would be dropped and abandoned though, the ride would always come together, but the code was tough, on the principle that if you didn't like it you didn't have to come back. That's where you find out about yourself, whether you want to stick it out until you can match the rest, or else sit up and say goodbye, it's not for you. They rode hard, Phil frequently in tears with the pain of holding on, trying not to get dropped, but there was great satisfaction attached to the small successes and they had a lot of fun. One time, miles from anywhere, one rider's wheel collapsed. They spotted a ruined old machine propped up against a farmhouse wall – more rust than bicycle – knocked at the door and asked the old woman who answered if they could borrow its wheel.

'Bike?' she said 'What bike?'

They made the swap, fixed the tyre and stuffed it with grass. They had to stop every so often to redo the stuffing but made it home.

The local racing fraternity wore leather jackets to and from the meets and Phil yearned for a leather jacket, to be in on that crowd. Curiously, the mate who got him into cycling had no interest in racing and Phil left the CTC club, joined the New Brighton racing club and got the leather jacket. He did 3 races before his 17th birthday, made it into 3rd category and got his first win – which catapulted him into first category. Alas, the club had no other first-category riders and only a team of three or more could enter races, so Liggett switched to the North End club and the wins started to come regularly. It was a punchy era for British racers. Brian Robinson had carved a brilliant career on the continent, and men like Vic Denson, Barry Hoban, Colin Lewis and probably the most talented of them all, Tom Simpson, followed where he had led. There was Michael Wright too, born in Belgium with Flemish as his first language. Pro cycling was a pipe dream in England, despite the valiant efforts of those road-race devotees, committed to the belief that time-trialling was an ultimately sterile exercise. France and Belgium offered the only chance of a real test of cycling talent and in the '60s there were unprecedented stirrings of ambition for a racing scene further afield than the Wirral, the Yorkshire Dales, the Peaks.

Liggett went to Belgium for a season's racing; the president of a local club liked his style and took him up. He got a bit of financial support, a mechanic to look after his bike and as much racing as there was on offer. Like all those who crossed the Channel in those days, he lived on thin commons. Beans on toast was the staple. In fact another Liverpudlian racer told me that he remembered those meals: tin of beans with the lid pricked in with an egg in the saucepan of boiling water. First time, he went to throw the water out and was reproached by the veteran: 'Hey-up, we need that to wash out our socks.'

The first race in Belgium, halfway through. Liggett is on the front, cruising speed, thinking: 'This is all right, not bad – easy,' when suddenly the bunch squeezes the acceleration like pliers on a cable-stop and he's at the back, gasping. That is always the way of it. The shock of racing speed. I haven't talked to a rider who didn't have the same experience.

There were, at the time, a considerable number of other Brits racing in Belgium, but no heed was paid them in the British cycling press. Liggett had been sending short pieces to his own local paper, the *Birkenhead News*, and now decided to quiz *Cycling Weekly* on its silence about the British contingent in Belgium. The editor, Peter Bryan, suggested he file some reports and they'd consider including them. They were accepted.

A while later back in England, Liggett applied for, and failed to get, a job on the weekly but the guy who got it left within a month or so and Liggett was offered the post. But he was told that it meant an end to his racing. He couldn't do both. I asked him about the switch from racing to journalism: he must have posed himself some hard questions.

'Yes, sure I did, but I was racing against guys like Merckx and I could see that I was never going to earn the sort of money he could on the bike. I needed a regular income, and I was still racing.'

Still racing – but clandestinely. It meant going straight from the regular Sunday dust-up into the editorial office to help lay out the magazine ready to be rushed down to Dorset for printing late on Monday morning. The strain began to tell, but then came the letters from readers saying how refreshing it was that *Cycling Weekly* was employing a journalist who knew the racing scene at first hand. Liggett was summoned to the editor's office:

'Okay, you can carry on racing,' he was told, 'but the minute you're late with copy you're on your bike, so to speak.'

The punishing round continued: an 80-mile race against guys who could train that much more; write reports, lay up magazine (often till past midnight); doss on the office floor; carry on in the morning – and then the whole office staff would go off mob-handed to the journalists' drinking HQ on Fleet Street, El Vino's wine bar, at midday. The winner of the weekend sweepstake on races paid for the champagne and all his resolutions to train more would dissolve in bubbles.

Even though pals would look after him in the races (relaying him, squashing daft attacks) it soon became obvious that he simply couldn't compete at anything like his full power. The editor suggested he should pick a record and beat it – a way of bowing out. Liggett flicked through the record books and came up with Winchester–Wantage. Curious idea.

Unfortunately, they picked a day of the Newbury Races. The by-pass was chock-a-block with traffic. The following car couldn't get through and had to double round, leaving Liggett without food or drink. With five miles to go he was ten minutes up on the record and hit the wall: *bonk*. Visions of four white lines weaving in and out through the wheels. Mars bars flying in echelon across the sky. General disintegration of mental and physical coherence. He made it but had nothing left for the welcome party holed up in the pub. It was a successful, if at the time unhappy, *envoi*.

Since then he has been a journalist, (snatched meals late at night, bad food and scant sleep), race director of the Milk Race for many years, and now of the Tour Down Under in Adelaide. But he is best known as the Channel Four commentator for the Tour de France. He and Paul Sherwen have consistently fronted what used to be the best popular coverage of the Tour available on television (perfect foil to the in-depth David Duffield comprehensive on Eurosport) and, almost incidentally, shown what a fantastic draw the race is, even to people who aren't bike fans, not only on the continent but in Britain. The Milk Race drew huge crowds; when the Tour came in 1994, the public went crazy. Given the prevailing attitude of the sport's national ruling body, the British Cycle Federation, to road racing (i.e. not really interested, thanks very much), this popular appeal of the great cycling spectacle is being denied to a huge audience. Liggett and Sherwen are just part of a team who produce a programme which, a year or so ago, won first prize for sports presentation (from *all* sports); and casual viewers who, in the normal run would never dream of watching a bike race switch on in their millions to watch the Tour de France.

'The thing is,' Liggett said, 'a football match is a football match – that's it. With a bike race it's a whole lot more: people gathering on the road before the race comes, a great party atmosphere – especially with the Tour of course, but it's the same with any race. And the odd thing is that it's almost an anti-climax when the riders do eventually come through.'

I agree. If you said to anyone, 'well . . . you get to see about 30 seconds of live action all told, or, if there's a break and the bunch are down, *two* bursts of 30 seconds. Exciting, eh?' they'd probably say they'd rather watch a croquet match. Yet if they see it they *know* what the excitement is: something scarcely definable but it's at the heart of the sport. And of course, razzamatazz aside, it is the riders who define the particular electricty of cycle racing.

Liggett makes no secret that his own particular hero is the man who embodies all that is best in cycling: Eddy Merckx. In 1975, already facing his first defeat in the Tour, he fell heavily one day and broke his jaw. He rode on, against the most vehement medical advice. Had he abandoned, Thévenet's fabulous victory over the man they deemed invincible would have been diminished. Every evening, Merckx turned up without complaint, on the press tribunal to answer questions – business as usual – but in such pain from the injury that he had to hold onto the stanchions of the stand to steady himself, the whole platform shaking with his effort – but still he would not pack the race in.

Even on the last day, the first time of finishing on the Champs-Elysées,

213

when someone asked him how he felt about losing his first Tour, Merckx, wearing the rainbow jersey of World Road Race champion, replied: 'What do you mean? It's not over yet,' and from the gun he attacked. Thévenet clinging to his wheel, red in the face with strain, Merckx hammered out 48 kph for 6 km; then he sat up and waved the Frenchman through: '*Now* you've won the Tour.'

Arrogance? No, just part of the Tour's mystique – the stature of champions and the chivalry of the code. It was just a great champion acknowledging publicly the courage and superiority of another rider.

There is, or was, a decidedly feudal element in the workings of the Tour *peloton*. Probably the last of the true patrons of 'the bunch', as the *peloton* is called in English, was Bernard Hinault. A rider of matchless ability and dominant will, whose capacity to win and to know he would win took on what can only be called a mysterious quality, he controlled a race in a manner largely unthinkable today. Given the huge demands made on riders by the Tour, there were days of unspoken truce – subdued racing to give sore legs a rest. If any rider grew impatient and attacked, Hinault was quick to send one of his own team men up to bring the fugitive back for a tongue-lashing.

'Never do that again, if you want to finish the Tour.'

Hinault was not acting in his own interests but for the *peloton* as a body; just as he was always prepared to act for the riders against the organisation. In his first Tour in 1978, he led a strike in protest against the excessive number of transfers by train, car and plane from stage finish to start. Fifty metres from the finish into Valence d'Agen, Hinault, in the tricolour jersey as French champion and flanked by two senior members of the *peloton* (Freddie Maertens in the green Points jersey and Michel Pollentier in the King of the Mountains polka-dots), dismounted and walked in. The stage was annulled. That solidarity among the riders, galvanised by the strength of a natural leader like Hinault, is rooted in a shared acceptance of the rigours and the dangers of life as a pro bike racer. It is a close-knit community with its own legal system and code of ethics. As Liggett put it:

> When Chris Boardman first joined the pro ranks he was never allowed to work at the front of the bunch. That was sacred territory and you had to earn your place there. As soon as he went up to the front he was pushed back into the bunch. He may have arrived with an Olympic gold and the world hour record, but still he had to win respect on the road. The day he was allowed to ride at the front, he said, was the day he knew he was a pro.

214

That is the kind of fealty which men like Hinault, brought up in the code, exacted; some riders simply do not understand it. The Americans, inclined always to behave like petty ambassadors for 'God, truth and the American way', have much to learn in this respect. The quarrel between Hinault and the young Greg Lemond who was nipping his heels, was none other than a clash between the old (I believe the born) aristocracy of the *peloton* and the brash *arriviste*. There was a conflict of interest, certainly. Lemond wanted to win the Tour and felt that Hinault was denying him a deserved victory – but where Hinault, undoubtedly as powerful an ego as any astride a bike, was deeply imbued with the ethics and responsibilities of pro cycling as rooted in almost a century of tradition and protocol, Lemond's self-interest effectively swept all that aside. He toed no line except the one which began 'I'. It is, in truth, the American way, by God, and Lance Armstrong seems to have a similarly blinkered view of the way things should be done (i.e. *my* way). And 'seems to have' is important here. Perception counts for much. Armstrong may well be a decent, straight, professional (if humourless) guy, but he comes over as arrogant, self-obsessed in the extreme and ruthless. Accused by one of his team men of treating them like slaves, he punished the offender by riding him into the ground until someone told him to ease up. This was at the very least shamefully insensitive and inconsiderate of the needs of the lesser men whose job it was to ride for their leader. They will only do so without complaint if the leader appreciates – and is *felt* to have appreciated – their devotion. Men like Hinault and Merckx are born to these duties. Albeit of *seigneurial* rank in the hierarchy of the *peloton*, like generals with superior moral power, they always saw to their men.

Even grandees like Merckx and Hinault honoured the tradition in the sport of being open to the press, giving interviews without payment – raw from the race, often still on the bike. Not Armstrong though: he is permanently surrounded by a ring-fence of envoys, advisors and myrmidons. Any approach to or from him is sanitised, manipulated; an exercise in PR rather than personal rapport.

Another significant change sponsored by a new breed of riders which Liggett deplores (and I absolutely agree with him) is the introduction of two-way radios. Many riders (not all) wear earpieces now. It means they are in constant touch with their team director. Whereas before they had to make decisions for themselves – judge the rhythm of a race, check attacks, decide when to follow and when to bide their time – they now need do little of this. Tactics have ceased to be a major part of their individual responsibility. In the 2000 Tour de France, it was quite apparent that Armstrong was under orders for the duration of the race, a stream of orders issuing from the team car. The attack up to Lourdes Hautacam, which effectively won him the Tour, seemed inhuman, not because of the power he unleashed, but because he didn't (or couldn't) repeat it subsequently. It came not from will but from the sizzle of a voice in his ear. Savagely attacked by Pantani in the Alps and hit by a near-critical depletion of blood sugar (*la fringale*, 'the bonk') he floundered and, had the Italian been in better form, Armstrong might well have *lost* the Tour. Bruyneel in the car talked him through. There's nothing wrong with help from the car driving alongside; that's part of the race. But Armstrong's reaction after the attack demonstrates how tactically numb he is. Pantani walked the plank, he said. The attack was absurd. Wrong. It was the attack of a man whose desire to ride himself out of his skin supersedes all reason; it is certainly deaf to advice or threat. Pantani wears no earpiece: he listens to his own inner voice – instinct.

Confidence, a wilful confidence which responds to the spur of passion – that is what Liggett most admires. Not every rider can be a champion. What counts is attitude, the attitude of a winner, the attitude of what the French call a *baroudeur* – the rider who consistently rides hard because that's his job, for sure, but also because it's embedded in his character.

For instance, Liggett believes that Hinault's definition of a champion (a rider who can win important races all through the season) still holds true today. Riders complain that it is impossible nowadays to win Classic one-day races at the beginning and end of the season *and* hope to win any of the big Tours too; that the demands of both genres of race are contradictory; that the season is too long – any excuse. Yet the fact is that riders face about 120 races a year today, whereas the pros in the '70s rode over 150. Contemporary riders get paid considerable sums for *not* racing (through sponsorship, appearances, trade advertising) and therefore do not shoulder the sort of pressure that went with having to race to supplement the team wage, which always was the case. In the past most Tour riders went from Paris straight into an exhausting round of criterium one-day races all over France, Belgium and Holland. Nowadays they don't bother because there are more prestigious rides to focus on and, more significantly, they don't need the extra money. They *are* required by UCI rules to enter a string of designated races in which they take points essential for their team's ranking (first or second division), upon which can depend entry into the bigger races. There is, too, a growing tendency (a regrettable trend) amongst riders in the *peloton* today to quit races when they're not going well, even to enter them fully intending to abandon before the end. For instance, Jan Ullrich pulled out of the 2000 Vuelta a España, when he was wearing the leader's *amarillo* jersey, offering the excuse that: 'riding the Vuelta wasn't ideal preparation for his preferred target, the Olympic time-trial'. Sadly he is not alone in regarding certain races as no more than training rides. That, decidedly, is *not* the attitude: it demeans the sport, it betrays the professional obligation.

This sense of obligation and devotion to the *métier* squares nicely with how Liggett feels about his own work, an attitude which colours his own standards.

'All my commentaries come from the heart. I admire anyone who takes his chance – a small guy taking the risk, beating the system if you like, against the chasing pack. That brings out the emotional response in me. You can, occasionally, throw out a wrong fact and that's always a pity. If in doubt I tend to leave it out. I *do* get emotional during the races, though never afterwards. But, above all, I try to bring to the public in their living rooms as vivid a picture of what they're seeing as possible: the atmosphere, the feel of the race. I have to think of the industry too: it's a considerable reputation on the line when we broadcast, whatever we broadcast. I'm very aware of missing what I wanted to do, just not quite getting it and it's like a bad performance on the bike. You feel you've let yourself and a whole lot of other people down. That's what kept me going on the Wantage record ride. But when you do an exceptional commentary, you do know – and it's great, you're on such a high you can't sleep. And again, it's like a hard race: you're so beyond the limit you're thinking *'never again'* but afterwards, you feel so good you just can't wait for the next time. How do you know when you're going to turn in a great performance? You don't. That's what makes it so irresistible. It's what I prize most about road-racing: the unpredictable nature of it.'

He added a nice story, about a time when they drove ahead of the Tour to a recommended restaurant for lunch. The place was packed, heaving and the *patronne* was completely run off her feet. However she ushered them in, found them a corner of a table. The kitchen was full of journalists helping get the starters out, serving and rushing around. Amazing. The Tour spirit spilling over. And, at the end of the meal, everyone settled the bill without being asked.

He added that this is a spirit which is in danger of being stifled by having big teams in the Tour de France. And he suggested it would make the race far more open and exciting if the organisation were to introduce eight-man teams (as against the present nine-strong ones), which would allow two more teams into the line-up. Indeed, the next day, word from the Tour presentation in Paris vouchsafed just that. Liggett has an exceptional understanding of bike racing and the pro scene, all aspects of the sport, and is forthright on the matter of doping.

'I hate cheats. I like honest performance, even if a rider is riding a bad race, at least he's doing it on his own terms. But a cheat . . . I won't be doing with it. If I've praised him for winning and then find out he's a cheat he's finished for me. Alex Zülle was incredibly brave to admit to taking EPO; he wasn't alone in taking the stuff, but there were very few who faced the music.'

The trouble is that cycling has always been riddled with doping; the authorities knew it but allowed it to go on for so long that it got ruinously out of hand. Cycling *is* making a valiant effort to clear its name; the fight against EPO has, probably, been won. As for the sport's infection with other drugs, Liggett believes that the only answer – the vital answer – is out-of-season testing. If national federations independently, and of their own will, imposed random checks with automatic two-year suspensions for cheats, and if enough riders were caught, the mental approach would change. At present it is one of deep cynicism and there is nothing more injurious to the sport. Liggett knows of Australian riders who arrived in Europe, were introduced to the needle and went home in disgust. Some even quit cycling because they saw no future in a sport where every winner seemed to have a 'doctor' in the car. Even when he was racing in Belgium, Liggett encountered the suspicion: he'd win a race only for his mates to say: 'What're you on, Phil? We dropped you in training. Where are you getting the form?' It's a tired jibe. You don't judge a good racer by what he does in the doldrums of training but how he performs in the high gale of a race.

The tragic death of Tommy Simpson, who had taken amphetamines, has heightened the drugs issue. There can be no doubt that his example soured many people at the time and it is unfortunate that his fatal collapse on the slopes of Mont Ventoux is indelibly associated with drug-taking. It feeds the cynicism. But Simpson was an exceptional athlete, a singular individual whose whole make-up demonstrated the power of mind over matter. His body was simply not strong enough to achieve what he yearned with every fibre to achieve. For him, said Liggett, the Tour was a disease, he *had* to be there. The will to succeed was terrifying in its concentration. But he could never climb like Jimenez, say – though he wanted to, and he drove himself so hard in the attempt that he

218

effectively broke himself. Someone with a less-tough constitution would have faltered long before Simpson actually gave out.

Probably the single most damaging aspect of the sport and a serious impediment to reform is the very nature of the way it is managed. The rules are far too complex and arcane, the machinery too cumbersome. Recent pettifogging over the precise specification of a permissible shape of a racing bike, for example, has been farcical. In 1994, Tony Rominger set a new world record for the hour on a bike which would, save for its unequal-sized wheels (the rear wheel was slightly larger), have passed present-day muster. Yet the UCI, with flagrant disregard of their own rules, erased all records set since that of Merckx – on a conventional track bike in 1972, at altitude. Despite prevailing proof to the contrary, they make no distinction between altitude and sea level. The fact is that the ruling body is too selfishly insular; they seek to run it as a secret sport, applying their own inner masonic regulations without any true passion for bike racing.

As for the British Cycling Federation, Liggett believes that their fundamental approach is too narrow. The great successes on the track – at the Sydney Olympics and the World's in Manchester – will have encouraged the 'no gamble, no risk' coaching practices reliant on the evidence of heart-rate monitors, straight-line speed and manageable achievement. Peter Keen, the coaching director, has this method down to a tee and will always work to the formula – the formula which equates medals won with money received from the lottery-funded Sport UK. But this is percentage coaching, working to rules stipulated by accountants. No wins, no money. Thus, riders are excluded from the squad because they don't train according to the stated pattern which is geared to monitored success. It is training governed by statistics, slide-rule objectives and results tailored by machines. It is redolent of all that was worst in the Soviet system of manufacturing athletic supremacy.

It is no less than a regression into the basic amateurism of time-trialling; the shaving off of seconds on the same piste over and over and over again. True, many riders have been lured into cycling by time-trialling but the narrow obsession has kept them hermetically sealed from *real* competition. The future of the sport emphatically lies in road racing. Track racing will do nothing to raise the profile of cycle sport; it is, essentially, a spectacle for the aficionado. Britain has produced a string of brilliant track racers: Reg Harris, Beryl Burton, Hugh Porter, Tony Doyle and the current bloods – Jason Queally, Yvonne McGregor and the rest of the team. Simpson began as a track racer, was a pursuit medallist, but the proof of his fame and the impact it had on the public was the very fact that when he died and was known to have taken drugs, parents discouraged their children from taking to the bike. Had he been a track rider, who would have known or cared beyond the enclosed fraternity of the track fans?

Track careers are, generally, short-lived. There are exceptions, but riders who reach the peak of their talent on the track (usually around 24 or 25 years of age) need to progress to the road: that is the forum where to excel is to reach the true heights of the sport. Look no further for proof than the effect of road-racing in the USA. Liggett brought the first ever American team to Europe for the Milk Race, of which he was director between 1972 and 1993. Their aim was simply to finish. The following year, Jim Ochowicz came with the team and won the Hot Spots competition. He went on to manage the great Motorola cycling team, for whom Lance Armstrong first rode as a pro.

Britain does not lack talent; it lacks promotion of talent. The BCF, rather than enter a team in the Milk Race, habitually sent a team to the Peace Race in the eastern bloc, for spurious diplomatic reasons, to the abysmal neglect of any ambition the home-born riders might have of making a career on the continent in the professional *peloton*. And in the time that the UK has been *talking* about getting a British team in the Tour de France, American riders have *won* it five times and have achieved hero status and astonishing publicity for the race in particular and the sport in general. The British, let's face it, love success, they love their own champions to succeed, but they cannot abide high heroes, such as the Tour de France lionises, for life – pride will have its fall but if you don't drop we'll sure as hell push you over.

There is, of course, more to life than cycle racing, but Liggett is emphatic about the way that a career as a pro cyclist affects life afterwards. To come through the pro ranks is a hard trial of any character; it is uncompromising, unsentimental. Early ambition may be fostered by admiration of a champion and the desire to emulate, but it is tested ruthlessly in the same forum which has always honed and tempered these champions. Survive that, and a rider will have found an unshakeable bedrock of confidence in himself. He will, quite simply, be a better person – ready for anything that life may throw at him. There is, I can attest, a powerful sense of self-assurance about the pro cyclists I have met and talked to. Men to have beside you in a crisis. Some testimony to the sport, and to the alchemy that takes place inside the *peloton*.